Securing
E-Business Systems

Securing
E-Business Systems

A Guide for Managers and Executives

Timothy Braithwaite

John Wiley & Sons, Inc.

This publication is designed to provide accurate and authoritative information in regard to
the subject matter covered. It is sold with the understanding that the publisher is not
engaged in rendering legal, accounting, or other professional services. If legal advice or
other expert assistance is required, the services of a competent professional person should
be sought.

ISBN 0-471-07298-2   ISBN 978-1-119-09093-9 (paperback)

10 9 8 7 6 5 4 3 2 1

Dedicated to
Florence Braithwaite

About the Author

During his career, Timothy Braithwaite has spent more than 15 years in senior security management positions and another 20 years in executive director positions for computer and communications services organizations in both the public and private sectors. He has also worked as a private consultant. Tim has previously published *The Power of IT: Maximizing Your Technology Investment* (Milwaukee, WI: Quality Press, 1996), and *Evaluating the Year 2000 Project: A Management Guide for Determining Reasonable Care* (New York: John Wiley & Sons, 1998).

Contents

Preface

As a reader interested in the uses of information technology (IT) to improve business productivity, create opportunity, and increase profitability, you have just clicked your way or have visually inspected a substantial list of "e-business" and "e-commerce" book titles. There are dozens of such books available today, and each offers a treatment of the advantages of pursuing an increasingly electronic path for the conduct of business in the "new economy."

New economy or old, and the "dot-com shakeout" of the last two years notwithstanding, these books are correct in advising a course of e-business activity for most enterprises. But a question to ask is whether the majority of these titles address the topics that are necessarily germane to the establishment and future success of an e-business initiative. For example, a major topic that seems to be missing from most other titles is a discussion of an e-business management model to guide the planning and implementation of a technology that can bring as many vulnerabilities and risks to an organization as it can benefits.

To be sure, most e-business and e-commerce titles point out the technical complexities faced by an organization seeking to use the technology, but few discuss methods for managing such complexity. And fewer still present management techniques to help prevent problems that arise from the technological uncertainties of the IT industry itself. Complexity and uncertainty conspire to threaten the e-business journey of most organizations, and yet methods for managing these problems are seldom being addressed in the e-business titles now available.

As an example, one of the most challenging problem areas for the e-business, one that is directly related to IT complexity and uncertainty, is that of security. The lack of adequate security with the majority of e-business systems and applications is most definitely a result of technological complexity and organizational uncertainty. The technology is so complex that attempts to secure systems seem almost futile as vulnerability after vulnerability continue to appear long after software products and systems have been tested and put into production. And uncertainty as to what is at risk and what adverse impacts may be experienced should a security breach occur makes the solving of this particular e-business problem one that goes far beyond most e-business titles.

Securing E-Business Systems: A Guide for Managers and Executives seeks to remedy this shortcoming by presenting the essential knowledge and methods needed to guide the securing of the e-business infrastructures currently being planned, designed, implemented, and operated by organizations. A successful business will be the one that is capable of managing the myriad emerging security risks associated with the B2B, B2C, and B2G interdependencies growing out of e-business applications. Security weaknesses inherent to such e-business applications and relationships can never be fully anticipated before implementation, so it is imperative that organizations concentrate their efforts on managing the ever-changing environment in which business is being conducted for security implications. This calls for more than a one-time effort to "fix" today's security defects. What is needed is the realization of executive management that security is an essential cost of doing business over the Internet—a price of admission to the "new economy."

The book has several unique features:

- It does not spend a great deal of time trying to convince the reader that there are security problems associated with the use of computer technology in business. It assumes that the reader is informed and concerned about the securing of e-business.

- It brings together the essential technologies needed to secure e-business but allows that specific implementations of a security technology will have to be studied in detail for it to be effectively employed in any specific business environ ment.

- It takes a pragmatic view of an extremely complex topic that has come to be dominated by vendor hype and self-serving information that is not always in the best interest of the user.

- It is about "process"—the creation of security management processes and procedures that will outlive the "security crisis" of the moment and establish a foundation for the "continuous" improvement of a corporation's e-business security posture.

- It will insist that e-business systems cannot ever be secured unless and until a corporation's IT is under control and being managed as strictly as any other component or support element of the corporation.

A design criteria for this book was to provide as many self-standing chapters as possible while pursuing the theme of "what it takes to manage" the securing of e-business applications and support architectures. Chapter 1 provides a definitional foundation to be used throughout the remainder of the book. Chapter 2 discusses the e-business model and how it has evolved from the traditional, pre-Internet business model. Highlighted throughout this discussion is the need to balance the perceived advantages of e-business with the associated risks to systems *integrity*, *confidentiality*, and *availability/reliability* from using e-business technologies.

It is a fact that as business and government commit more of their essential work processes to an electronic forum, there are accompanying vulnerabilities and resultant risks that must be addressed. These weaknesses, inherent with the use of computers, communications networks, and the Internet in conducting essential business functions, are described in Chapter 3 along with a catalogue of generic safeguard technologies and administrative actions that are commonly applied as part of a "best practice" countermeasures strategy.

Threats to e-business, however, are continually changing and the technology of countermeasures must change in response. Solutions for the security problems of today will not be adequate next year as e-business architectures evolve and new business applications are embraced. To get a handle on change, organizations must establish a formal e-business security management program that institutionalizes the necessary analytic processes for ensuring an "acceptable risk" security posture regardless of changes to the technical architecture or software applications. Chapter 4 (Part One) provides insights to some of the long-standing misconceptions concerning the use of IT that are incompatible with the goal of securing an e-business. It outlines fundamental IT and system management problems that, if left uncorrected, will only contribute to a continuing state of e-business insecurity. These are system management deficiencies that result in the realization that "you cannot secure what you are not managing." Chapter 4 (Part Two) describes the essential elements of a corporate security management program capable of establishing, maintaining, and continuously assuring an "acceptable risk" security posture regardless of future technological changes to e-business operations.

Finally, Chapter 4 will conclude with an outline of the functions, structure, staffing, and contracting considerations essential to the establishment of a successful e-business security management program—a program that will outlive the "security crisis of the moment."

The first order of business for most organizations probably will be the need to "jump-start" their security effort. Chapter 5 presents a "new" approach for quickly determining the security posture of an e-business environment by implementing intrusion detection technology on all existing networks that support e-business operations. This strategy provides empirical evidence of suspicious activity actually occurring on monitored networks and allows for the ability to take near real-time remedial action should a security breach occur. This "just-in-time" monitoring strategy, for the "just-in-time" e-business system, when combined with traditional security assessment methods will identify both real and hypothetical security requirements for which pragmatic security solutions can be designed and implemented.

While most organizations are presently playing "catch-up" in securing their existing e-business architectures and applications, they also must anticipate security weaknesses and incorporate security safeguards into systems and architectures now on the drawing board. Chapter 6 addresses the challenge of designing tomorrow's e-business application for secured operations. How can an organization go about defining, designing, developing, testing, and deploying systems to operate within "acceptable risk" tolerances? Who should participate, what methodology can be used to guide these efforts, and how can executives and managers effectively monitor such efforts? Appendixes A and B supplement Chapter 6 and offer assistance by providing a little history, a little philosophy, questions to consider, and a matrix to be used in milestone review meetings for new system development efforts where security is important.

Without a doubt, the greatest challenge faced by past computer security initiatives was the difficulty in justifying adequate funding. Historically, security programs have been "undercapitalized" and subsequently became "piecemeal" efforts with little or no thought given to sustainability. Because of the high risk associated with e-business systems and due to the rapidly evolving technologies of e-business, security cannot be viewed as a one-time thing. Security is forever. This means that security programs must be adequately funded to provide for "continuous" security monitoring, analysis, and safeguard improvement. Chapter 7 provides contemporary rationales to be used in justifying the increased funding that an e-business, security program will require to be effective. These "new" rationales supplement the historically inadequate "cost vs. loss" risk analysis with hard-hitting "nonquantifiable" business survival arguments that only the senior-most executives can properly weigh. Chapter 9 provides information about public and private sector efforts to protect the critical information infrastructure of the nation. Concerns about a national "electronic" Pearl Harbor underlie these efforts and support the nonquantifiable business survival arguments covered in Chapter 7.

Chapter 8 addresses some of the emerging liability issues for the e-business to consider. It offers a series of questions to be answered in proving that the corporation pursued a course of "due diligence" in the securing of their e-business systems. This is an area that requires constant scrutiny because of the speed with which it is evolving and because of the impact it has on the security strategies of the corporation.

Finally, in an attempt to be practical, the book offers a section that can be tailored to fit the needs of the reader. Appendix C provides a representative *Corporate Plan of Action for Securing an E-Business.*

Readers choosing this book will find they are in a good position to successfully pursue the management task of securing their e-business systems. If a reader already knows about the technology of e-business security, Chapters 4, 5, 6, and Appendix B will provide specific details covering the establishment of a security management and systems development structure that can ensure continued security for future e-business architectures and software applications. And for anyone needing assistance with justifying the resources needed for an effective security program, Chapters 7, 8, 9, and Appendix A are required reading.

Chapter 1

Electronic Business Systems Security

What is it?
What does it include?
How important is it?
How to get started?

INTRODUCTION

One of the major computing challenges in today's economy is the manifest lack of adequate security over the information, computers, networks, and Internet applications on which business, government, and the economy depend. Many computer security threats have been identified over the past 25 years, and each has spawned a special category of corrective actions to address it. For example, in earlier times, efforts to address the lack of automated security were variously known as computer security (COMPUSEC), communications security (COMSEC), emanations security (EMSEC), information security (INFOSEC), and information technology security (ITSEC). More recently, information assurance (IA), Internet systems security (ISS), and cyber-security have grown in popularity. Each of these areas in turn have grown subcategories of security knowledge and special safeguarding techniques that are needed to secure today's electronic business systems. There is no one security solution for an e-business system because the e-business application sits at the pinnacle of modern computing and is therefore susceptible to all the security weaknesses of the various foundation technologies.

For our purposes, e-business security acknowledges all the threats identified by each of these security categories and employs the technical security safeguards and risk mitigation techniques associated with each category as determined by the actual risks found to be threatening the business. E-business security also calls on the traditional disciplines of personnel and physical security to complete the picture of safeguards that will be needed when addressing threats to the electronic business.

Conceptually, e-business security represents an accumulation and consolidation of information processing threats that identify the need to protect the integrity and confidentiality of information and the need to secure the underlying support technologies used in the gathering, storage, processing, and delivery of that information.

But what is e-business security and why is it important? How do threats to electronic business impact the world of contemporary commerce and what must be accomplished to improve an organization's security posture—especially when it comes to "new" e-business systems?

HOW IS E-BUSINESS SECURITY DEFINED?

Some definitions:

- Assure—make safe, make certain, tell positively, give confidence.
- Information—knowledge.
- Information Technology (IT)—the technology of the production, storage, and communication of information using computers.
- Electronic Business—the application of information technology to business activities.

Using these definitions, e-business security can be said to be concerned with *making certain* that the *knowledge-value* of business information is *made safe* and is available for business processing when needed. Consequently, e-business security is concerned that the technologies used for the production, storage, and communication of information are *made safe* so that the *knowledge-value* of the information is *certain* and can be trusted when used. If information and the processing technology are *made safe*, users will have confidence that the information *positively tells* (i.e., accurately portrays) the reality of that which the information is supposed to represent. In different words, e-business security is concerned with the confidentiality of information, maintaining its *knowledge-value,* and ensuring its availability to *legitimate* users and customers when required to perform an *authorized* business activity.

By comparison, if information, and its *knowledge-value*, are not *made safe,* cannot *be trusted*, and are not readily available to legitimate users and customers, business and government activities will be adversely impacted. If by accident or deliberate action, information is stolen, becomes inaccurate or misleading, or is not available for use, business and governmental decisions and actions may become compromised, distorted, or wrong, and/or decisions cannot even be made and actions cannot be taken. When this occurs, executives, stockholders, users, customers, and citizens lose confidence in the information and may no longer trust the system, process, or organizations that make use of the information. They also lose confidence in the organization responsible for maintaining the information and the integrity of the business process. E-business security, then, is concerned with being able to assure trust in all information and the computing processes used to conduct e-business.

CAN E-BUSINESS SECURITY BE EXPLAINED MORE SIMPLY?

Perhaps it is helpful to view the scope of e-business security as including all those actions required to prevent, minimize, and recover from the universally appreciated threats summarized by the acronym GIGO—garbage in–garbage out. Within this context, e-business security is concerned with preventing those accidental and/or deliberate actions that may result in the introduction of inaccurate data or information to a system (GI) as well as any accidental or deliberate processing, storage, and communication activity that may produce inaccurate, false, or misleading outputs from a system (GO).

These concerns are addressed by taking action to assure the integrity and confidentiality of information and processes while at the same time assuring the ready availability of information, processes, and other system resources when required for use by legitimate users and customers. For example, "denial of service" attacks, such as those often experienced by Internet users, are currently being viewed as the number one threat to our highly automated and interconnected way of conducting business and executing the functions of government. This is because a successful denial of service attack destroys the ability of the e-business system to function at all.

In conclusion, e-business security is concerned with all aspects of how business information is collected and handled, how hardware and software process and communicate that information, how information is stored and protected from eavesdroppers, and how system resources are configured and *made safe* to ensure their ready availability to legitimate users and customers.

IS E-BUSINESS SECURITY REALLY SUCH A BIG DEAL?

To the extent that business information and the technology used to produce, store, or communicate that information are considered important to an organization's e-business operations, the definitions and discussions outlined in this chapter are consistent with the intent of Presidential Decision Directive-63 (PDD-63) on Critical Infrastructure Protection and other initiatives calling for the protection of the nation's critical information infrastructure. In a practical sense, if information and/or its processing were considered mission-critical or mission-sensitive for Y2K purposes, it should probably now be considered critical for the intent of e-business security.

Presidential Decision Directive-63 directs that information integrity, confidentiality, and availability be assured, not only for government systems but also for all information processing systems on which the nation depends. E-business systems certainly fall within this definition. The intent of the directive can be accomplished only if all aspects of information collection, production, storage, and communication are *made safe* (i.e., secured). By inference, this includes how e-business systems are designed, managed, configured, accessed, and operated. It also includes how software and databases are designed, programmed, and tested; how system changes are made and validated; how systems are monitored for incidents; and how critical information and backup systems are protected. By establishing information, computer, and communications security controls sufficient to prevent and mitigate anticipated risks, and by establishing a continuous security monitoring and security improvement process, the intent of PDD-63 can be satisfied.

All aspects of computing and communicating impact the objectives of assuring integrity, confidentiality, and availability and should therefore be within the scope of an e-business security initiative.

IS E-BUSINESS SECURITY MORE IMPORTANT THAN OTHER INFORMATION TECHNOLOGY INITIATIVES?

E-business security is an overarching business issue that, based on analyzed risks, establishes the threat acceptance and reduction parameters for the *safe* use of technology. As an overarching issue, e-business security can be thought of as being absolutely fundamental to the effective and efficient use of information technology (IT) in support of e-business. E-business security enables the operational concepts of e-business or e-government to become a viable way of conducting the affairs of the corporation and the government. Having built an electronic business or government world, our dependency on information and its confidential, accurate, and timely processing has grown to the point where compromises of information, loss of integrity, and/or failures of the underlying support technology may be catastrophic.

How much or how little security is required in any given instance is a "due diligence" issue for management. Determining what constitutes a "pound of security" and the associated costs are decisions that can be made only after considerable analysis—analysis that requires the direct involvement of senior executives of the corporation. If information and its supporting processing and communicating technologies are not important to your organization, little attention need be given to these issues. However, if information processing and its supporting technologies are central to the conduct of your business, a great deal of security work may be necessary. It all depends on your situation, how well you know your risks, and what has previously been done to address those risks.

The question that needs answering is "what risks threaten your e-business and how are your customers, employees, partners, investors, and shareholders impacted should any of those threats materialize?" The answer to "how much or how little security is required" must consider a great many variables that change over time and therefore require a continuous improvement mind-set and the establishment of security management processes that allow threats to be monitored so that continuous security posture improvements can be made.

HOW DOES AN ORGANIZATION GET STARTED?

First, an organization must know the actual security posture of their existing e-business processes so that management is aware of system vulnerabilities and how they may adversely impact business operations. Management can then intelligently choose, in the light of analysis, what degree of risk to accept. When was the last computer and network security assessment conducted? If your company is like most companies, it has been several years and does not reflect the new distributed e-business and Internet applications the company has been building or integrating from off-the-shelf products. Additionally, your organization was distracted for several years with the Y2K problem and all the work and expense that was needed to correct it. Consequently, most organizations must begin anew to determine an appropriate course of e-business security action for their company.

Beginning anew means to start with a formal assessment of the vulnerabilities, threats, risks, and potential adverse impacts associated with how information technology is now being used to support the electronic business processes of the organization. Such an assessment will identify ways in which information and processing integrity can be compromised, confidentiality breached, and availability of computing services denied (Chapter 3).

Questions concerning the cost of bringing e-business systems up to an acceptable level of security can be answered only after the security assessment has been conducted and senior management has contemplated the "quantifiable" losses and a series of potential adverse impacts that are generally "unquantifiable" (Chapter 7).

In addition to identifying technical security weaknesses, this assessment should attempt to discover the extent to which IT support organizations and/or contractors adhere in their daily operations to system management "best practices" and security "best practices" being advocated by security experts. Adherence to these practices is crucial if the e-business operations of the organization are to be executed in a well-managed, stable, dependable, and *safe* manner (Chapters 4, 6, and Appendix B).

Following an assessment of technical weaknesses and management practices, a plan of corrective actions or "road map" should clearly outline appropriate safeguard actions, their costs, and the anticipated costs needed to design and execute a security program of corrective actions and day-to-day management of that program (Chapters 4, 6, and Appendix B).

Security assessments for e-business systems come in many flavors depending on the complexity of the business and computing environment to be analyzed, the amount of time that has elapsed since the last assessment, and the dollars available to conduct the analysis.

E-business security assessments may evaluate the security posture of the entire enterprise, focusing on vertical "legacy" business systems or new e-business applications, or may determine the effectiveness of security practices at a system-specific operational level. A new aspect of a traditional security assessment growing out of the Y2K experience is an analysis that crosses all system interfaces of a "supply chain" made up of various interdependent businesses. This will be especially appropriate where just-in-time processing is occurring or where business to business (B2B), business to customer (B2C), or business to government (B2G) is a growing part of the business model. For corporations that are already heavily networked, an essential element of the e-business security assessment is to immediately begin monitoring current system traffic to discover what is actually going on at the systems and network level (Chapter 5).

Finally, a major question that most organizations should ask regarding e-business assessments is whether their employees have the technical, security, and "best practices" knowledge and experience needed to conduct the type of analysis that factors in all the technical innovations and associated threats that have been introduced into the e-business processing mix in recent years. Beyond the act of assessing (and even more important, what does an organization do with the findings from an assessment after it is completed?), the real measure of worth for an e-business security assessment lies in whether the findings and recommendations are feasible and capable of being implemented and administered. Are the recommendations truly practical or are they merely a collection of actions resulting from the use of checklists? Is there an attempt to integrate the recommendations into a set of system controls that is consistent with the way business is actually being conducted by the organization? Does management know how business is being conducted at the operational level? Is there a process for reconciling apparent conflicts between processing efficiency and the possible imposition of security and internal controls? Of equal concern, how does an organization plan to maintain the secured processing environment after recommendations are implemented and how will the continuing IA posture be monitored during daily operations?

If there are any doubts about the abilities of an organization's internal staff to conduct the security assessment, there also must be doubts about their ability to determine a course of corrective action, devise an implementation strategy, and maintain a secured environment in the face of rapid technological change. It is therefore essential to look beyond the assessment to the entire *security life cycle* to plan and budget sufficiently for the implementation of corrective actions and the maintenance of a secured operational environment.

There are many sources for conducting security assessments, but few that can provide follow-up on *security support services* based on standardized and repeatable methods recommended by the standard-setting bodies of the world such as the National Institutes of Standards and Technology (NIST) and the International Standards Organization (ISO) guidelines (Chapter 4).

INSTEAD OF PLAYING "CATCH-UP," WHAT SHOULD AN ORGANIZATION BE DOING TO DESIGN E-BUSINESS SYSTEMS THAT ARE SECURE IN THE FIRST PLACE?

The answer to this question begins with the system management practices of the IT support organization and/or contractor. The "Holy Grail" of security professionals has always been to influence systems while they are in development and to design security in rather than add it on after the fact. This has proven to be elusive for a number of reasons having to do generally with how IT is managed by the majority of businesses and governments and particularly how system development projects are often mismanaged. The bottom line is that security cannot be designed into an e-business system if these systems are not being defined, designed, programmed, tested, and deployed in a disciplined manner. Furthermore, security cannot even be effective as an add-on if systems are not maintained and operated in a disciplined manner. Put simply, *you cannot secure what you are not managing—and you cannot manage without enforcing the discipline of a "structured" software and systems engineering methodology* (Chapter 6 and Appendixes A and B).

Chapter 2

E-Business Systems and Infrastructure Support Issues

INTRODUCTION

In this chapter, the term *e-business* as it is commonly used is explained, and important issues concerning the hardware, software, and communications infrastructure needed to support an e-business architecture are discussed.

As a concept, e-business has many advocates and promoters; but, as with other previous "breakthroughs" in automating the business, it has its share of problems that need resolution. Most of these problems stem from the old saw that "the devil is in the details," and there are a good many *details* in implementing e-business that will bedevil.

E-business is the latest in the progression of automation applied to the conduct of business. At each step of this progression, more and more of the business process has been consigned to the computer with a smaller and lesser role being reserved for humans. With the exception of software programmers and their heavy involvement during systems development, integration, deployment, and problem resolution, most employees and users of an e-business system are merely passive observers of a business process as it moves along its automated path. Only when there is a "glitch" in the system are employees and users expected to do more than initiate transaction function keys. When there is a problem, software programmers become heavily involved but much of the workforce usually sits idly by until the system is back up and ready for more processing.

Exhibit 2.1 is from the book *E-Business Essentials* by Norris, West, and Gaughan (John Wiley & Sons, May 2000). Exhibit 2.1 is used here to illustrate the complexity of an average real-life business process and to make the critically important point that as a company automates such a process, it is the e-business software in its final version that will dictate *how* business activities will be performed and how the business must adjust. Where once company employees performed each activity, were directly supervised by experienced managers, and had many of their process actions reviewed for accuracy by other employees, today's e-business software has consolidated the majority of the processing steps and automated much of the review function. In many cases, only the software creator knows how the system works and, as is discussed in Chapters 4 and 6, poor information technology (IT) management and systems development practices make even this assumption uncertain. Software and IT management problems aside, Exhibit 2.1 also illustrates another major challenge, which is that unless an Exhibit 2.1-type diagram of the desired business process can be created, agreed to by all interested parties, reduced to software instructions, tested, and successfully deployed to the workplace, the enterprise is at risk of not being able to conduct business at all.

Additionally, a careful and conscientious application of the security definitions of confidentiality, integrity, and availability to Exhibit 2.1 will demonstrate numerous points in the process where safeguard actions may need to be taken to ensure the security of the e-business system.

E-BUSINESS DEFINED

While there is no universally accepted definition of e-business, this book assumes that e-business embraces all aspects of producing, buying, and selling products or services on-line. The essential characteristics of e-business are that dealings between two or more parties are conducted on-line where the key commodity being communicated is information about the transaction. There are many terms used to describe e-business, such as e-government, e-commerce, e-market, and e-trade. Systems are devised to be business to customer (B2C), business to business (B2B), business to government (B2G), government to citizen (G2C), and so on. In each case, private communication networks and the Internet are being used by organizations to establish cooperative strategies with suppliers, business partners, and the customer or citizen. These strategies expand the reach of the organization and improve the quality of their product or service, reduce inventories and overhead, and increase revenues and profits. These cooperative strategies comprise a complex, interdependent "system of systems"—in effect, a network-based alliance of business and government and customers and citizens who share a common goal, the electronic conduct of business and government activities. Exhibit 2.2, also from *E-Business Essentials*, portrays the "system of systems" that makes up an electronic business environment. This figure represents the culmination and almost 30 years evolution of the application of computer and communications technology to the conduct of business.

A SHORT HISTORY OF E-BUSINESS INNOVATIONS

For all the hype, there is little new about conducting business electronically. Since the advent of cost-effective storage that could house vast volumes of transaction and master file data and multiprogramming computing, businesses have looked to use these capabilities to reduce overhead, improve accuracy, and speed up delivery of goods and services. However, beyond the automation of backroom clerical record keeping, the first comprehensive applications of computers to business had to wait until a communications technology capable of handling high traffic

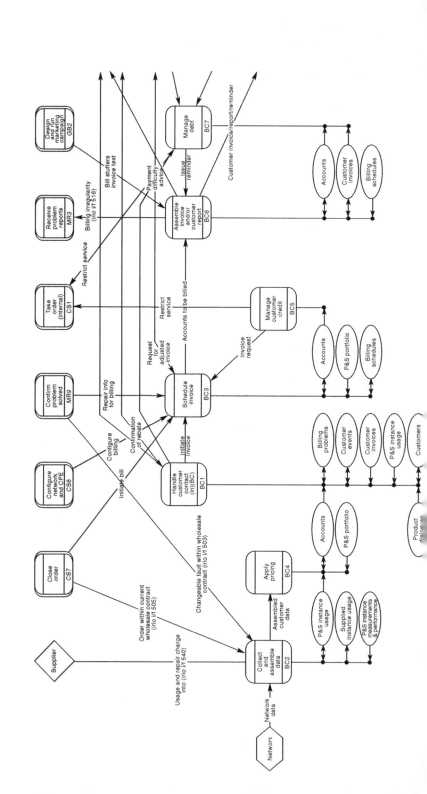

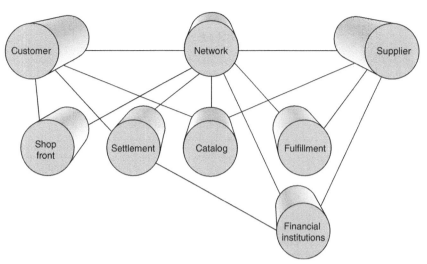

Exhibit 2.2   The Essential Elements of an Electronic Business
Source: Norris et al., *E-Business Essentials: Technology and Network Requirements for the Electronic Marketplace* (New York: John Wiley & Sons, 2000). Reproduced with permission.

volumes was developed. The convergence of these three technologies coupled with an evolving sophistication in information modeling, business process modeling, and software development allowed the first genuine e-business efforts to begin around 1970.

In the early 1970s, manufacturers figured they could save billions of dollars through materials requirements planning (MRP) systems. These systems linked various steps in a corporation's internal supply chain and were generally known as production control systems. For example, such a system would link bills of materials to inventory to purchasing and accounts payable. Also in the 1970s, manufacturers began to believe that the key to responding to Japanese competition was to increase the use of robots in assembly lines. The automobile industry spent billions of dollars, but many of the anticipated gains proved illusory.

In the 1980s, businesses, led again by the automotive industry, established a series of consortiums to set standards for linking themselves electronically with their top suppliers. The resulting system, known as electronic data interchange (EDI), was a technological next step for expanding MRP. EDI required dedicated communication lines to pass structured business data between the systems of the trading partners with no manual intervention. It was expensive, but it worked. Exhibit 2.3 depicts EDI in a supply chain of organizations. EDI is relevant to any business that regularly exchanges information such as client or company records and is especially relevant if you send and receive orders, invoices, statements, and payments. In the terminology of e-business, EDI provides a dedicated and easy way to secure means to communicate with members of a supply chain. EDI allows paper-based processes to be replaced and handled electronically. This is why the term EDI has come to be called "paperless trading." EDI is analogous to

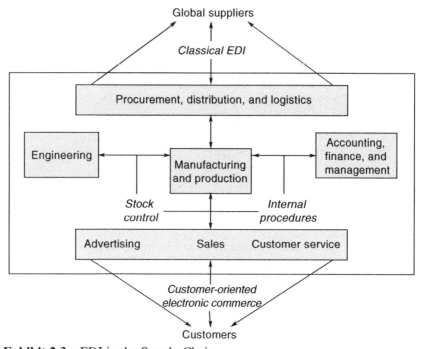

Exhibit 2.3   EDI in the Supply Chain
Source: Norris et al., *E-Business Essentials: Technology and Network Requirements for the Electronic Marketplace* (New York: John Wiley & Sons, 2000). Reproduced with permission.

e-mail except that it is much more structured in what can be communicated and how it is formatted. EDI communicates transactions directly between computers instead of between humans as done with e-mail. EDI networks are constructed between two or more trading partners to store and collect messages, provide audit trails, and resolve protocol differences. Known as value-added networks (VAN), they tend to be proprietary rather than open like the Internet. Since EDI has evolved within specific industries, industry-specific standards have been established that limit a network's capability to be expanded in attempts to lower transaction costs. Because of this, EDI remains rather expensive when compared to the Internet. It is salutary to reflect that despite 15 years of government and industry advocacy, EDI has attracted only around 100,000 commercial customers worldwide. The key stumbling blocks have been cost and infrastructure, specifically the fact that most EDI users must connect over dedicated proprietary communication lines or VANs. The Internet removes this impediment while allowing much of the benefits of EDI.[1]

Also during the 1980s, lean manufacturing techniques were introduced to keep inventories to a minimum. As Toyota and other Japanese companies

---

[1]Norris et al., *E-Business Essentials: Technology and Network Requirements for the Electronic Marketplace* (New York: John Wiley & Sons, 2000), p. 141.

established factories in the United States, Detroit realized that just-in-time (JIT) techniques were important and moved to embrace these concepts and systems. Just-in-time systems expanded the MRP concept across the supply chain from raw materials acquisition to delivery of component parts just before they were needed on the assembly line.

In the 1990s, companies began trying to tie together more of their internal systems using products from IT software vendors like SAP, Oracle, PeopleSoft, and Baan. But, it was not always possible to eliminate older legacy systems and the new software failed to create fully integrated companies. The 1990s also saw computer-aided design and manufacturing (CAD-CAM) mature. With these systems, manufacturers were able to greatly improve the speed with which they introduced new mock-ups, eliminating clay and wooden models. Organizations also began to use software to implement collaborative methods for other product development and for geographically dispersed project management.

Finally, in the late 1990s, business and government began in earnest using the Internet in an attempt to link their customers, dealers, suppliers, and citizens with improved internal systems and with an Internet-enabled supply chain. Specifically, the Internet has allowed companies to invest in many more on-line business initiatives. The following are examples of where companies are putting their dollars and the projected payoff:

- *E-Marketplace*. Transactions at e-marketplaces expect to reach $2.8 trillion by 2004 according to AMR Research. Defense contractor United Technologies bought $450 million worth of metals, motors, and other products from an e-marketplace in 2000 and claim prices were about 15 percent lower than they usually pay.

- *E-Procurement*. As a part of the estimated $2.8 trillion cited, Eastman Chemical is buying about 20 percent of its supplies on-line today, up from almost nothing three years ago. That has helped boost productivity 9 percent a year.

- *Knowledge Management*. Companies will spend $10.2 billion to store and share their employees' knowledge over the Internet by 2004, says the IDC Corporation. Electronics manufacturer Siemens has spent $7.8 million to create a web site for employees to share expertise to help win contracts. This is claimed to have resulted in new sales of $122 million.

- *Customer Relationship Management (CRM)*. Corporations will invest $12 billion by 2004 on linking customers, sales, and marketing over the Internet, says the META Group. Lands' End converts more than 10 percent of its web visitors to buyers—compared to the average of 4.9 percent—in part because it offers live chat and other customer service extras.

All of these uses of the Internet constitute an aspect of e-business, and some require transaction process of a sensitive and financial nature. E-business methods and systems must be able to meet these demands.

THE NEED FOR SECURE E-BUSINESS SYSTEMS

The progression of technology applied to business just catalogued shows the inexorable creep of business activities from the physically secured traditional back office to the openness and accessibility provided by today's contemporary technologies. While this movement to openness and greater accessibility promises increasing the *reach* of a business, it also exposes the business to an entirely new world of risks—a worldwide exposure that increases as growth of the Internet reaches exponential proportions.

The need for secure electronic systems has never been greater and is covered in Chapter 3. For now, we are concerned with understanding the constituent parts of the physical hardware and software infrastructure that supports an e-business architecture. What are the essential technical components of an e-business and transaction processing system that are susceptible to security risks?

Exhibit 2.4 depicts the fundamental component parts of a technical e-business system. This diagram provides the basic foundation for discussions in the remainder of this chapter, Chapter 3, and Chapter 6. Exhibit 2.5 extends the communications component of Exhibit 2.4 to include dial-in capabilities, dedicated VANs, and the Internet. Both diagrams allow important technical processing

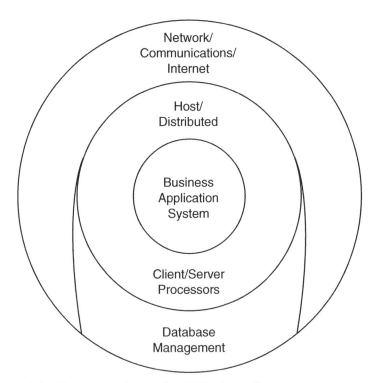

Exhibit 2.4   Component Parts of an E-Business System

relationships to be portrayed and examined as they exist in contemporary e-business computing environments.

Exhibit 2.4 shows a business application system and its relationship to the technical level support systems that are usually provided by a heterogeneous mix of hardware and software vendors. From the corporate executive's perspective, a functioning business application system can be viewed as the sum of hardware, software, databases, communications, and other specialized technologies such as presentation systems working together to produce a desired business output and atmosphere. A business application system, the only system in Exhibit 2.4 that actually accomplishes a revenue-generating function, is depicted as centered within the other technical supporting systems of hardware, software, and communications because it must rely on them to create a secure operating environment so that its output products can be "trusted." A business application system carries out a business function and executes in software the logic of a design that best performs the function in a programmed manner.

A business application system is constructed to perform a designated business function according to a defined set of specifications. These specifications describe the *quality* and *operational* characteristics of the software and the parameters within which its output will be "trusted" for use. Exhibit 2.6 shows that application software systems must be described in the quality language of correctness, *availability* and reliability, *integrity*, usability, *confidentiality*, testability, and maintainability. Without these specifications being expressed in measurable terms, a programmed software function has no expressed "success criteria"

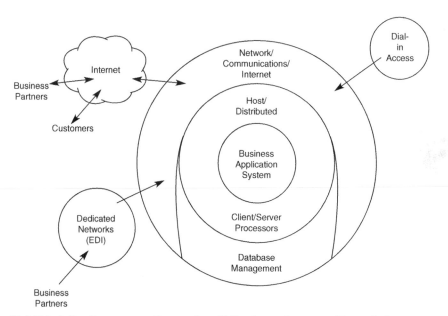

Exhibit 2.5   Component Parts of an E-Business System—Extended

except to be able to pass through a compiler and run without aborting. Without this degree of specificity, no manager, programmer, user, or customer knows the necessary and desired parameters within which the final software application must perform the business activity.

For example, it is one thing to state that the design goal of a business application system is to "pay the suppliers" and quite a different thing to specify paying each authorized supplier the accurate amount on the proper day of the month and according to the specific "discount" accounting rules of the company. Without this degree of precision, stated as a set of software specifications, the software programmer must, and will, *make something up*. Without this degree of precision, the system cannot be audited and probably does not satisfy the rules for business record keeping.

Even when properly designed, however, the e-business application still needs a stable operating environment in which to perform its function and meet the quality demands of the specification. To do this, each individual application system must look to each of the other components of Exhibit 2.4 to perform their respective computing functions in a reliable and trustworthy fashion. The quality specifications of maintainability and testability express critical software management requirements of an e-business application system. These two specifications are essential for the long-term quality of the application system and are possible with well-designed, well-developed, and well-documented software. Chapter 6 addresses the design of secure applications software.

If, then, the purpose of the business application system is to execute a programmed business activity within the parameters of a precisely defined set of

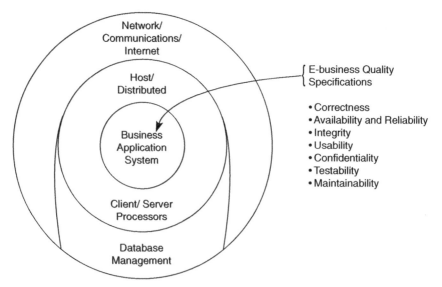

Exhibit 2.6   E-Business Quality Specifications

quality specifications, what are the functional purposes of the other components of Exhibit 2.4? In discussing each other component, the software and hardware comprising the component must be viewed as a single entity working in tandem to successfully accomplish its assigned computing task. Each component can perform only as well as its weakest element, and the weakest element of all the infrastructure support components in the figure is software.

In other words, the ability of business application systems, processor platforms, database management systems, and communication and network systems to operate in a reliable and trustworthy fashion is greatly compromised by the generally unstable and "buggy" condition of software. All software—everywhere.

SOFTWARE: THE VULNERABLE UNDERBELLY OF COMPUTING

Computer processors, database management systems, and communication and network systems are the electronic foundation on which business applications depend to carry out their function. For example, computer processors that include mainframes, servers, and PCs are the "traffic cops" of computing that allocate and control the *computer system resources* needed by the application system during its execution. Database management systems (DBMS) perform a similar function regarding the information storage and retrieval task, keeping the ever-growing volumes of business data under control. Likewise, the task of communicating with other systems and processors is managed and controlled by the software of local area networks, wide area networks, and, most recently, the Internet. Each of these support systems, in turn, depends on tremendous amounts of software to perform their distinct computing functions. It has been estimated that between 80 and 90 percent of all executed software instructions are of the "traffic cop" variety. These instructions are considered to be overhead—merely providing the system's performance and stability required to reliably execute the business application software. "Traffic cop" functions are performed by the operating system (OS) of a processor, the DBMS, and the network; as such, they are huge. The OS of WIN 2000 from Microsoft is said to have over 40 million lines of code—just to provide a productive and stable platform to operate a business application.

If ever there were an IT blame game that appears truly unwinnable, the incessant squabbling over defective software is it. Customers complain that buggy code from software vendors expose them to system crashes, time wasted recovering and devising workarounds, and overly expensive IT projects in which software products simply do not work as advertised. It is estimated that defective code accounts for as much as 45 percent of computer system downtime and costs U.S. companies about $100 billion a year in lost productivity and repairs. The estimated cost for fixing the Y2K problem was $100 billion. It appears that American business and government are destined, for the foreseeable future, to experience annual losses of a Y2K magnitude due to buggy software.

It is not the intent of this book to deal directly with the problems of software quality. The fact remains, however, that the lack of quality software, whether developed in-house or purchased, represents very serious vulnerabilities to the viability and security of the e-business system. This is because buggy software is the principal cause of system instabilities and "crashes"—posing a constant threat to system availability, reliability, and uptime. Remember, when an e-business system is down, a good portion of the business is essentially down. The losses may be sizable. Buggy software also possesses the type of defects that can be easily exploited by insiders or outsiders. This threatens the *integrity* of business information and the *confidentiality* of customer private or business proprietary data. Finally, because buggy software is unstable and "crashes," programmers commonly equip software, especially operating systems, with secret "backdoors" to be used in emergencies to override misbehaving code. Unfortunately, "backdoors" do not always remain secret and are among the first avenue of attack from hackers and those wishing to seize control of a system for their own purposes.

Just how bad is the underlying software quality problem? Estimates vary, but experts agree that just 3 or 4 defects per 1,000 lines of code can make a program perform erratically. Factor in that most programmers inject about 1 error per every 10 lines of code they write, multiply that by millions of lines of code in many systems, and then figure that it costs software developers at least half their total development budget to fix errors during testing. While most software people claim to care about quality, the problem is that the software management and development methods used on most projects are not designed to produce quality code. Vendors usually like to bang out code and then try to fix it during testing. At some point, testing must cease and the software is shipped to meet a market schedule whether all bugs have been found and corrected or not. In fact, software vendors are known to ship software with known defects just to meet a release schedule. Defects are then corrected in the next "upgrade" or through emergency "patches."

This attitude toward software development continues despite the fact that software quality assurance methods have existed for at least 20 years and that the economic and maintenance arguments for their use have long been proven.

The foregoing discussion concerning the condition of contemporary software is true for all component parts of Exhibit 2.4. Application systems, operating systems, database management systems, and communication and network systems are all threatened by software defects. This means that organizations are attempting to build and secure e-business systems while being forced to depend on computing infrastructures that are inherently flawed and insecure.

How did IT get into this mess? A large part of the current problem stems from the rapid rise of client-server processing systems in the 1980s and 1990s that exposed business to the "quick and dirty" PC culture. In the 1960s and 1970s, businesses buying mainframe technology could count on reasonably dependable OS code and predictable hardware and software from vendors such as IBM, Burroughs, Univac, and Honeywell. These vendors controlled the pace of technology introduction and could take the time to build dependable systems. When there were problems, user groups were able to exert considerable pressure to get them fixed. Even under these conditions, there were embarrassments.

But the PC industry, built on high volume, low prices, and frequent upgrades, made a joke of most quality assurance and quality control efforts. The PC user was initially very tolerant of defective software. Insidiously, the PC user began to believe that buggy software was the norm—something that had to be accepted. Early PC users were on an adventure to learn and master a "new" technology—technology that appealed to the "tinkerer" in many. After all, you never knew what caused a "crash," you, or the system itself.

Over time, users became conditioned to expect not only bugs but also the associated loss of time as system and work product recovery became a part of everyday life. This same conditioning has resulted in a later tolerance to system outages and corrupted work products, as client-server and distributed e-business applications began to appear enterprise wide.

The gradual creep toward serious IT dependency has not been accompanied by an equal improvement in system software quality and reliability. Increasingly complex IT architectures are increasingly subject to system instabilities and security vulnerabilities because of their highly heterogeneous software nature and poor integration testing record. Nearly everyone who makes or uses commercial software says it is impossible to test for all possible combinations of e-business products that customers have been led to believe they can create. Compounding the problem is the rise of computing paradigms such as Microsoft.net, which encourages companies to build more and more distributed applications. This means that software problems created by the customer can very quickly affect a large number of users unless strict control over development and testing is exercised. Just last year, Oracle grew so weary of customers who ran into problems with its application development suite that customer customization was discouraged. Chief executive officer Larry Ellison advised, "If you start heavily modifying our software and we come out with a new release a year from now, you can't take it. You call us on the phone with a problem, we really don't understand the problem because a lot of that system you've written . . . not us."

The results of poor quality software can make IT managers dyspeptic. Nike, for example, blamed a sales shortfall of as much as $100 million for its third quarter ending February 28, 2001, on a botched implementation of supply-chain management software. The athletic footwear and clothing maker says it double-booked orders, producing millions of unwanted shoes, and fell short of supply of popular models after the software rollout went bad. The software vendor claimed that Nike pushed the $400 million system into production too quickly and went live with too many suppliers and distributors at once.

In 1999, Hershey Food went live after two and a half years of development with a $112 million order-taking and distribution system that touched nearly every facet of its operations. When Hershey's system started delaying orders by as much as a week, the company missed crucial Halloween candy deliveries to retailers, forcing big chains such as Wal-Mart and Kmart to stock up on competitors' products. Hershey estimates the problems cost $120 million in sales.

A few months earlier, eBay suffered a 22-hour-long outage of its e-commerce website traced to a bug in Sun Microsystems' Solaris operating system that corrupted an Oracle database. Sun acknowledged that a known bug caused the problem.

Using the definitions of e-business security from Chapter 1, the Nike experience is the result of a software integrity problem. The Hershey experience is also the result of an integrity problem, while eBay suffered from a lack of systems availability. And not a "hacker" in sight! But, an outsider or insider might have been able to exploit such problems for fraudulent purposes, and when systems are in such disarray it would probably go unnoticed.

So where do IT and business managers go from here? Again, it must be stated that e-business security efforts are generally "hamstrung" by the fundamental instabilities found in each component of Exhibit 2.4 that supports the business application system. These instabilities are often due to poor quality and insufficiently tested software. For this reason, organizations must take a two-pronged approach to securing their e-business systems. First, businesses must manage IT for quality improvements. This means improvements to internally designed systems and improvements to vendor-supplied software. More information on this issue is found in Chapters 4 and 6. Second, businesses must establish management and technical control processes and procedures that will achieve the highest level of continuing e-business security possible given prevailing software conditions and commensurate with acceptable risk.

For our purposes, it does not matter what the exact hardware or software in Exhibits 2.4 and 2.5 are at any given moment. It does not matter because corporate managers must learn to deal with this ever-changing problem through control systems that can continually assess the inherent risks of pursuing an e-business strategy regardless of architecture or specific vendor configuration. Executive management must not become mired in today's technical security problem—it will surely change tomorrow—but must focus on establishing appropriate management and control mechanisms to prevent future problems. In Chapter 3, classes of e-business threats are presented and generic examples of safeguards are catalogued for each threat. But this is done only so senior officials can become familiar with the classes and language of system vulnerabilities that threaten their e-business operations.

The real-world exploitation of system vulnerabilities is possible in many ways that change daily, depending on the exact hardware, software, and network being used; the existence of a genuine threat agent; and the attractiveness of the target system.

THE INTEROPERABILITY CHALLENGE AND E-BUSINESS SUCCESS

There are several distinct but related interoperability challenges facing the implementation of an e-business strategy. Each challenge, in turn, affects the achievement and maintenance of a state of e-business security.

Although some enterprises, consultants, and software vendors are talking up end-to-end Internet-enabled real-time supply chains, they will be difficult to realize for many reasons.

First, there is an overall lack of technological capability, especially in small to midsize companies, to execute such a complex system. Newly announced intentions by large corporations at the top of various supply chains to build supplier enablement systems will eventually help, but small companies will still be expected to build their own back-end (i.e., internal) processes capable of ensuring accurate information exchange according to some industry or manufacturer's standard and business processing model.

Second, there are global issues that will hamper adoption of real-time supply chains: issues such as laws, technology preferences (i.e., European Union vs. the United States), culture, and language.

Third, real-time supply chains require real-time system management infrastructures that can respond to requests from supply partners and react to things that go wrong. Most enterprises, including those that have installed supply chain management and enterprise resource management systems, are having difficulty providing business partners with this kind of integrated real-time information domestically, much less globally.

Fourth are the human factor considerations including the issue of trust. To get supply chain participants involved in real-time Internet-enabled processing, promoters must present a win-win argument. It is not enough to say "do it if you want to remain in my supply chain." Business process mapping across components of the supply chain and education about how each member will benefit are required. Additionally, data, format, process, and information content standards will be needed to raise the level of trust among all partners. These standards will indicate a willingness and openness to benefit all. Such standards are largely lacking today or are immature.

Fifth, there are also privacy and data confidentiality concerns. Organizations have traditionally believed that to share information meant giving away intellectual property, market insights, and proprietary business data best kept in the company. Not until supply chain partners can demonstrate to each other that such information will be protected from access by competitors will trust be established. Then, collectively, business partners can come to an understanding of where their competitive advantage lies and work together to leverage, through Internet-enabled supply chain processes, those advantages.

Last, there are purely technological challenges to interoperability. As stated earlier, using the computer to enhance business activity is not a new idea. Companies have been exchanging business documents for years using EDI. But EDI is expensive to implement, requires special networks or VANs, and is therefore used only by the very largest organizations. The ubiquitous Internet, however, seems to offer an economic alternative for electronic commerce to evolve between companies.

One of the first technological challenges of B2B integration is deciding which data or format and language to use between systems. Choices range from simple

ASCII files to high-level formats such as EDI or XML (eXtensible markup language). If you want to exchange XML documents with another company, you both must agree, not only on XML, but also on what version or flavor of XML.

Contributing to the technical interoperability problem is the fact that there are hundreds of vertical-market B2B central exchanges exploding on the Internet. On-line exchanges and electronic marketplaces provide an alternative solution for enabling dynamic B2B commerce. Such exchanges provide a centralized point for commerce to be conducted. Rather than having to connect to each partner, an organization only needs to connect to the exchange. The exchange generally provides common services such as partner relationship management, security, auctions, reverse auctions, product catalogs, order processing, and billing. An exchange may also provide inventory management, shipping tracking, financial services, logistics procurement, and other services.

Of the many vertical-market exchanges appearing on the Internet, however, few of them tie back to the back-end system of each partner that would provide true automated B2B operations. The challenge of e-business, from an interoperability perspective, is to be able to communicate with a variety of systems without having to change any of them or without a series of separate intermediate conversion steps being required. According to David Linthicum, CTO at Saga Software Inc., "There's a lot of confusion in the market with a variety of standards. There are different points of integration, and managing them over the Internet in a reliable and scaleable manner is a very difficult task." According to Ross Altman, research director at Gartner Group, "Most people are focused on building functionality for auctions and reverse auctions; this is a simple part of the problem. There are many higher level functions that are necessary for on-line business to business selling." For example, the B2B process includes the handling of requests for proposals, questions, and quotations. This requires the ability to broadcast the proposal request to all supply partners who have indicated an interest in the procurement, answering questions to all, collecting responses, and channeling them back to losing partners after an acquisition decision is reached. This process must have high integrity because supply partners must "trust" the process to be open and fair. According to Altman, " methods and mechanisms for automating the process . . . are generally not available now in exchanges focused on auctions and reverse auctions." Therefore, such systems do not meet the actual B2B requirement.

Another major interoperability challenge of a technical nature is the fact that many e-business applications are evolving to be vertically focused. Because of this, large companies will need to participate with multiple "smokestack" systems, each functioning with different standards and perhaps with different languages and equipment. Again, according to Saga Software's Linthicum, "We will truly get to a connected worldwide economy when trade can happen instantly without someone having to pick up a phone or use a web page." This vision will come only as a by-product of solving the interoperability and security problems so prevalent today.

E-BUSINESS SECURITY: AN EXERCISE IN TRADE-OFFS

Exhibit 2.7 identifies five additional specifications that directly affect the cost-effectiveness and operational efficiency of an e-business system and the design of its supporting infrastructure. Whereas the *quality* specifications of Exhibit 2.6 are considered essential to the functioning of a "trusted" business application, the specifications in Exhibit 2.7 are considered to be very desirable for achieving the best possible cost-effective and efficient design and integration of the supporting system of processors, databases, and communications. There is conflict between the two sets of specifications.

When the quality specifications of Exhibit 2.6 are satisfied, the e-business application system will be used as designed to conduct business in an acceptable manner. If, however, the specifications are not satisfied, system users and business partners will be *forced* to devise "workarounds" to accomplish their job and in doing so will introduce unplanned security vulnerabilities into the business process. A "workaround" is generally thought of as a creative, perhaps even ingenious, way to carry out the business activity when the automated system is not responding or when it is known that the automated system is producing untrustworthy results. This is dangerous because "workarounds" often, out of necessity, skirt security and integrity controls to get work done. "Workarounds"

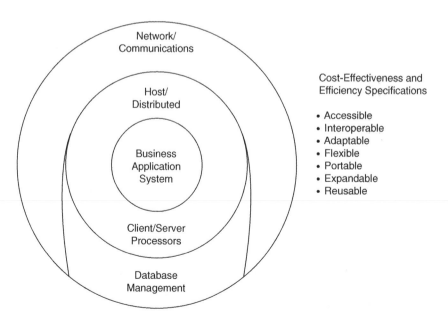

Exhibit 2.7   Desirable Cost Effectiveness and Efficiency Specifications

often exploit existing system "backdoors" to keep the business application running. Sometimes the originators of "workarounds" create their own "backdoors" and then leave them in the system for use during some future emergency.

The solution, of course, is to ensure that the business application system is clearly and concisely specified in quality terms and then thoroughly tested. As the stability, quality, and reliability of application code improves, the need for "workarounds" will diminish and the associated vulnerabilities will be reduced.

Striving to satisfy the specifications of Exhibit 2.7 poses a different threat to an e-business system. Each of these specifications, as a goal, is highly desirable, and vendors aggressively market their proprietary solutions for achieving them. But these specifications are often in direct conflict with the previous quality specifications for ensuring "trusted" systems.

There are three problems posed by cost-effectiveness and efficiency specifications. First, these specifications are very difficult to specify. How is their achievement measured? They are open-ended with no real endpoint that can be defined except in the most vague terms:

- *Accessible* to whom, to what, why, for how long, and for what purpose?
- *Interoperable* with what, when, and where?
- *Adaptable* to what—new systems, lines of business, new partners?
- *Flexible*—does that mean knowing that software and systems must be precisely defined and programmed?
- *Portable* to what platforms—compatible with what standards?
- *Expandable*—how far, how wide, and in which direction?
- Finally, *reusability*—the elusive goal of programming—the coding of software modules to be utilized again and again regardless of proprietary limitations, programmer knowledge and skill, or even appropriateness to the problem at hand.

Second, to be successfully implemented, each of these cost-effectiveness and efficiency specifications must have one simple thing in common—the ability of an enterprise to plan ahead and then control their technology efforts in accordance with those plans, an ability that is too often in short supply.

Without a long-range business plan, an e-business strategic plan, an IT architectural strategy, and an IT infrastructure acquisition and implementation plan, there can be no satisfactory answers to the questions posed concerning each specification. Without answers, these specifications can become "red herrings." Much time and effort can be expended arguing the best ways to satisfy each specification, but without a working knowledge of the organization's future business plans, such arguments lead nowhere and may actually be detrimental to building "trusted" and secured e-business systems for today.

Third, the greatest danger posed by these seemingly desirable system characteristics is that management may become overly enamored of their achievement and not understand or appreciate the compromising trade-offs, against security that will be made if these specifications are driving the system's design and implementation. For example, the first six specifications of Exhibit 2.7 require an openness of the planned e-business architecture that is counter to the more constrained approach needed by most organizations to achieve an adequate level of security. The threat lies in the erosion of operational stability that each of these six specifications brings to a system that also must meet the quality specifications of Exhibit 2.6. *Correctness, availability and reliability, integrity, usability, confidentiality, testability, and maintainability* each require that the e-business process and software be precisely defined and expressed in concise and measurable language. The system should not be "sort of" correct, available and reliable, trustworthy, testable, maintainable, and used. At the same time, however, a system can be "sort of" accessible, interoperable, adaptable, flexible, portable, expandable, and reusable, depending on a great many factors including the vendor communities' ability and motivation to actually deliver on the *vague* promise each specification implies.

So there exists a series of trade-offs between meeting the specifications required for a quality and "trusted" e-business system and meeting those specifications that are desirable in the name of cost-effectiveness and future efficiencies. In other words, specifications in Exhibits 2.6 and 2.7, by their very nature, conflict with each other. For example, the business desire for ever-greater systems accessibility will always conflict, to some extent, with the business need for confidentiality, integrity, and system availability. The simple fact is that the more accessible a system is, the harder it is to secure—especially if the system is *too* interoperable, adaptable, flexible, portable, and expandable. This is the *crux* of the Internet challenge to e-business security. The Internet seems to meet virtually all of the cost-effective and efficiency specifications, but at the cost of opening up e-business systems to a torrent of attacks that put at risk the essential quality of "trusted" business processing. Chapter 4 and Appendix E propose feasibility studies and risk management as the techniques to employ in conducting these types of critical trade-offs.

FEW SYSTEMS ARE DESIGNED TO BE SECURE

The challenge facing the corporation pursuing an e-business strategy is that of constructing, deploying, operating, and maintaining systems that satisfy all of the specifications in both Exhibits 2.6 and 2.7. It is difficult, in light of the fact that most software vendors chose to talk up and concentrate on the list from Exhibit 2.7. They sound good and speak of future efficiencies and cost-effectiveness but are not precise. Who wouldn't want an e-business system that could adapt and expand, forever providing broad accessibility because it is flexible, portable, interoperable, and made up of code that can be reused during future expansions? It is hard to hold anyone accountable should these lofty and vague expectations not be realized.

While the specification list from Exhibit 2.7 is exciting and much easier to sell because of its future focus, a system described in the terms of Exhibit 2.6 is more mundane. Who could get excited about a system that merely does what it is supposed to do—be available, reliable, accurate, and easy to use and deliver "trusted" confidential outputs. Isn't that what all systems are expected to do?

Because of these realities and dynamics, secured e-business systems are not and cannot be made available "out of the box." They must be "cobbled" together out of heterogeneous hardware and software possessing security features of varying effectiveness. It falls to the corporation and the e-business implementers to "cobble" together a secured system and a safe reliable infrastructure. This must be done in a computing environment where potentially hostile programs are continuously arriving across the Internet to run on potentially vulnerable computers. Securing e-business is much like trying to construct a 747 while in flight.

CONCLUSION

The technical backdrop against which e-business systems are being constructed is full of holes. The multiple quality and operational specifications that e-business systems strive to satisfy are themselves contradictory and usually force a compromise of desired security objectives. In Chapter 3, threats to which the e-business model and infrastructure are exposed are catalogued, the principles of protection are defined, and industry safeguard "best practices" are presented.

Chapter 3

Security Weaknesses in E-Business Infrastructure and "Best Practices" Security

INTRODUCTION

Corporations and government organizations are embracing the use of contemporary distributed on-line computing to conduct their affairs. In Chapter 2, applications of e-business were discussed and the prevailing conditions of "buggy" software and interoperability problems that contribute to fundamental instabilities in the supporting technology were explored. Understanding the existence and extent of such conditions is important for *setting realistic expectations* for an e-business initiative and in establishing the need for proactive and adequately capitalized e-business security programs—security programs that are chartered to provide the best possible protection, given the underlying instabilities, within a range of acceptable risks.

It is also very important for managers and executives to understand and appreciate that vulnerabilities, threats, risks, and safeguard actions are dynamic, and that they change at the rate of technological and business innovation. In addressing e-business security, it must be recognized that there are no lasting solutions, just a continuously played chess game between attacker and defender. Of course, the term *attacker* does not denote merely a human entity motivated to perform nefarious acts, but acts of nature. Also included would be the actions of other connected systems that may adversely impact the *integrity* of information and processing, the *confidentiality* of information, and the *availability/reliability* of a business system when needed for legitimate use.

It is the purpose of this chapter to introduce managers and executives to the general categories of threats that make e-business systems vulnerable. Each threat is defined in lay terms, and typical behaviors exhibited by a threat are noted. Exhibit 3.1 provides the frame of reference for this discussion. It illustrates the common infrastructure elements associated with an e-business system using the Internet as the principle means of communications. It depicts the internal corporate systems of research and development (R&D), human resources, finance, and order processing. The corporate system is connected through the Internet to service providers, remote offices, business partners, remote corporate offices, and consumers. The system also communicates using wireless devices—again, through the Internet.

Following an overview of generic threats and a discussion of the special vulnerabilities posed by the Internet, the principles of protection are presented. On this informational foundation, commonly employed "best practice" safeguards to counter each threat are presented.

This chapter does not identify vendor products or endorse the use of any one safeguard technique to the exclusion of another. It is hoped that the reader will understand the importance of analyzing e-business risks, using a "defense in depth" strategy and the need to invest staff and other resources to stay knowledgeable about all new moves of the chess game.

FUNDAMENTAL TECHNICAL SECURITY THREATS

The first category of threats to the e-business system deals with malicious actions and is comprised of seven subcategories—malicious software, spoofing, scanning, snooping, scavenging, spamming, and tunneling.

Malicious Actions

Malicious Software

- *Virus*—software that attaches itself to other software, such as a bogus "patch" to an application that is really designed to implement itself to other applications for which it was not intended. In this way, virus software replicates within the computer system, attaching itself to all applications to which it can gain access. A virus may be innocuous, humorous, data-altering, and/or resulting in a denial of service (DOS) or other catastrophic behavior. All computers, from mainframes to personal digital assistants (PDA) and cell phones, are threatened by the virus phenomenon.

- *Worm*—software application designed to propagate through a network rather than through a single computer. Multitasking computers using open network standards are especially vulnerable to worms.

- *Trojan Horse*—software hidden in other software that is being distributed as a useful program. The Trojan horse may be a virus or a worm, or it may be surveillance software, such as a *cookie,* which communicates information back to a perpetrator. A Trojan horse will not execute unless the user runs the "covering" software in which it is hidden.

- *Time Bomb*—a virus, worm, or other malicious software code designed to activate at a certain date and time. Enough lag time is usually allowed, following introduction of the *bomb,* to ensure widespread dissemination of the code throughout the organization before the trigger date and time.

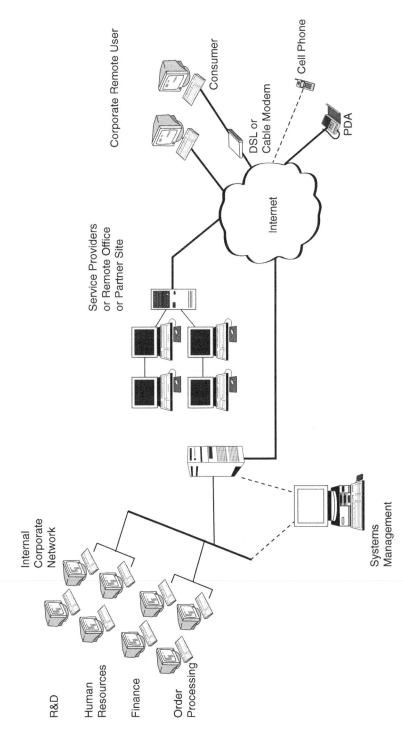

Exhibit 3.1 E-Business Security

29

- *Logic Bomb*—a virus, worm, or other malicious software code designed to activate under certain conditions. For example, code to purge certain critical files and their backups upon notification to payroll to cut a termination check for Tim Braithwaite.

- *Rabbit*—a worm designed to replicate to the point of exhausting computer system resources by consuming all processor cycles, disk space, or network resources. Systems left on 24 x 7 are especially vulnerable to this threat as the rabbit can run all night or all weekend with little interference from other programs.

Spoofing

- *Spoofing*—getting one computer on a network to have the identity of another computer, usually one with special access privileges, so as to gain access to all other computers across the network. The originating computer for the spoof often does not have access to certain privileged commands, so attempts to use automation-level services such as e-mail or message handlers are employed. Automated services adhering to open standards are most vulnerable.

- *Masquerade*—accessing a computer by pretending to have an authorized user identity. Obtaining an authorized user ID is commonly achieved by placing false log-on prompts on a target computer. The techniques of snooping, scanning, and scavenging are often successful in obtaining such IDs.

Scanning

- *Sequential Scanning*—running a software program that sequentially attempts potential passwords and authentication codes until successfully accepted by the target computer system. Scanning attempts are often indicated by the presence of a high number of multiple rejections of sign-on attempts or logged attempts to execute system administrator privileged commands.

- *Dictionary Scanning*—scanning through dictionaries of commonly used passwords and authentication codes until successful. Dictionaries are composed of commonly used words, names, and dates—so-called "Joe Accounts"—the passwords and codes that every other "Joe" uses.

Snooping

- *Digital Snooping*—electronic monitoring of digital networks to uncover passwords and other data. Unprotected data links, laptops, and wireless devices are especially vulnerable to passive monitoring by devices that can receive electronic emanations from such equipment. Snooping is also performed by "trusted" but curious system users. Indicators include unusual system access activity during off-hours.

- *Shoulder Snooping*—direct visual observation of monitor displays to obtain information necessary for gaining system access. "Sticky" notes used to record account and password information, password entry screens that do not mask the typed text, and "loitering" opportunities combine for successful shoulder snooping.

Scavenging

- *Dumpster Diving*—accessing discarded trash to obtain passwords and other data, such as system administrator printouts of user logs and "sticky" notes in the office trash. Indicators of a problem would be a noted increase of successful accesses from the norm.
- *Browsing*—usually semiautomated scanning of large quantities of unprotected data to obtain clues as to how to achieve access to protected data. The information available is open to a general class of trusted users and is assumed to be safe, but it can give clues to passwords (e.g., spouse's name).

Spamming. Overloading a system with incoming messages or other traffic to cause a system crash or to open system access "holes" as the system crashes. This is the favorite way to launch a denial of service attack, and all systems attached to the Internet are especially vulnerable.

Tunneling. Any digital attack that attempts to get "under" a security system by accessing very low machine-level commands or functions such as executing "root" or operating system "privileged" instructions that control all computer activity. Such commands control the computer at its most primitive level and can be used to bypass security controls. Tunneling attacks often occur by creating a system "emergency" that causes the system to "reboot" or initialize, at which time the perpetrator seizes control. Often, perpetrators are aware of and exploit "backdoors" left by developers for debugging purposes

Unintentional Threats

The next category, unintentional threats, addresses equipment and software malfunctions and how well the e-business system handles human error. This category of threats goes directly to the generalized problem the IT industry has with quality and reliability of software. As discussed in Chapter 2, software is the vulnerable underbelly of computing, and unpredictable software is often the first avenue of exploitation by hackers or others wishing to seize control of a computer and its e-business processes. Premeditated attacks aside, unpredictable and unreliable software also pose considerable risk as a cause of system downtime and the loss of on-line availability during periods of business processing.

Comprehensive testing of all software to reduce the likelihood of software defects and extensive testing of the system's ability to successfully handle human error is essential to preventing this type of threat.

- *Equipment Malfunction*—hardware operates in an abnormal, unintended mode, destroying data and preventing normal business operations until it is fixed. Often peripheral equipment, such as printers and storage devices, are more vulnerable than computers because of their more mechanical nature.

- *Software Malfunction*—the dreaded "glitch" or "bug" that results in system lockup, loss of data, loss of computing capability, and loss of business activity until the software is analyzed for causing the defect and is corrected.

- *Human Error and Backdoors in Code*—system access, usually to the "privileged" instruction set of the operating system, can be used to override or bypass security controls and checks. While categorized as human error, in reality backdoors are deliberately built into operating systems and other software to allow programmers to directly access powerful operating system "privileged" instructions that will allow them to overcome emergency problems. Anyone who has knowledge of a "backdoor" and has the requisite skill can seize the operating system of any computer whenever he or she wishes and bypass all security controls. This is a gaping security hole that can be exploited by anyone with access, the knowledge of an operating system, and the ability to write "root" and/or "privileged instruction code."

- *User or Operator Error*—the inability of software to "gracefully" process an inadvertent or deliberately created error condition experienced during normal operations. This is the result of not adequately testing the software against the problems that may be created by an improperly trained operator or user or those who would "play" with the system. In the military this is known as a failure to make the system "sailor-proof," referring, of course, to the temptation of bored folks on the midnight shift to "play" with a system to see how it will respond.

Physical Threats

This last category deals with the familiar "acts of nature" that threaten the infrastructure systems supporting e-business computing.

- *Fire Damage*—computer environments are highly susceptible to fire because of the high concentration of electrical equipment. Electrical fires destroy not only through heat but also through the generation of toxic gases caused by the combustion of PVC cable insulation and wire covering. Locating computing equipment in cramped, out-of-the-way, and poorly ventilated "wiring closets" contributes to the likelihood of a fire and delays their discovery. Many systems can often be found in basements next to furnaces and fuel storage areas.

- *Water Damage*—physical destruction due to water coming into contact with computing equipment. Computers are often located in the lower floors of buildings, where seepage can occur due to water leakage or due to fire fighting in higher parts of the building. The presence of water will often be discovered only when it comes into contact with the electrical wiring of the computer. Computers housed in regular office space are usually vulnerable to sprinkler systems being used as the primary fire suppression method.

- *Power Loss*—computer or vital communications and support equipment, such as air-conditioning, fail due to a lack of electrical power. All e-business capability may be lost until power is restored. Files and in-process processing may be lost. Computers that are dependent on aboveground power lines are particularly vulnerable.

- *Civil Disorder or War*—destruction of computing capability due to civil unrest or regional wars. Of special concern to multinational companies.

There are endless permutations and combinations of the technical and physical threats just listed. The actual manifestation of each threat depends on many factors, including the complexity of the e-business application and the number of different software packages and hardware components making up the application. The manifestation of threats also depends on the care with which the underlying software was created, tested, and documented. With regard to the threat to communications, the number of possible penetration paths is becoming exponential as the Internet continues to grow.

Without doubt, the greatest challenge facing an organization pursuing an e-business strategy is the task of keeping up-to-date with the ever-increasing number of technical threats and how to formulate and apply protective strategies in such a dynamically changing environment.

While physical threats and solutions are considered well known, an element of caution is advised because of the existence of "unknown" business dependencies that have grown up in the era of client-server and Internet operations. Organizations not only must guard their own physical computer infrastructure against "acts of nature" but also must be prepared to continue operations in an emergency should physical harm beyond their control befall computing infrastructure components. This calls for proactive and realistic continuity of operations plans that are periodically exercised with all business partners and kept current to reflect changing e-business configurations and processing dependencies.

Special Threats Posed by the Internet

E-business as an operational and economic reality has "legs" because of the Internet. The World Wide Web has provided communications concepts, protocols, and an infrastructure to enable a much broader *reach* for both business and government activities. Coupled with the personal computer (PC) and messaging systems, the Internet has allowed an explosion in communications around which entirely new business models are being built. Business to business (B2B) and business to customer (B2C) models have been quickly followed by government initiatives to create government to citizen (G2C) and citizen to government (C2G) models. Each of these interactive models depends on the Internet to provide the backbone infrastructure to communicate anywhere in the world 24 x 7.

The financial stakes involved in having reliable and secure Internet processing are enormous. Forrester Research estimates that worldwide B2C revenues topped $100 billion in 2001, while a separate report by eMarketer estimates that B2B revenues reached nearly $500 billion. While these numbers represent a mere fraction of total domestic economic activity, the major thrust for the future of business has been determined. The ubiquity of PCs and Internet access means that successful digital business models will emerge, the dot-com crash of 2000 notwithstanding. As these business models evolve, dependency on the Internet will grow in the extreme. Many technology executives believe that someday soon we will live in a truly digital world transformed by Internet technology. We will come to see the Internet protocol embedded with the uniform product code in and on everything we purchase—our cars, appliances, even supermarket products—to form a virtual "bubble" of information surrounding our lives. The purpose? To allow business to anticipate and address our needs as consumers. Also, mobile commerce will be possible through wireless networking, and this will expand the "bubble" of information far beyond anything known today.

Whether such a vision is desirable from a privacy and individual freedoms perspective is debatable, but clearly unacceptable threats to either privacy or freedoms will exist if adequate security controls are not implemented to "make safe" future manifestations of the vision. From a strictly business perspective, such systems will need to be secure in order to avoid economic losses and major corporate embarrassment.

To understand the security issues surrounding business and government use of the Internet, its origins and intended use must be recalled. When it was created nearly 30 years ago, the Internet was a collaborative effort between industry, government, and academia. It was designed to be an open, borderless medium for communicating and sharing research information. It was designed to be expandable and to survive natural or artificial catastrophes by using "packet switching" technologies. It was not programmed with security features since open sharing of information was the design objective. *It was not intended for sensitive commercial or government use.* Yet we find that business and government are both deeply committed to the Internet regardless of its inherent inability to provide even a modicum of security beyond enhanced survivability. Both the IT industry and Internet users are playing security catch-up and it is late in the game.

Since the underlying design of the Internet is to facilitate the easy access and exchange of information, it is inherently public. This is simultaneously the Internet's greatest strength and its greatest weakness, especially when it is used as an access method to sensitive information and business processes or when it is used as a method for transmitting confidential data. Unless someone erects barriers around the content they place on the web, the material is accessible to all comers. Although barriers can be made to work, they run counter to the whole idea of openness. If information is sensitive and should not be easily accessible, why put it on the web at all? Why not mail it to a select list of people or use secured dedicated data links?

In reality, business and government are attempting to accommodate conflicting e-business demands using a *flawed* communications medium. The Internet is great for projecting the image of a citizen-friendly and open government even though using it may compromise personal data. It is great for presenting a product line to the cyber-consumer in the comfort of the home even though financial transactions are vulnerable to eavesdropping and exploitation. It appears to be great for providing on-line 24 x 7 access to critical business processes but not until the infrastructure is sufficiently robust to not suffer damaging system outages.

The Hacker's View

To fully understand the security shortcomings of the Internet, it is helpful to view it through the eyes of a "hacker" or a professional industrial espionage agent (hacker-spy).

First, the Internet is unbelievably large in terms of addressable connections. For example, the number of logical connections of a single 32 bit machine is 65,536, and the Internet, which is composed of thousands of 32 bit machines, exists for the sole purpose of making connections.

Second, a hacker or hacker-spy, depending on his or her motivation and the purpose for the hack, will depend on the following "facts of Internet life":

- Networks contain homogeneous components with incompatibilities that are easy to exploit.
- Users choose utility over security—meaning that security controls are not to impede access or productivity.
- Firewalls can be penetrated and require daily maintenance to be effective.
- Host systems behind firewalls generally have weak security.
- Virus detection software is always behind the power curve.
- Automated tracing software is not up to the demands of the on-line business environment.
- There exist innumerable intermediate host systems that can be used as "zombies" to overwhelm a target system.
- Social engineering tricks still work well.
- Denial of service scenarios are plentiful, available to download, and easy to use.

Additionally, the origin of an attack may often be difficult to determine. By all appearances, it may seem that an attack is coming from a single point in the network aimed directly at you (Exhibit 3.2). But more likely, to protect the originator, the attack is coming from a single point(s) that has been commandeered by the originating attacker to run the attack software (Exhibit 3.3). This is usually unknown to the owner of the commandeered computer. Finally, in a denial of service attack, hundreds or even thousands of computers can be commandeered to simultaneously submit requests for service, thus overwhelming the target system (Exhibit 3.4). The systems involved in the attack are acting like "zombies" carrying out the programmed instructions of the hacker all at the same time. Many times, a denial of service attack provides the planting of surreptitious software to be used by the hacker at a later time. Also, as the target system begins to "fall apart" under the attack, many system safeguard secrets may become known and may be compromised by the hacker.

Relying on these "facts of Internet life" and the ways in which attacks can be camouflaged, hackers commonly employ the following popular methodology to penetrate and compromise e-business systems and its sensitive proprietary data:

Step 1. Hack a remote site to launch the attack

Step 2. Scan college research web sites

Step 3. Find out who they are doing research for—your corporation

Step 4. Plant "sniffer" software to capture passwords

Step 5. Get user ID and password of a researcher

Step 6. Act like a user and enter your corporate system—your firewall will allow this because it is a permissible access

Step 7. Plant software to gather data even when hacker is not on-line

Step 8. Retrieve gathered (stolen) data

Step 9. Export it, sell it, and use it

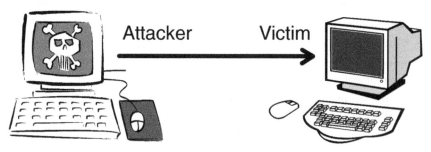

Exhibit 3.2   Appearance of an Attack

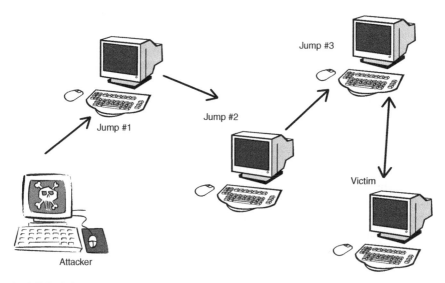

Exhibit 3.3   Reality of an Attack

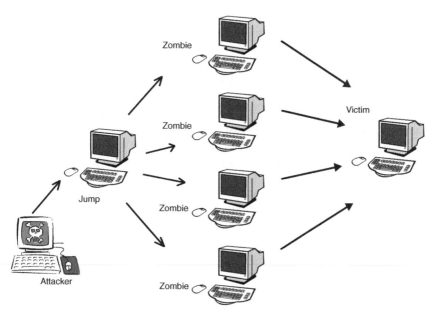

Exhibit 3.4   Distributed Attacks

As if this situation were not bad enough, hackers have joined together to combine and improve attack strategies and publish them in "script" form on the Internet for anyone to use.

While the Internet has expanded the reach of corporations and government beyond anything imaginable a decade ago, it is nevertheless a dangerous place to conduct business. Now that the Internet is essentially built and being used, the task of securing it remains. It is as if a superhighway has been constructed through the high mountains. It has been opened to traffic, which is steadily increasing, and suddenly it is realized that "guardrails" would be a good idea.

THE GUIDING PRINCIPLES OF PROTECTION

Before examining specific *integrity, confidentiality, and availability and reliability* "best practices" that can be used in an attempt to counter the threats of the previous section, the guiding principles of protection must be presented. Whether the challenge is to secure a "legacy" mainframe environment, an Internet-dependent e-business, or a stand-alone PC, there are fundamental protection concepts around which security should be built. The following six principles of protection, when properly mixed and matched, provide a "defense in depth" that can prevent, detect, and allow the timely recovery from almost any security incident.

Principle #1: Integrity.   This principle of protection includes controls placed on the e-business system and supporting infrastructure systems to ensure completeness, accuracy, consistency, and confidentiality of information, software, communications, and processing results. Controls are also used to assure that stored information cannot be tampered with, thus becoming accidentally misleading or deliberately fraudulent.

Integrity controls extend to all steps of a business transaction, from data collection and entry to final output preparation and presentation for use. For each transaction and information flow through a system and between systems, potential sources for error introduction must be identified. At key points in each flow, specific data verification and validation checks should be made and copies of the data made for backup and process recovery purposes. For example, during a long and involved process, intermediate results should be generated, captured, and stored using a checkpoint and restart utility. This allows for the efficient restarting of the process should a system outage occur. Rather than losing many minutes or hours of processing, the program can be restarted at the nearest checkpoint using the stored intermediate results. *Integrity* is also assured by placing validation and verification checks on sensitive or valuable data being input to a system or when communicated between systems.

Protection against data and file contamination is assured by the proper combination of identification and controlled access technique (see principles #3 and #4) coupled with a clearly defined and enforced set of rules covering the processing permissions granted to a user after gaining access to a file or software program. Permissions include the ability to "read/write," "read only," "write only," "execute," "append," and other restrictive limits. Such permissions are usually decided after analyzing the authorized work requirements of an employee or business partner once they are granted access to a system, information, or software program.

Integrity of a communications signal is assured by the liberal use of error detection techniques such as "hashing" methods to highlight when data or "packets" have been lost or changed during transmission.

The *integrity* and confidentiality of the contents of a transmission are assured through the use of encryption techniques. Encryption can be implemented in hardware and/or software.

Traditional encryption methods employ "keys," which are kept secret to all but the transmitter and the recipient of the transmission. Using a "key," messages are scrambled and made unintelligible to any recipient not possessing the same "key" to unscramble the message. This technique has been used with military and diplomatic systems since the time of the Romans. But as the volume of sensitive automated transmissions has grown, traditional encryption has become very difficult to administer because it requires the secure transporting and storing of many, many "keys." As the age of digital communications became mainstream, the old way of scrambling messages would not do. A new method was needed for millions of people to communicate in private and with the cyberspace equivalent of an authenticating physical signature. The solution to the problem of traditional encryption was to *split the key*. This has become known as public key cryptography.

This revolutionary new technique lets each person have his or her own mathematically related "key pair"—a public "key" to be distributed freely and a private "key" to hold closely. To transmit a confidential message, the sender gets the "public key" of the intended recipient. Using the recipient's "public key," the message is scrambled—now even the sender cannot decode the message. Only the recipient can unscramble the message using the second or "private key." Since a secret trapdoor is built into the message, the "private key" acts as a latch that springs open the trapdoor and lets the holder of the "private key" unscramble and read the message. No more worries about transporting secret "keys." This same technique can be used to authenticate the sender of a message and acts as a *digital signature*.

The support organization needed to administer this scheme is known as PKI—public key infrastructure. While less costly to administer than traditional encryption, PKI still requires considerable investment in time and effort to implement and administer successfully. Traditional encryption and PKI will solve data integrity and confidentiality problems associated with the communications of transactions and other sensitive data, but both must be carefully planned and budgeted for ongoing expenses.

When applied to the communications medium of the Internet, the use of public key encryption provides a "virtually" secured transmission path. Known as virtual private networks (VPNs), they provide the equivalent of a dedicated transmission line for sensitive information using the Internet.

Software *integrity* is a function of the quality assurance practiced during development and the amount of testing conducted before release of the software to production or sales status. Once software is in actual production, control techniques must be utilized that can discover if the code has been changed or tampered with since last considered "clean." Typically, this is accomplished by simply conducting a "bit" count of the stored program to determine if anything has been added or deleted. If there has been a change, there should be documentation authorizing such a change and certifying that proper testing was conducted and completed successfully.

Software *integrity* is a major operational overhead expense when done correctly. For software to possess integrity, there are multiple IT management control practices that must be enforced during the process of software development and then maintained during the life of the software. These IT control practices are discussed at length in Chapters 4 and 6.

Hardware *integrity* is assured by taking configuration and physical security precautions that guarantee system availability. Such precautions include duplicate system components at points of critical failure and the redundant posting of data to parallel storage devices that are individually powered. Separate power sources and uninterruptable power supplies are required when continuous on-line processing cannot be disrupted. These integrity actions deal with the overall soundness of the e-business system's supporting infrastructure, the operational environment of "supply chain" business partners, and the employees and contractors staffing the system complex.

A final element of *integrity* is the trustworthiness of the people who program, operate, and use the e-business system to conduct business. Keeping in mind the Computer Security Institute and Federal Bureau of Investigation caution that the majority of security breaches originate from inside an organization, this aspect of *integrity* takes on great significance. Because of this reality, human resource specialists and traditional personnel security professionals must become more involved in recruitment and in observing employee behavior after hiring. Monitoring and observing personnel behavior, however, is a subject of great sensitivity—one that can affect employee relations and the reputation of a corporation as a desirable place to work. It is interesting to note that in most of the contemporary cases of government espionage, early significant indicators of problems have generally gone unnoticed. Indicators such as the ability of individuals to live beyond their means with no visible source of legitimate additional income or irregular behavior, such as drug abuse, had gone unnoticed. These are behaviors that go beyond the competence of IT managers to notice or, when seemingly small infractions are observed, there is a reluctance to act for fear of disrupting what appears to be an otherwise functioning employee.

Depending on the damage an individual IT user employee can do to an organization, there should be graduated levels of background checks, bonding, lifestyle checks, and separation of duties to govern hiring decisions and operational duty assignments. While some perpetrators of computer crime are motivated by the traditional temptations of money, sex, drugs, and revenge, there are those motivated by the "hacker code." "Hacker" profiles are under development, and this is an area that will increasingly require HR and IT management familiarization in the years ahead.

Principle #2: Isolation.   This principle of protection requires the construction of physical and electronic barriers between the sensitive elements of an e-business system and the other less sensitive support aspects of computer processing. These barriers enforce a separation of employee duties and/or computer processes deemed necessary to ensure the integrity of particular business activities and/or the confidentiality of sensitive data.

Before the computerization of business, many individual clerks routinely and repeatedly executed specific transaction processing steps and had their work validated by other personnel. For example, with a payroll system, clerk A would examine collected timesheets for completeness, clerk B might validate the authenticity of charge code, and the section supervisor would review and sign off on the "batched" time sheets for his or her area of responsibility. The time sheets would then be consolidated at the next higher organizational level, where additional checks and validations by professional administrative personnel would occur. Finally, all time sheets for the entire plant would be checked, recorded, and approved for payment by a finance official. Checks would then be cut and all accounts reconciled with the paying bank.

A typical payroll process may well have employed over a dozen separate processing steps and validation checks, each performed by a different clerk. This "separation of duties" ensured better accuracy, and it made fraud difficult by forcing a great deal of collusion. In a computerized business, however, the performance of separate checks and validations by different people has been slowly eliminated, consolidated, and consigned to the "software." Much of the integrity of the payroll process, and many other business processes for that matter, now depends on the efficacy of the software and the reviews by harried supervisors and clerks who were told "the new payroll software package will do the work." Automation has all too often compromised the traditional practice of "separation of duties" and with it the protection principle of *isolation*.

For the principle of *isolation* to be effective with e-business systems, the requirements for processing consistency and auditability must be accurately defined and incorporated into the design of the system. Just how an e-business system should satisfy the criteria of consistency and auditability is well documented in the audit community. Software designers familiar with generally acceptable accounting practices know the necessary checks to build into systems so that sufficient validation and verification actions occur during the processing of transactions. In Chapter 6, the stakeholders to an e-business systems design are identified and representatives of the audit community are included on the list. Creating physical and electronic barriers to prevent unauthorized access to sensitive data and computer processes also ensures isolation (see principle #4).

At the level of the computer's operating system, barriers are constructed by "privileged" machine-level commands that are used for isolating elements of the system's resources from the average user. These "privileged" commands themselves are "off limits" to all except the operating systems programmer and are supposed to be protected. However, as previously discussed, "backdoors" often exist, and where this is true all security can be negated.

With the exception of "backdoor" operating system exploitation, effective isolation is only as good as the security system's ability to control access to system resources and e-business applications and files. Controlling access in turn depends on the ability to identify all system resources and system users desiring to access those resources and systems to accomplish their business function.

Principle #3: Identification, Authentication, and Nonrepudiation. A successful e-business strategy depends largely on the effective implementation of the protection principle of *identification* and *authentication*. Unless all users, software, system resources, business process software and files, and all hardware capable of accessing the system and each other can be identified, there can be no controlling access. Without controlled access, sensitive elements of the overall system cannot be isolated from nonsensitive elements, and integrity cannot be assured.

Identification and *authentication*, as a protection principle, applies to all aspects of the computing environment, is fundamentally essential to security, and poses a formidable administrative challenge for most organizations. The *identification* of all objects (i.e., software, files, system resources, etc.) in a system and all the subjects (i.e., users, programs, etc.) seeking access to objects, is central to the construction of access lists and tables that control such access and then limit processing activity (i.e., read, write, execute, etc.) once access has been granted. Identification is usually accomplished by assigning a unique number to an entity. For example, employees are assigned a unique "user ID" during in-processing. This number is usually used for all human resource functions during the person's term of employment. It is also used to identify an employee to the computer-processing environment for various security purposes.

Authentication is the process of determining whether someone or something is who or what it is declared to be. The most common form of *authentication* is the use of passwords. But since passwords are easily compromised, other more sophisticated techniques often must be employed. These techniques include:

- badges (i.e., photo and smart card technology)
- biometric devices such as fingerprint readers
- personal data given during a sign-on session in addition to a password (i.e., wife's maiden name)
- computing device with "embedded" ID code (i.e., token)

Such approaches are generally based on something a person knows (password), something a person is (fingerprint), or something a person has (badge). Each of these techniques authenticates a person as unique and authorized to have access to certain objects after a confirmation check of an authorized access list or table.

Since the protection principle of *identification* and *authentication* extends to the physical arena, these same techniques are often used to control access to facilities or to sensitive areas within a facility.

When communicating business or other sensitive data, there is often an additional requirement to be able to prove that a transaction indeed took place. *Nonrepudiation* is the affirmation, with a high degree of confidence, of the identity of a sender (or recipient) of a digital message using digital signature procedures. It is intended to protect against any subsequent attempt by the signer (or recipient) to deny the authenticity of a transaction. A digital signature is the electronic equivalent of a written signature, providing evidence that the original document is authentic, unaltered, not forged, and *nonrepudiable.* For e-business applications, digital signatures almost always use the public key strategy and PKI structure.

For an Internet-based business, then, the task of identifying and authenticating all subjects requesting system access requires that ever more sophisticated and costly techniques be used as technological advances are made. Communicating business transactions over the Internet opens the e-business system to an entire world of the curious, the mischievous, and those bent on fraudulent activity.

The task of identification and authentication, however, is very difficult to accomplish because of the decentralized, distributed, and mobile nature of today's evolving computer environment. To be secure, a system must be able to accurately identify thousands of users, originating from hundreds of locations, and thousands of pieces of computing equipment running the gamut from PCs to laptops to wireless access devices. Each user, from whatever equipment source, needs to access scores of software programs, each of which in turn requires access to files and stored data. To effectively control access, all rosters of users and inventories of equipment must be accurate, physical locations known, software systems known and certified to be "clean" of unauthorized modification, and all network connections known and under the control of a qualified systems administrator.

Finally, all users must be *authenticated* to the system, confirmed to be authorized to carry out the business functions they are requesting, and with certain transactions need mechanisms to make then *nonrepudiable.*

All of these requirements demand an amount of internal administrative support that is generally neither understood nor appreciated by most business managers. Adequate staffing is imperative if this fundamental protection principle is to be performed effectively. It cannot be just another task expected of an already overworked systems administrator.

Principle #4: Controlled Access.   The protection principle of controlled access is essential for assuring that unauthorized access to system resources and e-business applications does not occur. Controlling access is necessary for attaining and maintaining the degree of *isolation* deemed appropriate to safeguard computing processes and data files that are critical to the e-business. Controlled access cannot occur unless the principle of *identification* and *authentication* has been successfully implemented for all entities and computing components of the e-business processing environment, including partners in the supply chain.

Access should also be controlled to facilities and workspaces where computing platforms, terminals, and workstations reside. Lock, keys, badges, biometric devices, and visual recognition can be used to *identify* and *authenticate* entry into workspaces.

Determinations as to who should have access to a physical workspace are made based on examining the necessary work assignments of the individual. This is referred to as "need to go" and is considered a first-line security defense.

Depending on the sensitive or critical nature of work tasks being performed in the workspace, electronic access controls are employed to govern who can have access to what e-business applications and files and who can execute computer processes or modify data. This is referred to as "need to know" and "need to execute." Controls may also be placed on the ability of an individual user or computer process to direct outputs to distance locations.

Access is controlled through the input, by an individual or a requesting computer process, of a valid unique identifier and some form of authentication code. Authenticators may be typed or may be incorporated into devices that can be read by hardware such as an ATM card or a token of some sort.

Once an individual or computer process has been identified, authentication takes place against an access table or list to determine authorized rights to use system resources. Depending on what has been authorized, permission to read, write, execute, and so on is granted or denied.

It must be remembered that all of the software that performs the access-controlling task is considered to be a security support program operating under the control of the host computer's operating system. In addition to any defects in the access control software that may be open to exploitation, a successful penetration of an operating system will almost certainly negate the effectiveness of any access control scheme. For example, passwords and authentication codes are among the first targets of anyone seizing control of an operating system using known or unknown flaws or the presence of any "backdoors."

When communicating between networks, and especially when using the Internet as the principal e-business communications medium, "firewalls" are an essential implementation of an organization's access control policy. Firewalls are hardware and software systems specially designed to grant or deny network access attempts from other internal networks and the Internet. Within heavily networked corporate environments, a firewall should also be utilized to enforce access policy between distributed elements of the Intranet as well as just being used to block attempts from the Internet.

Access control of mobile computing components such as laptops and wireless devices pose special challenges to the e-business environment. While firewalls can be "tailored" to protect the corporate system from undesirable mobile access, two other significant threats exist. First, since the exact location of the mobile component is always in doubt, authentication of the user as authorized becomes critical to having some assurance that proper physical "handling" of outputs will occur. Second, since mobile computing components, especially wireless devices, are open to electronic eavesdropping, encryption is essential if sensitive data are being transmitted. Encryption, however, does not protect eavesdropping while working with the laptop at a remote location—only when data are in transit.

Corporate policies should be developed as to whether sensitive data, such as R & D, contract bid data, costing data, and customer-sensitive data should ever be allowed to be kept, processed, or communicated from mobile computing devices. Of course, the greatest violators of such a policy would undoubtedly be the corporate executive team—for whom an exception can always be made.

Principle # 5: Surveillance.   The protection principle of surveillance, while seeming to be passive in nature, may actually bring an aggressive element to the security equation.

Since the vast majority of computer security actions are recommended and implemented based on the *possible* existence of theoretical threats impacting your e-business system, only proactive *surveillance* of the system provides "hard" evidence of what is actually occurring in the workaday environment for which safeguard actions must be taken.

Surveillance, as a principle of protection can be conducted in three ways—around-the-machine, within-the-machine, and within-the-network.

Around-the-machine *surveillance* treats the computer and the e-business software application as a "black box." Inputs are created, introduced into the system or software "black box," processed, and then output from the "box." Auditors judge the efficacy of the processing that occurred within the box by comparing the output against previously prepared results arrived at by using the input and independently calculating what the results should be. The limitations of this approach to *surveillance* are severe when dealing with on-line applications, so more automated methods are needed.

Around-the-machine *surveillance* can also take the form of accounting reviews and security assessments to determine if the manually processing side of a system is being conducted correctly and honestly.

The within-the-machine approach introduces the need for special audit software to monitor and build an accounting of system activities for independent review by the audit staff. With this approach, attempts are made to record actions of the business application software, thus looking into the "black box" to determine what is actually transpiring as the e-business application executes its on-line processing.

Within-the-machine *surveillance* provides a way for the auditor to confirm the effectiveness of integrity controls within the business application software by submitting test accounts and test transactions to see how well the software is performing. Fictitious transactions can also be created and then processed by the system to ascertain the effectiveness of controls to prevent fraudulent or abusive activity by employees, customers, or business partners. Within-the-machine *surveillance* has an associated overhead that can sometimes interfere with processing throughput times.

Within-the-network *surveillance* invokes the use of intrusion detection technologies to monitor, in real time, access attempts by or to the various networked systems making up the enterprise Intranet or the supply chain Extranet. Intrusion detection systems (IDS) provide many benefits to security control implementation efforts because an IDS reports on what is actually happening within the networked environment, including accesses coming from the Internet. Such information can be used to lend a degree of factual evidence to the whole proposition of security policy formulation, security safeguard selection, implementation, and maintenance of a secured processing environment. Until now, security decisions concerning protection mechanisms have been based largely on the supposition that something could happen because it had happened to others. Anecdotal evidence of security incidents and vulnerabilities were presented and safeguard actions were taken based on the inference that the same type of incident could adversely affect your business. This contributed to two problems, overkill and underkill. *Overkill* occurred when unnecessary controls were placed on the processing system and business productivity suffered. This has not happened often, but it has occurred. *Underkill*, conversely, is very likely to occur because a lack of "hard" evidence that a system is under attack contributes to the undercapitalization of security initiatives and a fragmentation of efforts.

With the use of IDS, supposition can be either dismissed or reinforced based on the gathering of evidence of what is really happening at the e-business system and network levels. Intrusion detection systems not only reveal information about outside attempts to gain unauthorized access to e-business processing, but also can report on what "trusted" employees are attempting to access within the company. Chapter 5 is dedicated to a deeper discussion of the IDS concept and its powerful importance to the securing of e-business systems.

Within the allowable range of privacy regulations and intelligent customer and employee relations, the use of IDS to conduct network and host-server *surveillance* can reap immediate benefits. By helping to determine the magnitude of threat to e-business operations from unauthorized access attempts, immediate corrective actions can be taken such as redefining "firewall" access rules to reflect a "new" more stringent or less stringent security policy based on demonstrated need. This is turn can propel the security undertaking forward with a new sense of realism and meaning.

Principle # 6: Incident Response and Recovery. The last principle of protection is the creation of well-thought-out plans for responding to detected security incidents that will limit the extent of damage and speed recovery of the e-business system back to full operational efficiency. These efforts are within the scope of corporate "crisis management" programs and should not be delegated solely to the IT department to prepare.

Detection of a potentially damaging security incident may occur in many ways. A system may crash due to a virus, a communications or internet service provider (ISP) may experience an outage and go down, business applications software may fail, and so forth. Whatever the cause of the incident, detection should occur as early as possible so that an impact analysis can determine the appropriate preplanned emergency response and recovery actions.

Incident response and recovery, as a principle of protection, must encompass all aspects of the e-business system, both automated and manual elements and up and down the supply chain. This means that the complete flow of transactions, data, and goods or services to be delivered must be known so that analysis of the incident can be quickly performed and impacted areas identified. At a minimum, this requires that all critical data flows and processing paths be fully documented and kept up-to-date. Incident notification "trees" and specific recovery activities are based on an intimate knowledge of how the e-business system and its supporting infrastructure systems are configured, who is responsible for what, and what recovery actions are to be taken when, where, and by whom.

To be most effective, *incident response and recovery* must be designed into the very fabric of the e-business system. It is not enough to merely back up files periodically and hope for the best. Systems must be designed to be "fault-tolerant"—designed to survive the security incident with little or no noticeable impact on operations and no loss of data.

Incident response and recovery requires that significant resources be dedicated to plan preparation and to the daily maintenance required for effective use. These are sizable efforts, but they are absolutely essential if the objectives of minimizing damage and speeding business reconstitution are to be realized.

"BEST PRACTICE" PREVENTION, DETECTION, AND COUNTERMEASURES AND RECOVERY TECHNIQUES

This section identifies the "best practices" being commonly used to prevent and detect the technical security threats previously catalogued. It also includes proven countermeasure and recovery techniques.

Malicious Actions

Malicious Software—Safeguards

- *Virus—Safeguards*
    - *Prevention*—limit unnecessary connectivity and downloads from the Internet. Enforce mandatory access policies using traditional access control techniques. Use "firewalls" to limit external network access to system resources. Inventory and control all software and versions being run on mainframes, servers, PCs, workstations, and laptops. Use only authorized

(i.e., known) media for the loading of data and software. Educate users not to "open" attachments or run programs from sources unknown to them.

- *Detection*—monitor for changes in file sizes or date and time stamp since last authorized software modification. Look for unexpected or frequent system failures, slow running or starting of computers, and unexplained reductions in available memory.

- *Countermeasures/Recovery*—use antivirus scanners to look for known viruses and antivirus monitors to look for virus-related behaviors. Attempt to determine source of infection, contain the spread, and issue an alert to all system users.

- *Worm—Safeguards*

  - *Prevention*—limit connectivity and downloads from the Internet. Enforce access control policies using traditional access control techniques. Use "firewalls" to limit network access to system resources. Inventory and control software versions being run on mainframes, servers, PCs, laptops, and workstations. Use only authorized media (i.e., known) for the loading of data and software.

  - *Detection*—computer is slow during start-up and slows while running. Look for unexpected or frequent failures and unexplained reductions in available memory. Monitor for changes in file sizes or date and time stamp of last authorized software modification.

  - *Countermeasures/Recovery*—attempt to determine source of the attack, attempt to contain damage within the host network, and issue an alert to other networks.

- *Trojan Horse—Safeguards*

  - *Prevention*—since user cooperation in running the host program is necessary for the "hidden" code to execute, users must be educated to not run programs from sources unknown to them.

  - *Detection*—computer is slow during start-up and slows while running. There may be unexpected failures while running previously reliable code.

  - *Countermeasures/Recovery*—enforce policy against running foreign programs. File and program size should be frequently checked against last recorded authorized software or version release. Date and time stamp should also be checked. Determine software housing Trojan horse code, contain damage, and issue alerts to all networks, users, and system administrators.

- *Time Bomb—Safeguards*

  - *Prevention*—update and run antivirus software immediately after it is made available from the vendor.

  - *Detection*—correlate reported user problems to discover patterns indicating possible date- or time-related problems.

- *Countermeasures/Recovery*—identify source program containing time bomb and determine if there are other embedded time bombs. Contain damage and issue alert to users of the source software housing the time bomb.

- *Logic Bomb—Safeguards*

  - *Prevention*—limit connectivity and employ "firewalls" to reduce threats from outside sources. Enforce access controls on internal system accesses, possibly using "firewalls" in addition to traditional methods.

  - *Detection*—check software and file sizes frequently for unauthorized modifications. Correlate user problem reports indicating possible logic bomb experience.

  - *Countermeasures/Recovery*—identify source program containing logic bomb code and disable. Contain damage and issue alert to other source program users.

- *Rabbit—Safeguards*

  - *Prevention*—limit connectivity and employ "firewalls" to reduce threat from outside sources. Enforce traditional access controls internally within the corporate Intranet. Consider use of an internal "firewall."

  - *Detection*—check software and file sizes frequently for unauthorized modifications. Computers slow to start or slow while running may indicate that a runaway rabbit program is consuming system resources.

  - *Countermeasures/Recovery*—identify source program containing rabbit code and disable. Contain damage and issue alert to other users of the source program.

Spoofing—Safeguards

- *Spoofing—Safeguards*

  - *Prevention*—limit system level privileges to the minimum necessary to perform the computing functions required of each particular computer system. Update all software security "patches" as soon as received from the vendor.

  - *Detection*—monitor transaction logs of automated services processing on specific computer systems, scanning for behaviors unusual from those normally associated with the particular service.

  - *Countermeasures/Recovery*—disconnect the compromised automated service and computer system. Monitor access points at the network level. Scan for the next "spoof" in an attempt to trace back to the perpetrator.

- *Masquerade—Safeguards*

  - *Prevention*—strictly limit user access to network administrator command functions. Those used to manage network resources should be reserved only for the system administrator. Staff with at least two levels of network administrators, each with different privileges.

- *Detection*—correlate user identification with shift times or increased frequency of accesses. Correlate user command logs with network administrator command functions used during a specific time frame.

- *Countermeasures/Recovery*—change user passwords and authentication codes frequently. Use standard network administrator functions to capture access path ID and then trace back to perpetrator.

Scanning—Safeguards

- *Sequential Scanning—Safeguards*
  - *Prevention*—enforce effective organizational password policies. Make even system administrator access to password files difficult.
  - *Detection*—correlate user identification with shift times or anticipated work hours. Correlate user problem reports relevant to possible masquerades.
  - *Countermeasures/Recovery*—change entire password file or use honey pots to capture access path ID and then trace access path back to perpetrator. A honeypot is a fictitious system asset/file designed to attract intruders and then capture information about the intrusion.
- *Dictionary Scanning—Safeguards*
  - *Prevention*—enforce "robust" organizational password policies.
  - *Detection*—correlate user identification with shift times or anticipated work hours. Correlate user problem reports relevant to possible masquerades.
  - *Countermeasures/Recovery*—change entire password file or use honey pots to capture access path ID and then trace back to perpetrator.

Snooping—Safeguards

- *Digital Snooping—Safeguards*
  - *Prevention*—employ data encryption. Limit physical access to network nodes and communication links.
  - *Detection*—correlate user identification with shift times or anticipated work hours. Correlate user problem reports. Monitor network for intrusion attempts.
  - *Countermeasures/Recovery*—change encryption scheme. Use employee intrusion detection technology to identify perpetrators. Use honey pots to capture access path ID and then trace back to perpetrator.

- *Shoulder Surfing—Safeguards*
  - *Prevention*—limit physical access to computer areas and work areas where PCs and workstations are being used. Require frequent password changes by users. Mask passwords on computer screens.
  - *Detection*—correlate user identification with shift times or increased frequency of access. Correlate user command logs with administrator command functions used during a specific time frame.
  - *Countermeasures/Recovery*—change user password and use standard administrator functions to determine access point and then trace back to perpetrator.

Scavenging—Safeguards

- *Dumpster Diving—Safeguards*
  - *Prevention*—shred discarded hard copy, degauss magnetic media used to store sensitive information or log data. Enforce sensitive document accountability procedures and organizational destruction policies.
  - *Detection*—correlate user identification with shift times or anticipated work hours. Correlate user problem reports relevant to possible masquerades.
  - *Countermeasures/Recovery*—change entire password file or use audit tools to trace back to perpetrator.
- *Browsing—Safeguards*
  - *Prevention*—destroy discarded media. When on an open source network, disable ability to free-roam through the system. (Of course, many Internet applications are based on browsing, so sensitive business functions must be isolated from the portal function.)
  - *Detection*—correlate user identification with shift times or increased frequency of accesses. Correlate user command logs with administrator command functions.
  - *Countermeasures/Recovery*—change user password and use standard administrator functions to determine access point and then trace back to perpetrator.

Spamming—Safeguards

- *Prevention*—require authentication fields in all message traffic.
- *Detection*—monitor disk partitions, network connections for overfill conditions.
- *Countermeasures/Recovery*—analyze message headers to attempt trace back to perpetrator.

Tunneling—Safeguards

- *Prevention*—design security controls and audit capabilities into even the lowest level software, such as device drivers and shared libraries. Either the operating system is designed this way or it is not. Assume that it is not.
- *Detection*—audit for changes in date and time stamp of low-level system files or changes in sector and block counts for device drivers.
- *Countermeasures/Recovery*—"patch" or replace compromised device drivers to prevent repeated unauthorized access. Monitor suspected access points to attempt trace back to perpetrator.

Unintentional Threats

Equipment Malfunction—Safeguards

- *Prevention*—replication of entire e-business system including transactions, intermediate calculations, final results, and transmitted and stored data. This requires "parallel" processing systems and storage running at separate locations from separate power sources. Use with mission-critical on-line operations or for life-critical systems. In less critical situations, system components susceptible to mechanical failures may be duplicated to be brought on-line in emergencies. All memory should be backed up as frequently as is necessary to ensure a smooth and rapid recovery after an equipment failure. All equipment should be on an enforced preventive maintenance schedule.
- *Detection*—is primarily performed by running hardware diagnostic systems during normal operations and preventive maintenance.
- *Countermeasures/Recovery*—(1) parallel processing system running from separate power source, (2) on-site availability of critical processing components, (3) off-site availability of processing system configured for immediate use, (4) reciprocal processing agreements with business partners.

Software Malfunction—Safeguards

- *Prevention*—strictly enforced software version/release program, comprehensive testing (i.e., clean) and software designed to "degrade gracefully." Control access to software to prevent tampering or infection by virus, worms, and so on.
- *Detection*—software diagnostic tools to compare resident software to last "clean" copy according to version/release records.
- *Countermeasures/Recovery*—backing up last "clean" copy of software on separate storage device and having a "robust" operating system (i.e., designed

to gracefully handle software failures) will facilitate quick recovery. Activate contingency plan.

Human Error and Backdoors in Code—Safeguards

* *Prevention*—enforce defined software development and security testing policies for all in-house software efforts. Tightly control access to the operating system and double-team those who do have access in order to attain a degree of mutual surveillance and to reduce risk by forcing collusion.
* *Detection*—audit trails of "privileged instruction" usage tied to user identification logs.
* *Countermeasures/Recovery*—close backdoor (can usually be done only with a systems "patch" from the vendor). Attempt to monitor "privileged instruction" usage and trace back to offending program or user. Activate contingency plan.

User or Operator Error—Safeguards

* *Prevention*—require up-to-date operator instructions, enforce security training policies for users and operators. Enforce separation of programmer and operator duties.
* *Detection*—review audit trail of system transaction. Run audit software that attempts to carry out illegal actions.
* *Countermeasures/Recovery*—making back up copies of software and transaction data provides ability to recover should user or operator errors cause equipment malfunction. Activate contingency plan. See *Equipment Malfunction.*

Physical Threats

Fire Damage—Safeguards

* *Prevention*—off-site system replication, although costly, provides immediate backup capability for critical on-line or life critical systems. Properly designed and constructed computer space meeting fire insurance specifications. Enforce fire prevention "housekeeping" rules.
* *Detection*—on-site alarms to detect the by-products of combustion—under-floor alarms for electrical fire gases, and above-floor alarms for normal smoke.
* *Countermeasures/Recovery*—Halon gas or FM200 fire extinguishers mitigate damage to electrical equipment caused by water. Caution: Halon can be toxic

to humans in certain concentrations. Backup and COOP plans to provide guidance for speedy reconstitution of systems operations.

Water Damage—Safeguards

- *Prevention*—off-site system replication for critical on-line and life support systems. Placement of computer spaces above floodplain. Properly designed and constructed computer spaces to limit likelihood of ceiling leakage and equipped with under-floor drains.
- *Detection*—water detection devices.
- *Countermeasures/Recovery*—equip computer spaces with emergency drainage capabilities. Backup and COOP plans to provide guidance for speedy reconstitution of system operations.

Power Loss—Safeguards

- *Prevention*—off-site replication of critical systems. Dual or separate feeder lines for computers and communications equipment from different power grids.
- *Detection*—power level alert monitors.
- *Countermeasures/Recovery*—Uninterruptable power supplies (UPS). Full-scale standby power facilities for critical on-line and life support systems. Backup and COOP plans to provide guidance for speedy reconstitution of system operations.

Civil Disorder or War—Safeguards

- *Prevention*—off-site replication of critical systems. Tighten facility security and keep a low profile to prevent hostile targeting.
- *Detection*—deploy physical intrusion detection devices and work with local police "intelligence" network.
- *Countermeasures/Recovery*—harden site, employ stringent physical access restriction, and have riot contingency plans in addition to regular backup and COOP plans. Ship critical files to off-site (i.e., out of country) location daily.

Putting It All Together. Using Exhibit 3.1 to illustrate an unprotected e-business-processing environment, fundamental technical vulnerabilities have been identified and today's commonly employed safeguard techniques explained. Each of these techniques implements one or more of the six principles of protection previously covered.

Exhibit 3.5 depicts each of the following technical safeguards and where they would reside on the network:

- Virtual Private Networks (VPN)
- Intrusion Detection Systems (IDS)
- Virus Detection Software
- Honeypot System
- Encryption /Digital Signature & PKI
- Firewalls
- Certificate Authority
- Token/Smart Cards

Beginning in the upper left hand corner of Exhibit 3.5, the corporate network systems for R&D, Human Resources, Finance, and Order Processing are being protected at the workstation by *anti-virus software*, and by the use of *tokens/smart cards* to authenticate access by employees. Just below the workstations is a secured computer functioning as a *Certificate Authority* for digital signatures used within the company for internally encrypted transmissions and authenticated messaging.

In front of each individual corporate network, a *firewall* has been configured to control access to each network from internal corporate access attempts. These *firewalls* also act as a second "filter" for accesses that may have been able to get through the more permissive corporate firewall—seen at the center of the figure—whose primary function is to impose rather "open access" policies on traffic coming by way of the Internet. Directly below the internal *firewalls,* a bogus system known as a *honeypot* has been purposely constructed to attract illegal accesses so that information about perpetrators may be captured.

Just to the right of the honeypot, a systems management console is shown which is controlling both the corporate and internal *firewalls* and is managing the *intrusion detection system* and *anti-virus* software placed between the corporate firewall and the internal networks.

At the center of the figure is the corporate *firewall* acting as the first line of defense against unauthorized accesses via the Internet. Between the firewall and the Internet, "cloud" transmissions are being *encrypted* to create a virtual private network or *VPN.* Along all communication links, then, as long as the data remains encrypted, we have the security of a *VPN* using the public key encryption method. Facilitation of the public key encryption method, and an integral part of the public key infrastructure, or *PKI*, is the secured computer and console found in the lower right of the figure. This computer is functioning as a "trusted third party" *certificate authority* authenticating all parties of an encryption to each other and vouching for their digital signatures. This is occurring with all communications when a *VPN* has been established for purposes of transmitting sensitive data to and from any corporate system, business partner, or remote corporate user.

Below the corporate firewall and tapping into the communications link to the Internet is an ethical hacker, under contract to the corporation, to perform a

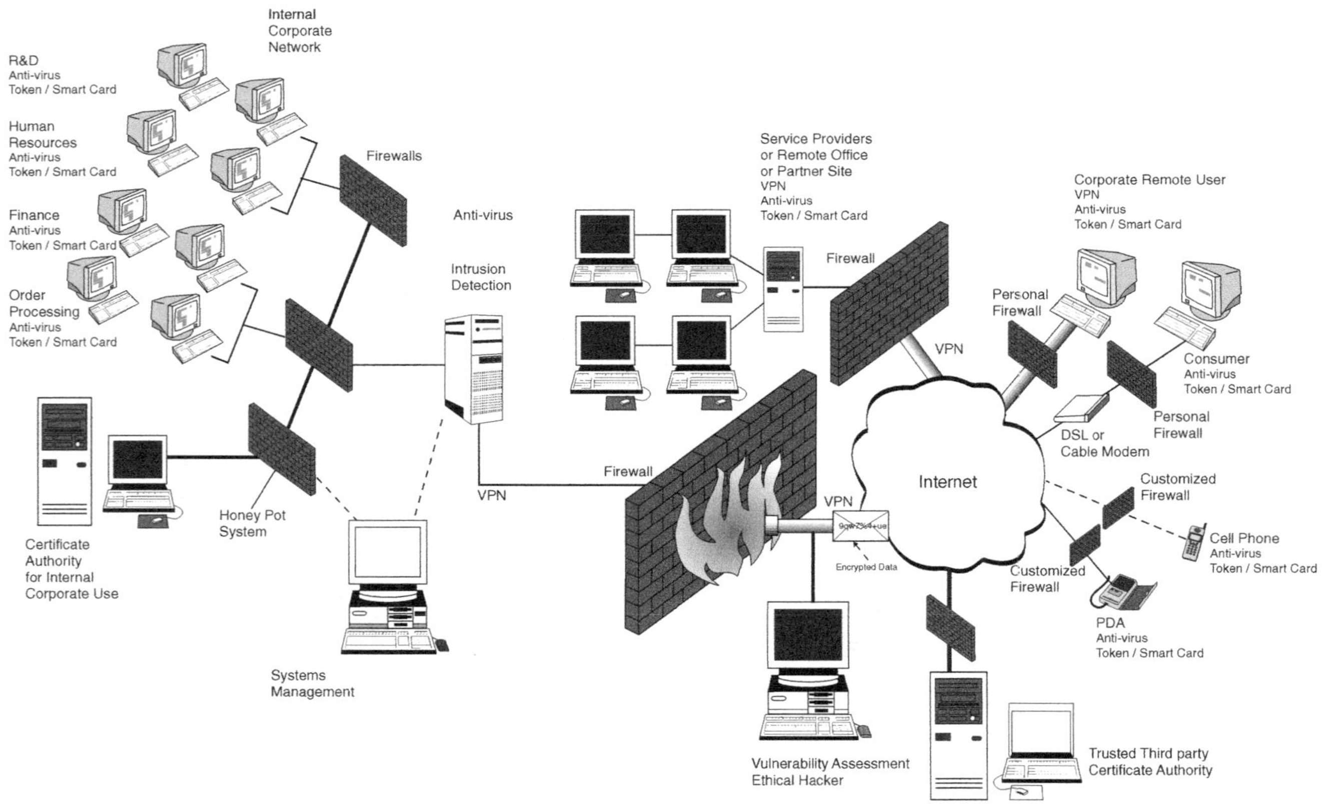

Exhibit 3.5 E-Business Security

vulnerability assessment by attempting to penetrate the secured corporate environment.

Directly above the corporate firewall, a properly secured service provider, remote office, or a business partner's site is depicted. They have the same security controls as the corporate environment and can be viewed as a "safe" partner with which to conduct e-business.

To the right of the Internet "cloud" the world of remote and mobile corporate users and the customer is depicted. Each is vulnerable to the same types of attacks as those directed at large corporate systems and each needs to take similar precautions even though they are probably not as visible nor as attractive a target. Extra procedural care must be taken, however, because the safeguard techniques used for remote and mobile users are not nearly as well evolved or tested as similar techniques used to protect corporate systems.

Chapter 4

Managing E-Business Systems and Security

INTRODUCTION

During the past decade, the use of information technology (IT) has shifted from its traditional role in backoffice accounting toward one that increasingly pervades and influences the fundamental core business activities of the corporation, government agency, or nonprofit organization through Internet-based on-line processing. Today, IT not only affects how the "core" business must be managed but also is greatly influencing how corporate resources are being allocated. For example, according to *Fortune* magazine, during calendar 2000 total spending by business on IT surpassed total spending on other capital goods.

Keeping with this trend, the business executive in recent years has been inundated with advice and theories regarding the promise of IT and how IT can be used, indeed must be used, for a company to compete and thrive. The latest *moniker* for all this technological progress has been e-business, with every step of the journey coming ever more quickly and with business executives being constantly cautioned against falling behind their competitors. Always the promise of essential "new" and mind-bending capabilities, never a mention of limitations and the often-experienced "blown" project estimate. Always talk of the strategic use of IT to dominate a market with the "killer" application, never a caution to check into a software vendor's reputation and dedication to testing and complete documentation. Always articles about exploiting the next technological breakthrough, never a warning that the IT staff may be becoming overwhelmed by complexity and how to tell if they are about to walk out the door.

Then, in 1997, corporate executives learned about the Y2K "date" problem and how long-term inattention and procrastination coupled with decades of undisciplined systems management and operation could threaten their company's very existence. It is said that "the devil is in the details," and the Y2K experience proved the statement to be true.

And now corporate executives are faced with the security threat to their "fledgling" e-business systems. While not tied to a "drop-dead" date, as was Y2K, when failures would definitely occur, security threats are open-ended and limited only by the day-to-day malignant interest of the perpetrator and the vigilance of the organization in protecting their e-business systems and other critical IT assets. If undisciplined systems management contributed to Y2K becoming the all-consuming obsession that it was, how much do the same undisciplined conditions contribute to the e-business security threat? If the "details" were not being attended to with regard to a well-known two-digit date field problem, what other "details" are not being attended to right now, today, tomorrow, and next year? If Y2K caused such an operational uproar and great unnecessary expense because of a previous lack of disciplined systems management, what must be done to remedy the management situation before security threats cause similar chaos and expense?

First, corporate executives must recognize that the challenge of bringing discipline to the use and management of IT, like it or not and for the foreseeable future, must be their responsibility. As previously stated, for many corporations, IT investments now exceed all other forms of capital investment, while information itself is coming to be seen not only as the "glue" that holds an enterprise together but also as central to the knowledge base that gives a competitive advantage. In short, management decisions concerning information and the technology that captures, processes, and delivers it are far too important to delegate very far from the executive suite. And until confidence returns that IT is being capably managed, the security aspects will need intimate executive oversight. This is not because everyone else is incompetent, but because for too long, critical IT decisions have been made without the appropriate level of involvement by those executives who legally run the corporation and are answerable to a variety of stakeholders and special interests for decisions that affect all aspects of a business. The importance and critical nature of such decisions have simply "crept up" on most organizations as the evolution of their IT usage has progressed.

According to Peter Drucker in *Management Challenges for the 21st Century*, change has become the norm and the job of executives is to lead change. "Being a change leader requires the willingness and ability to change what is already being done just as much as the ability to do new and different things. It requires policies and practices that make the present create the future"[1] In the case of the systems management problem, change leaders must change what is already being done (i.e., how IT is currently managed) if they hope to be able to do *new and different things.*

This is because the new and different things will almost certainly find their origins in IT and ways to exploit it.

Again, according to Drucker, "Whatever an enterprise does, both internally and externally, needs to be improved systematically and continually: the product or service, the production processes, marketing, technology, the training and development of people, and the use of information."

From Drucker's list, I would delineate and emphasize (1) those processes used in managing IT systems as a corporate resource, (2) the methods used to manage an e-business security program, and (3) the methods used to develop new

---

[1] Drucker, Peter F., *Management Challenges for the 21st Century* (New York: Harper-Business, 1999).

secured uses of IT. The first two topics are addressed in Part 2 and Part 3 of this chapter; the development of secured systems is covered separately in Chapter 6.

But how should a corporate executive act as a change leader seeking to take control of the IT future? What is required? What must executives undertake to improve the future tapestry of systems management required to assure the future security of their e-business systems?

The first order of business is for corporate executives to become familiar with some of the misconceptions concerning IT that have had an adverse influence on past uses of IT and its success in the business arena. The identification of some of the prevailing myths, half-truths, and previously uncritically analyzed assumptions about IT will equip executives to make better decisions concerning e-business systems and the environmental conditions needed for them to be operated in a secured fashion.

PART ONE: MISCONCEPTIONS AND QUESTIONABLE ASSUMPTIONS

Associated with the use of IT are stated and oftentimes implied expectations and assumptions that profoundly influence the course of systems development and the task of securing e-business applications and systems. These expectations and assumptions, if not understood for their fallacy and resulting adverse impact, can submit an organization to some very real dangers when pursuing an e-business agenda. Before addressing the fundamental management of e-business systems, the development of these systems, and the management program needed to secure and maintain the security of these systems, let us turn our attention to some of the misconceptions and poor assumptions that often lead IT projects astray.

Technology: A Silver Bullet for All Business Occasions?

Although somewhat tempered by the recent Y2K experience, the belief that technology is a silver bullet runs to the heart of our technological society. In the face of all implementation challenges, we *believe!* We believe that any technology is worth the effort to develop and implement. In the abstract, and over time, this may be true. But company executives are not presiding over the abstract—they oversee the reality of today's corporation striving to succeed in a highly competitive world. They must be pragmatic. The traditional tests of feasibility (Chapter 4, Part Two), if performed with any degree of diligence, will support that pragmatism.

The trouble with the silver bullet mentality is that it tends to see technology and technological products in a mystical light, and this in a sense *gives permission not to plan and manage the technology with enough rigor.* After all, today's business problem, whatever its cause or nature, will be solved by tomorrow's "breakthrough" technology or "killer apps." Someone will figure out a solution. The marketplace will rise to the occasion. The next software announcement will hold the answer. If thought to be true, each of these statements helps relieve the "believer" from having to take action to control and manage the systems environment. Why go to all that work when a "silver bullet" solution is just around the corner?

Outside the research laboratory, the silver bullet mentality reflects a lazy approach to technology management and sets up the believer to be exploited by the skilled marketer who prefers management by magazine.

Technology: Management by Magazine

"Management by magazine" is the phenomenon where technology decisions are overly influenced by the announcements of new technology products in IT and/or business journals, followed by pronouncements of great benefits resulting in breathtaking profits. Again, because of the almost mystical way in which technology is sometimes viewed, decisions to embrace a "hyped" product are often made without a full understanding of the complexity involved and with little regard for risk.

Just for today, consciously evaluate what the great preponderance of published and net-based technology articles pertaining to your line of business are saying. Exclude from this evaluation IT advertisements because they are obviously marketing pieces. Obvious advertisements have companies overcoming the "dark side of the force" if only you will buy the product or employ the advertiser as a consultant. Interesting and exciting, yes, but hardly the materials on which corporate IT and e-business decisions should be based.

The articles to be evaluated generally are presented as the subjective account from a fellow business manager singing the praises of a "new" IT product or e-business processing technique using "new" IT products. In the article, implementation difficulties are seldom mentioned, and the overall impression is one of great satisfaction with the product or new e-business processing technique. The "hidden message," the reason for which the article was written, especially if secretly commissioned by a product vendor, is that today's business processes and uses of IT are threatened by this new, better, faster, and highly profitable way of doing business.

Articles of this type are written mostly to promote corporate interest or self-interest and to generate sales for a fledgling idea or product in early stages of development. Only after many months will news articles and evaluations appear that critique the product or the new processing technique. In most cases, the trigger for follow-up articles are rumors of trouble that are considered newsworthy.

There is a very good reason influential business executives are never shown the inside of a wiring closet, the back of a personal computer, or the rat's nest of cables and wires under the raised flooring—they may perceive complexity and risk, not simplicity and profits. Complexity and risk may promote caution and analysis, while apparent simplicity promotes sales and higher revenues for the vendor.

While making technology appear overly simple in order to get sales is a risk, the great threat posed by Management by Magazine is that new ideas and products are *legion,* and there is a great risk to business processes that are working if they are *tinkered* with too frequently. There is even greater risk to a new e-business system under development if it must accommodate endless changes and new technical ideas brought about from what people read in too many magazines.

IT: Capabilities vs. Limitations

Early in my career, I was member of the faculty of a pioneering organization designated the Department of Defense Computer Institute. The institute had been chartered in the late 1960s by then Secretary of Defense Robert McNamara to instruct general and flag officers and comparable senior civilian executives in the *capabilities and limitations* of automatic data processing. It was recognized at the secretary's level, and through the urgings of such IT notables as then Captain Grace Hopper, USN, Dr. Carl Hammer of UNIVAC, and others, that senior government officials needed to be grounded in what computers could realistically be expected to accomplish. Thus equipped, they would be able to make intelligent decisions concerning this new technology.

It was acknowledged early on by the sponsors of the institute that nontechnical managers and executives could be susceptible to the unfounded claims of proponents of the fledgling technology and be taken advantage of. Executives, it was thought, needed to be educated and familiar enough with computer basics to be able to determine fact from at least gross fiction. To accomplish this, a course of instruction for senior executives was developed to convey the following critical concepts.

Concept 1: Computers Are Exacting.   At the institute, this point was demonstrated by having executives actually program computers using the BASIC language. This demonstrated that although computers were amazing machines, they were extremely demanding in their use. This exercise, interspersed with classroom instruction, required the generation of a logical flowchart, the development of a means to test the program, inputing of program language statements to the computer, and initiation of the computer to execute the program. Those executives learned a great deal about the exacting nature of computers and gained the valuable insight that computers *do exactly* what they are instructed to do, nothing more, and nothing less.

Today, an introduction to computing for senior executives would likely have them executing a preprogrammed routine in which they are invoking, through an icon and a mouse click, thousands of lines of fully tested code. Such an exercise may illustrate the capabilities of the computer but nothing of its inherent limitations and the discipline required to make it operate properly.

Concept 2: Computers Do Some Things Well, Other Things Not So Well.   With an executive's new knowledge about the limitations of computers came the realization that the division of labor and task assignments within an organization had to be carefully allocated between computers and staff. Exhibit 4.1 illustrates this division of labor.

Dissatisfaction with automated systems that have been imposed on operational business settings has been running consistently high since surveys were first taken. When asked, most employees working with computer applications and systems in the performance of their business function score the systems as follows:

- 20 percent are considered successes
- 40 percent return marginal gains
- 40 percent are considered failures

These percentages from *Information Technology and Organizational Change* by Ken Eason (London: Taylor & Francis, 1988) have been substantiated in many follow-on studies, most notably those done by the U.S. General Accounting Office (GAO).

This perspective of computing reality is crucial for executives to appreciate because it illustrates a continuing business consequence of executives not being involved in the next round of e-business decision making. While there are many contributing explanations for the dismal showing depicted above, one crucial reason may be that the *limitations* of computers and software applications to the actual conduct of business are not taken fully into account before system decisions are made and implemented. Without this important perspective, executives are often persuaded to accept the hope of the silver bullet instead of embracing the rigors of management needed for IT systems to be successful.

Elements of Work That People Do Well:	*Tasks That Computers Perform as Instructed:*
Taking Physical Action	Capturing Data
Creative Thinking	Transmitting Data
Decision Making	Storing/Retrieving
Communicating Ideas	Manipulating
Recognizing Patterns	Displaying
Processing Information	

Exhibit 4.1   Division of Labor Between People and Computers

Concept 3: Rigorous Methods Are Required to Manage IT. Because of the exacting nature of computers, the ease with which they can be misapplied to a human workforce, and the difficulty in achieving successful technical implementations, the institute's executive students were introduced to the solution: the discipline provided by a systematic engineering process for systems development. Exhibit 4.2 defines the generic phases of a systems development process (SDP). There is a lengthy discussion on the SDP, its uses, and its importance to e-business security in the next two parts of this chapter.

The SDP, in whatever representation, provides the mechanism, structure, and engineering discipline needed to solve the challenge of successfully applying IT to a business opportunity or problem. The SDP is recognized throughout the IT industry as the fundamental work process of software and systems developers. It is taught in all university programs and is available in commercially marketed automated versions. Whether the steps are performed sequentially or conducted according to one of several iterative models, it is the thought process that is important. But this thought process and the engineering discipline are all too easily abandoned in the rush to get some code working and into the hands of the customer.

Mergers and Acquisitions (M&A) Lead to Greater IT Efficiencies?

On paper, mergers and acquisitions always appear successful. Greater profitability results from greater market share and improved efficiencies in executing business processes. In reality, an M&A usually follows a troubled path, having a direct and adverse impact on the various IT departments of the merged or acquired companies.

First is the issue of systems compatibility between companies. Second is the issue of duplicate staff overhead, which eventually requires the downsizing of some or all of the IT departments of the various companies. Third is the threat posed to the ongoing conduct of e-business of the merged companies while issues one and two are being sorted out.

The predictable course of events when there are M&A is the short-lived enthusiasm for the M&A followed by the realization that overhead is soaring while profits are falling. Whenever an increase in profitability is required or desired, the easiest way seems to be through cost-reduction strategies, and the most likely area for reductions still seems to be in the personnel area. This initiates a round of downsizing, which poses special threats to the IT organization supporting e-business operations and hence the business itself.

After a downsizing, the risk of corporate memory loss looms as a very real threat, especially in areas where IT has replaced more manual and labor-intensive ways of conducting business. The truth of this reality came home to many companies as they worked up contingency plans for possible Y2K outages and processing problems. During 1999, when many companies were beginning to build their plans, it was often stated that previously automated workloads would be accomplished manually in a crisis. There seemed to be some appreciation for the

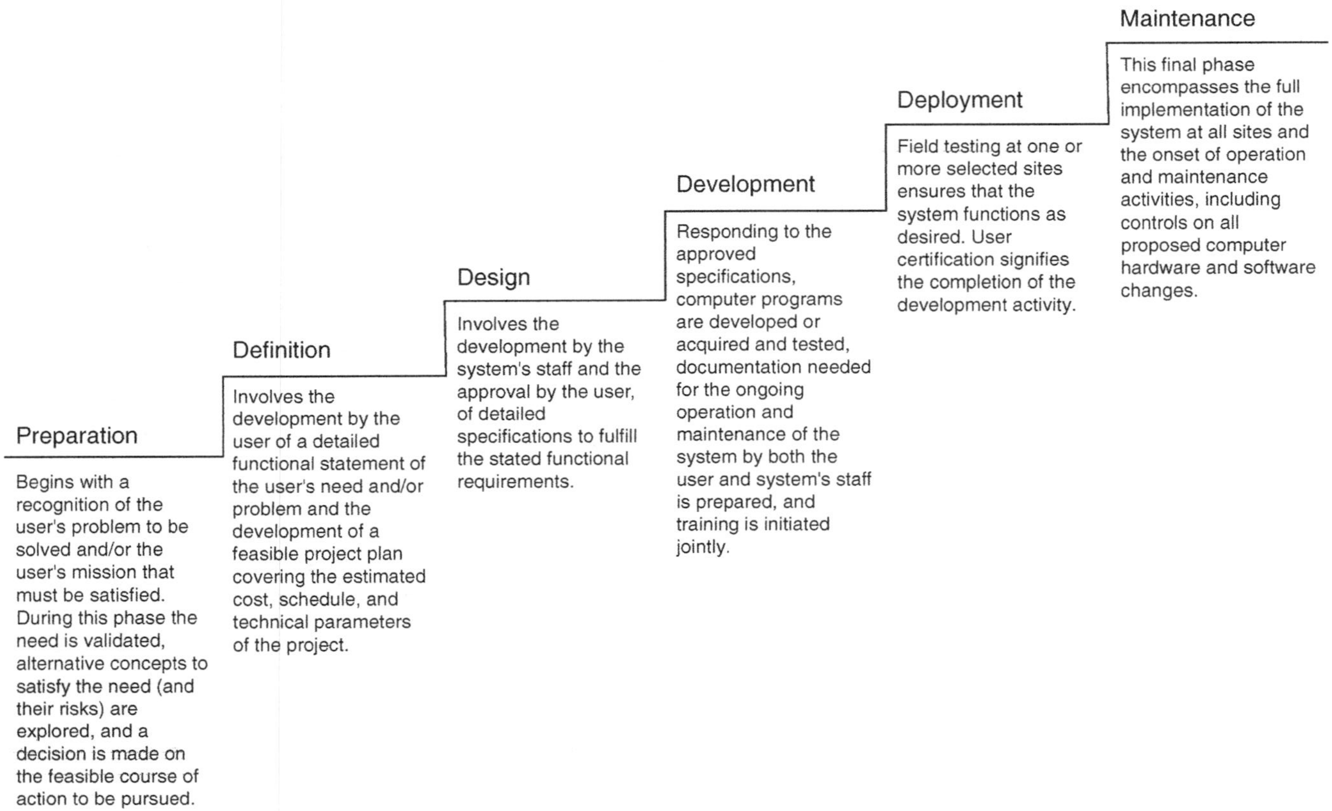

Preparation

Begins with a recognition of the user's problem to be solved and/or the user's mission that must be satisfied. During this phase the need is validated, alternative concepts to satisfy the need (and their risks) are explored, and a decision is made on the feasible course of action to be pursued.

Definition

Involves the development by the user of a detailed functional statement of the user's need and/or problem and the development of a feasible project plan covering the estimated cost, schedule, and technical parameters of the project.

Design

Involves the development by the system's staff and the approval by the user, of detailed specifications to fulfill the stated functional requirements.

Development

Responding to the approved specifications, computer programs are developed or acquired and tested, documentation needed for the ongoing operation and maintenance of the system by both the user and system's staff is prepared, and training is initiated jointly.

Deployment

Field testing at one or more selected sites ensures that the system functions as desired. User certification signifies the completion of the development activity.

Maintenance

This final phase encompasses the full implementation of the system at all sites and the onset of operation and maintenance activities, including controls on all proposed computer hardware and software changes.

Exhibit 4.2 Systems Development Process

general slowdown in business processing that might result from having to invoke the manual processing contingency, but the inability to conduct business at all was rarely or never questioned. What is now being realized is that a good many automated business processes that have evolved over the last two decades have no manual processing predecessor system on which to fall back. Also, it is apparent now that organizations that failed to demand that IT systems be strictly documented pay a heavy price when they have to figure out how business is actually conducted—especially the electronic portion.

To make matters worse, downsizing not only threatens the ability to maintain the "essential" e-business systems but also result in morale problems, where employees are spending more time looking for their next job, just in case, than attending to their duties. Remember that an IT employee can launch a secret and comprehensive job search through the Internet and never leave his or her cubicle.

Outsourcing: Panacea or Potential Threat?

A questionable practice for companies that are highly computer-dependent for e-business processing is the wisdom of excessive outsourcing of IT support functions. Ranging from complete IT facilities management and total processing by contractor, to the use of an application service provider (ASP) for specific e-business workloads, the practice of outsourcing solves some problems while creating serious business risks that must be carefully mitigated.

A critical problem faced by organizations seeking to outsource their IT functions and activities is that they do not have the necessary policies and metrics in place to manage the contractor or an understanding of the detailed specification language it will take to keep a contractor responsive to core business needs.

Before outsourcing, many of the details of how a business system was processed were kept in the heads of employees who understood the core business and its unique demands and characteristics. These employees were perhaps present when the system was built and were answerable to the same corporate leadership so that problems could be "worked out." With the advent of outsourcing, all system nuances and working relationships must be reduced to the language of a contract. It is significant to note that negotiations become very complicated as businesses and potential outsourcers struggle with how to reduce such complexity to contract language. Outsourcing merely because the IT task has become a headache for the company only results in a bigger headache once contract officials and lawyers become involved. If the IT task was a headache for the company, it may well prove to be a major problem for the contractor as well. The reasons IT was difficult for an organization to cope with do not disappear just because an outsourcer is now tasked to do the same work under a contract arrangement.

All too often, outsourcing has become the downsizing implementation strategy of choice and, as such, has added a new dimension to the threat of corporate memory loss and with it a new threat to the security of business systems. Depending on which IT functions are to be contracted out, the threat may be slight or potentially catastrophic. Early on, candidates for outsourcing centered on repetitive action and monitoring activities such as data entry, tape handling, and computer operations. More recently, outsourcing agreements have included network and systems administration and maintenance functions where vendor certification of operating personnel is needed to provide the improved levels of proficiency required for increasingly complex environments.

The latest IT strategy is to outsource the entire information processing activity or major elements of it to the extent that dependence on contractors can become near total and very dangerous. This latest phenomenon must be examined from a broader perspective than the economic arguments used to justify downsizing. Downsizing implies that a "core" capability will be retained in-house, with employees doing at least supervisory work. With outsourcing, companies are, for whatever reasons, washing their hands of an IT activity and allowing an entirely new set of risks to be introduced into the business.

The question of premiere importance is what constitutes the "core" functions of the business and how dependent is the core on the IT activities being considered for outsourcing? For example, many local governments plan to outsource their data center, network management, applications development, and help-desk services. In determining an acceptable level of contractor dependency, core government functions would need to be categorized as to citizen-related criticality, and then a public service judgment would need to be made as to whether contractors can be counted on to be as responsive to public needs as would a civil service workforce. Politically, this may not be an easy thing to decide since it brings into question the issue of privatization, which has powerful proponents. But all things being equal, the real question comes down to whether IT outsourcing contracts can be written to provide the flexibility, responsiveness, and dedication we expect of civil servants. Or does the state of IT contracting realistically lend itself to the demands of a situation where elected officials need to have direct control over employees, not just over a contractor's project manager working within the confines of a contract that is generally written to protect the interests of the contractor?

The same question must be asked of corporate plans to outsource IT activities. If the contracted IT support function is critical to the core revenue-generating business, can executives, the "board," and stockholders rest easy knowing that the primary recourse for obtaining the accurate and timely completion of an e-business task is through the enforcement mechanisms of a contract? Most contractual penalties for nonperformance are meager by comparison with the loss of revenue and goodwill should business fail.

Just-in-Time (JIT) Designs: A Weak Link Threat to Business?

To a great extent, the prosperity of the late 1990s can be attributed directly to the successful use of computers to reduce operating inventories and the traditional expense associated with warehousing. The design of just-in-time (JIT) manufacturing, inventory, and distribution systems would not be possible without the close integration of many different IT systems up and down a "supply chain." The essence of a JIT e-business application is the rapid and accurate exchange of order entry data, inventory status data, manufacturing status, raw materials and parts data, shipping data, invoicing, and accounts receivable data among multiple companies held together by a common desire to reduce costs.

The nature of a JIT system is one of mutual dependency and is only as strong as the "weakest link" in the chain of systems. Great efficiencies have been realized through JIT architectures, and they will continue to be central to the business model of the future. There are, however, many risks inherent in such designs, and care must be taken to identify vulnerabilities that could incapacitate a processing link so that design modifications can be made to mitigate such threats. The threats discussed in this section are in addition to the technical vulnerabilities covered in Chapter 3. These threats may be even more difficult to address because they are inherent to the design of such systems and to the intercorporate arrangements that must be worked out for a JIT system to function properly. The IT trade press has reported numerous difficulties of this nature over the last several years, most notably those experienced by Nike Corporation and Cisco Systems Incorporated, where supply line and inventory disconnects resulted in multimillion dollar losses. The "weakest link" threat is real and poses a "new" type of systems *availability and integrity* vulnerability to those engaged in e-business.

Just-in-time business strategies must be supported by carefully designed automated systems that span many different corporate organizations. *This is a task far too important to leave solely to the IT departments of the separate corporations.* Just-in-time designs invoke a multitude of automated cross-organizational interactions each time the system is activated. Speed and accuracy are paramount. Each corporate link in the chain of processing actions has a responsibility to all other links according to predefined design and contractual obligations. It is imperative that these obligations be based in a sound JIT design and spelled out in business—and technical service-level agreements incorporated into those contractual arrangements. Service-level agreements are negotiated definitions, with tolerance metrics for scoring, that spell out the exact technical interactions that must occur for a JIT business transaction to be considered successful.

To a great extent, a JIT e-business design requires a jointly executed feasibility study accomplished with the participation of all involved parties to the supply chain. To reduce overall risks, the essential activities leading to JIT business and technical service level agreements should include:

- The establishment of an intercompany business process review committee to ensure the mutual benefits to each partner in the supply chain and to establish the business process service-level agreements that are to be reflected in contractual arrangements between companies.
- The establishment of a technical support review committee that reports to the business process review committee to ensure that the hardware, software, and communications infrastructure to support the business process service-level agreements are designed properly and are sufficient to the task.

- A design of the JIT business process to be executed among the individual supply chain partners. The design should include agreement to a standardized representation of the data to be exchanged and clear definitions of what each element of data means across the supply chain.

- The expected "timing" of transactions from initiation to final product delivery must be stated clearly and concisely. The critical processing paths of transactions must be subjected to feasibility studies and a *security* risk assessment to uncover points of vulnerability.

- Problem scenarios must be developed and problem resolution procedures established to be periodically exercised. Scenarios should concentrate on potential disruptions (e.g., accidental or deliberate denial of service outages) to the JIT process flow. The results of this analysis will provide guidance to business continuity planning efforts.

- Since supply chain disruptions can destroy a JIT manufacturing and/or distribution business, a business interruption risk analysis should be conducted before design is finalized. This study will justify any necessary extra expense needed to build a JIT system with quick recovery characteristics.

Such actions will require the direct participation of senior corporate management. These are issues and questions of corporate survivability that can no longer be delegated without frequent, active, and documented executive review. The mission critical nature of JIT systems means that stockholders, the board, investors, and others will expect this level of "due diligence" executive involvement.

PART TWO: MANAGING E-BUSINESS SYSTEMS AS A CORPORATE ASSET

This part of Chapter 4 identifies improvements that are needed if organizations are to manage IT and especially e-business systems with the same degree of discipline as any other aspect of the business. Without basic IT management discipline and accountability being established and enforced, e-business systems cannot be secured.

Establish Executive Ownership of All IT Systems and Computing Assets

The prevailing view of IT and its uses has traditionally been one of sophisticated clerical activity. Until recently, except for applications of science, research, manufacturing process control, and military command and control, most uses of IT have dealt with the record keeping and reporting that accompanied normal business activity. This early reality of business computing as principally providing administrative support did not command the deep respect or involvement of senior management except to approve budgets for hardware systems that were also seen as status symbols. Under these conditions, the gradual creep of business dependencies on IT went unnoticed until Y2K surfaced. In many cases, not until organizations had to deal with the Y2K problem and were forced to prioritize, due to time constraints, the systems requiring corrective action, was the true extent of the dependency recognized. Until then, and because of the mistaken view of systems as merely administrative and clerical in nature, many non-IT managers and executives believed that business could be accomplished manually if need be. The unrealistic nature of this belief became clear when organizations began to develop contingency plans for Y2K interruptions. As an example, it quickly became clear that it was not practical to plan for the writing of millions of checks by hand or that the volumes of daily transactions processing through a web site could be serviced manually without a severe loss of revenues and customers.

Today, in light of well-documented security threats, the result of the same erroneous thinking is likely to be the undoing of businesses that have become dependent on e-business processing, and where executives have failed as change leaders to take ownership of IT, the e-business process, and the risks inherent in that mode of operation. Years of creeping dependency and inadequate computer system management practices have put many mainline business processes at risk and will similarly affect e-business systems unless executive managers take ownership of IT, control the e-business application, and manage the risks inherent in these systems.

Contemporary computing decisions must anticipate the collective needs of all business components and their requirement to interoperate. More and more, this requirement will extend to business partners and supply chain companies. The requirement to interoperate is at the center of e-business as information comes to be viewed more as a source of intelligence to be analyzed and less as mere clerical recordings of financials, sales, and inventories. E-business information needs, and therefore system design and implementation decisions, will likely extend outside the corporation to others with whom the company must coordinate complex collaborative product designs and JIT schedules.

The "new" reality of building efficient and secured e-business systems requires that information systems and the uses of IT be more highly standardized so that future e-business applications communicating up and down a supply chain are not plagued with interoperability problems that can overwhelm the ability to coordinate rapid and secured system changes necessitated by fluctuating business needs.

Corporations must design their own intrasystem and external communications around corporate business standards and then present a uniform IT architecture and operating environment for dealings with the outside world. A standard and uniform IT environment managed from the executive suite treats business information and the IT processing system as valued corporate assets and is risk-sensitive in making e-business decisions and in setting strategy.

Best Practice #1: Establish and/or reinvigorate the executive IT management committee chaired by the chief executive officer (CEO). Depending on how troubled the IT management function of the business appears to be, this committee must dedicate significant time to getting systems, especially e-business systems, under management control. If serious Y2K problems were experienced or if other IT projects continually experience expectation, budget, or delivery difficulties, this committee may need to meet frequently to review all aspects of systems management. Outside consultation is recommended to facilitate such a review. Of special concern would be the processes used to define, design, program, and test e-business systems—especially the security and integrity controls of such systems. This is the topic of Chapter 6 and Appendix B. In addition to the CEO, membership should be comprised of the chief information officer (CIO), the business unit directors, the chief financial officer (CFO), general counsel, and contracting. If the company offers IT products or services for sale, the director of marketing and sales must also be on the committee.

The executive IT management committee will be required to approve the statement of goals and roles and responsibilities of the e-business security management organization (discussed later in this chapter).

Best Practice #2: Based on current inventory data, ensure that all e-business systems (backroom and on-line), e-business software applications, and IT infrastructure support systems are the direct responsibility of a member of the executive IT management committee. This means that all systems-related prioritization and conflict resolution can take place in the committee. It is imperative that IT be viewed as a collective asset to be utilized by the business as a whole and not islands of computing in competition with each other. Even if the corporate management philosophy includes competition between business units, care must be taken not to let such competition result in noncompatible IT systems and databases sprouting up throughout the company. This would only compound the serious interoperability problem already existing in many organizations.

Determine Appropriateness of Pursuing IT Projects Through Comprehensive Feasibility Studies

Something is feasible if it is "capable of being managed, utilized, or dealt with successfully," according to *Webster's Third International Dictionary.* If something is feasible, it is generally considered to be reasonable and possible. There are three factors of feasibility: (1) technical, (2) economic, and (3) operational. Each factor is important in its own right, but it is through their collective trade-offs that they provide a process of elimination whereby the "best possible" course of action is determined.

A common attitude of many IT-intensive organizations has been that any application of the technology must certainly be good and that the long-term upside will always overcome any short-term difficulty and inconvenience. It has almost become a tenet of faith that new technology is always better than old technology and must therefore be embraced. The business sponsor for the new technology pushes hard, the technicians push hard, the cost-benefit studies *always* look positive, and few counsel for caution. And yet the track record for delivered

IT projects does not impress. A commonly accepted statistic, quoted in Part One of this chapter, is that some 40 percent of projects fail, another 40 percent are considered marginal, and perhaps 20 percent are acknowledged to be full-blown successes by the end users of the system.

Aside from the economic repercussions of such a dismal showing, the operational impact on systems security is significant. Failed and marginally successful systems throw users and system administrators into confusion, and in an attempt to continue doing their job they are forced to devise system "workarounds." Workarounds often "go around" whatever security and integrity controls were built into the system, thus negating their effectiveness. *Therefore, continuing to use an unsuccessful system poses especially urgent security risks.*

A principal explanation for poor system success rates is that at some level the proposed technology system was not an appropriate use of IT when all the variables necessary for user acceptance are considered. Feasibility studies are undertaken to account for those variables.

For example, if an IT project is being pursued to determine its future potentiality, it would be best planned and developed as a "pilot" from which the principal dividend would be knowledge. If, conversely, the IT undertaking is to address an operational business problem or seize upon a definable opportunity, then the analysis should be more rigorous, with an eye to developing a practical e-business solution. Of the tools available to make these determinations, none is more powerful than the feasibility study. Historically, feasibility studies have seldom been conducted in their entirety, and when they have been performed, they usually are biased toward the technical and are less concerned with operational issues. *And e-business security is nothing if not an operational issue.* Feasibility studies have also generally tended to portray an incomplete economic picture because all items of expense that are usually experienced over the expected life of a system are not considered in the analysis.

What corporate executives are usually presented with, when asked to make systems decisions, are analyses conducted by technicians to further advance their vision of the company's technical path. The operational impacts of new systems on customers and users are generally not considered to the same degree that technicians factor in their own future prospects by ensuring that they will be working with new technologies.

In the wake of recent e-business system failures, the critical eye of practicality should fall on all future e-business system proposals, with the practice of the feasibility study receiving new life as the disciplined method for determining what is truly practical. The need to balance the technical aspects of an IT proposal against operational and economic issues will finally be appreciated. This is how the balancing should take place.

Technical feasibility seeks to determine the probability that a proposed IT solution will work reliably at the technical level and questions whether there is a viable IT industry support infrastructure to allow the smooth implementation and maintenance of the proposed technology during business operations. Is it a tested technology, or will the company be put into guinea pig status by pursuing the proposal? Can the proposed technology be supported in the IT marketplace? Do third-party software packages exist? Are there people trained in the technology? How many and can they be afforded? If the proposed technical solution puts the company into a guinea pig situation or if the technology cannot be easily supported by the local IT industry and it is still selected as the solution, then there must be careful planning so that expectations are kept in line with reality and risks are known and consciously accepted by management.

Operational feasibility concerns itself with whether the proposed IT solution can be smoothly assimilated into current business processes and practices and what actions must be taken to prepare the workplace, employees, and customers to successfully use the new technology. Operational feasibility asks that we balance the often-overstated benefits of a new technology with the practical problems associated with productively using the technology with our customers, in our workplace environment, and with our employees. The desired e-business application must function in a specific corporate work environment, with specific employees at their level of technical competence, and with customers and their degree of acceptance. The desired application must enhance overall quality and performance of business activities in very specific ways and should in no way be disruptive.

While it understood and desired that new technologies change the ways in which business is conducted, management must decide how much and how fast the company, employees, business partners, and customers can absorb such change. To help make this series of judgment calls, the following should be considered.

Be sure to proceed with a clear understanding of the current level of customer and business partner satisfaction. Take care not to risk losing good relationships by pushing an e-business system that is unproven and may have questionable customer and partner acceptance. Remember that any change in the established business process forces change on others. Let someone else test the waters, and learn from their mistakes.

Determine the competitor's technology competence. Do not risk market share and satisfied customers unless there is a clear advantage in doing so. Remember that a company usually has a couple of years before it must begin worrying about falling behind competitors in the adoption of most technologies that end up changing how business is conducted. Most of today's successful dot-com companies are second- or third-generation adopters of the Internet for e-business. They let the early dot-com-everything fad run its course, learning from the mistakes of others, and then wisely integrated the concept into their existing "brick and mortar" business process.

Consider employees' level of technology sophistication and their ability to adapt to the new e-business system. Adequate training dollars should be factored into this part of the evaluation. Paul Straussman, noted IT consultant and former assistant Secretary of Defense for Information Systems, Department of Defense, has estimated that overall training costs should approach $2 to $3 for each dollar spent on hardware and software. This may seem high if the technical solution being examined is a commonly available desktop software package; but sophisticated and tailored e-business systems may exceed this estimate when training for all aspects of system use, administration, life cycle maintenance, and security are considered.

Factor in a dollar level of effort estimate to administer and maintain the system over its anticipated life cycle. Often this critical operational cost is missing from economic consideration, and yet it is generally accepted that as high as 70 percent of all IT budgets go toward maintaining systems after they go operational. Many will argue about what is included in maintenance, but regardless of what items are finally determined for costing purposes, this category of systems support workload must be considered an operational expense and must be consciously acknowledged. Remember that any unfunded aspect of the system's life cycle will force corners to be cut elsewhere to make up the difference. Improperly capitalized systems maintenance will only introduce an element of security threat that can jeopardize even a well-designed and well-developed e-business system.

Determine the difficulty of expanding each proposed solution to meet anticipated business growth demands. Promoters often use the words "ease of expansion" to market the idea that the proposed solution can be easily expanded to meet changing business requirements and increased volumes. Such claims should be carefully examined based on quantitative estimates, not just vague generalities. A specific area of concern is whether security controls can be as effective after periods of system expansion or whether security becomes a "drag" that interferes with productive work. Experience shows that security controls that slow down productive work will eventually be disabled in the name of efficiency. Proposed configurations to satisfy expanded volume projections can be evaluated through research or simulations for operational and security impacts.

Evaluate the capability *and* desire *of potential solution providers to support the proposed solution after acquisition and for the anticipated life cycle of the system.* Obviously, these two considerations are difficult to address with any certitude, but they must be evaluated openly. Determining *capability* and *desire* becomes a problem of divining the future of another company. For example, the highly regarded capability of a provider company to meet a firm's support needs today may be seriously jeopardized tomorrow following a buyout or merger. As is well known, buyouts and mergers tend to eventually destroy much of the capability of the purchased company as "key" people often leave or are forced out. Determining the future capabilities of a provider company involves anticipating its business plan. It is important to determine whether the technical solution being considered is on the provider's critical path for business growth. To buy a solution today only to discover a year or two from now that it must be changed-out because the provider no longer *desires* to support the system can lead to great unexpected risk inconvenience, and expense.

Determine the condition of systems documentation. Perhaps the most effective way to judge the soundness of a proposal for an off-the-shelf system is through the quality of the documentation generated and provided for customer use. Documentation functions as the blueprints and engineering drawings of a system and are absolutely essential for systems operations, maintenance, and upgrades to be carried out smoothly. Most software and systems documentation appears to be written by technical people for technical people, not for system users who are trying to do their primary job. Failure to evaluate the reputation of a provider for usable documentation can undermine the most elegant and productive technical solution.

Factor into the evaluation each of the changes to the current way of doing business that will be required to interface smoothly with each proposed solution. Operational feasibility should address all topics seen in the two right sectors of Exhibit 6.7. Typically, these employee-user-customer interface activities and work condition adjustments have not been given adequate attention, resulting in the likelihood of unnecessary business disruptions and eventual adverse customer impacts. Operational feasibility also surfaces many more items of expense than a mere technical analysis will identify. This increasingly accurate picture of overall costs will result in a more representative and meaningful economic analysis.

Exhibit 4.3 summarizes the totality of costs typically associated with an e-business system. If these costs are not identified and factored into the systems decision process, unrealistic expectations regarding system return on investment and cost-benefit will be created. Unreal expectations about system costs and break-even points will eventually put the system developers under great pressure to field a system before it is fully tested or else cut corners in the design and development. Historically, the corners cut are security and integrity controls, system availability and reliability safeguards, training, and documentation. It is therefore essential to have a complete cost picture of the e-business system before commissioning its development or short-term expediencies will undermine security and perhaps even system functionality.

Economic feasibility is conducted last in the sequence of studies in order to prevent choosing a proposed IT solution based on marketing materials, hype, and an incomplete portrayal of total cost of ownership. Too many so-called benefit analyses have painted overly optimistic benefit sides of the equation and woefully inadequate expense sides. The result is that many IT projects are initially under-capitalized and at the same time entered into with completely unrealistic expectations regarding business savings and break-even points. When cost-benefit expectations are unreal, a project is in trouble from day one. This usually results in a series of project compromises (usually in security and training) that end up satisfying no one while still costing a great deal more than initially estimated.

In summary, something is feasible if it is "capable of being managed, utilized, or dealt with successfully." The emphasis on feasibility is essential to securing the e-business system because an infeasible system is by definition unmanageable and therefore incapable of being secured.

Best Practice #3: Establish policy that all IT proposals be subjected to a full feasibility study conducted in the sequence of technical, operational, and economic analysis. This policy will ensure a standard method for comparing a

	Acquisition Costs	Operating Costs	Upgrade Costs
Hardware equipment	Equipment purchase or lease and installation	Maintenance/warranty Annual lease/rental security	Hardware replacement or upgrades
Software	Software One-time license Initial charges	Annual licensing Maintenance fees	Software replacement or upgrades
Personnel	Recruiting Salaries and Benefits Training and education	Routine monitoring and operations Training Problem determination and correction User liaison and administration Programming maintenance	User changes Software changes and upgrades Training and education Programming Contract programming
Communications	Initial hardware and hookup	Monthly charges Hookup Security Tariffs	Additional lines and equipment
Facilities	Facilities development Wiring Security Plumbing	Floor space Power Air-conditioning Security	Incremental wiring Incremental space Increased security

Exhibit 4.3   Items to Consider in Cost Analysis

variety of IT proposals, coming from different organizational components, for overall benefits and impact on the business. The recommended sequence of the study will help to ensure that uses of IT will not be overly biased by technical promises but have been balanced by workplace/employee/customer and sustainability considerations. It will ensure that realistic overall costs are forcing a well-thought-out statement of benefits covering the anticipated life of the system. This policy will help set more realistic expectations on the part of all *stakeholders* to the proposal and will lessen pressures to compromise on project goals and development discipline in an effort to salvage an ill-defined undertaking.

Best Practice #4: Require that return on investment and cost ownership studies not be considered a substitute for the full feasibility analysis. These two popular studies, often used to determine a cost-benefit profile of an investment in information technology, do not necessarily provide the same insights as the cumulative picture provided by the technical, operational, and economic analysis performed in that sequence. Again, experience indicates that most system failures derive from technical infrastructure support difficulties and internal business integration problems. Until such potential problem areas are given a full measure of attention, the complete extent of potential implementation and maintenance expenses cannot be factored into any form of economic justification.

Establish Executive-Level IT Risk Management Review Process

Risk management is *the total process of identifying, controlling, and eliminating or minimizing uncertain events that may adversely affect system resources and subsequently the business process.*

Risk and risk management, to the extent that it has been considered at all, has usually been associated with computer security, confidentiality, and perhaps fraud, waste, and system abuse issues. This is good, and while these are obviously valid concerns, they must be addressed within the much larger framework of information and processing infrastructure "availability." This is because the traditional look at computer risk was generally not as comprehensive as today's on-line e-business systems demand. The Y2K experience, directly and indirectly, forced organizations to acknowledge a far broader range of risks than those traditionally recognized. Y2K forced organizations to contemplate the loss of the technology infrastructure supporting the business—not just the concerns of information secrecy and the possible unauthorized or illegal manipulation of data or processes. For example, before Y2K, few corporations gave much thought to the viability of the technical network that facilitates their supply line of raw materials or component parts. It was pretty much assumed that, short of fraudulent activity, labor unrest, or natural disaster, suppliers would make good on their commitments and honor their contracts. Today, it is known that something as seemingly insignificant as the absence of *two digits* can cause far-reaching problems both up and down a vertical manufacturing line, a manufacturing to retail distribution chain, or a government benefits distributions system. The interdependencies among businesses have become much more evident, and in the future, prudent management would seem to require methods to address the inherent risks arising from those interdependencies.

"Acts of God" always constitute a threat to continued business operation and, as such, usually have been covered by some form of interruption insurance. After Y2K, it is highly probable that insurance companies will be much more circumspect when writing coverage for IT-related risks. Insurance carriers will likely become increasingly interested in exactly how IT-intensive businesses manage their IT-related risks and what they are doing to prevent and/or mitigate the adverse effects of certain risk scenarios.

Many previously neglected management disciplines must be applied to the uses of IT by those businesses with significant dependencies on the technology. Expanded-focus risk management is one such discipline that, when implemented, must be able to identify and monitor IT risks far beyond the traditional concerns of confidentiality and fraud, waste, and system abuse. This new expanded focus on risk will consider all facets of IT project and systems development risks (Chapter 6 and Appendix B) and other environmental business conditions that could threaten successful implementation of an e-business system. This expanded focus will start with any risk areas identified during the feasibility analysis and continue to monitor each risk area for changing conditions that could affect the project's outcome.

Appendix D, E-Business Risk Management Review Model, presents a guide for executive involvement in the management of risk associated with corporate uses of IT, suppliers or vendors, and operational factors that could adversely affect the business. In addition to the traditional computer risk areas of data *confidentiality* and *integrity*, special efforts must be made to identify and manage risks in at least nine other areas because each may pose special threats to infrastructure viability and therefore systems *availability*. Appendix D promotes the monitoring of identified risks so that increasingly appropriate actions can be taken to prevent or mitigate any adverse consequences of the risks occurring. The topics outlined in Appendix D are only a sampling and are in no way exhaustive of the totality of risks an e-business project may face.

Best Practice #5: Establish a policy that all corporate IT and e-business systems in current operation or under development, processing environments and support infrastructures (in-house and/or outsourced), and new contemplated technologies be assessed and continuously monitored for potential adverse impacts on the business. Such action will signal that preventive thinking and responsible risk-reduction actions are as valued as risk-taking behavior and will encourage a more balanced view of IT throughout the organization.

Such actions should be viewed favorably by the board, stockholders, insurance carriers, and business partners. Those in the stock-growth-at-any-price crowd may not immediately appreciate this type of conservative management and may not understand a risk management approach to IT. Those who learned from the Y2K experience will see the necessity and support the effort.

Make Improvements to the Management of IT

The IT industry as a whole has a poor track record when it comes to delivering successful implementations of the technology. While some of the difficulties can be rightly attributed to technical factors and to supplier or vendor failures, most problems must be laid at the feet of ineffectual corporate and project management of information assets and the enabling IT. The most penetrating audits of IT management and unsuccessful attempts to utilize organizational informational assets have been conducted over the years by the U.S. General Accounting Office (GAO), usually at the request of members of Congress. Note that not all GAO audits are of government systems and that a good number report on private sector companies developing or operating government systems under contract. From an overall management perspective, the GAO has consistently identified the following problems as fundamentally contributing to IT management and project failures:

- Lack of top management commitment to project success
- Inadequate project planning and execution
- Abandonment of the project plan
- Inexperienced project managers
- Flawed technical approach
- Failure to anticipate changes in support technology
- Failure to satisfy user needs
- Inadequate documentation
- Acquisition problems

While each of these appears to be a separate area of difficulty, they all concentrate their impact and directly affect the IT manager, who must somehow orchestrate these and other myriad issues to deliver a successful e-business system.

Information technology managers have generally been ill-prepared for the duties and responsibilities of the job. In the world of IT managers, few have formal business management training and even fewer are educated in the disciplines of IT best practice management. Since successful IT management is learned primarily by working on successful projects, not in the classroom, there is a shortage of managers who know how to be effective. Poor practices are simply passed from one project to the next because so few managers have ever been associated with a success. Or, as is often the case, a manager comes in during the middle phases of an already troubled project when there is little he or she can do to change the outcome short of starting over.

Often, IT managers have been promoted to such positions as a reward for technical excellence, to retain them with the company, or to demonstrate promotion policies. Many people become IT managers without proper preparation at subordinate management positions. Then there is the problem of recruiting managers from outside the company. This is a course of action fraught with danger, for in this age of "résumé inflation," it is very easy for prospective employees to misrepresent themselves, knowing how difficult it is for past employers to give candid appraisals for fear of legal action.

Conversely, it is not necessarily the best course of action to put a generalist business manager or an MBA in charge of an IT organization or project. Information technology is definitely an area where the manager must have a working knowledge of the technology to be managed. In the case of IT, this means that the manager must, in addition to business experience, have an understanding of the capabilities and limitations of the technology and the difficulties encountered in systems development and systems integration of an e-business system into the culture and operations environment of the corporation. This means "hands-on" time dealing with the weaknesses noted by the GAO in the majority of their studies. While managing to the "bottom line" works for most other corporate undertakings, it may not always be appropriate as the sole indicator of success when it comes to the uses of IT in critical business systems. There is an overhead "cost of doing business" reality that must be appreciated when making IT management decisions. Security and quality assurance (QA), for example, are costs that must be borne if the e-business system is to have long-term success. Security and QA generally cannot be justified solely through the financial thinking of the generalist or MBA manager without using the tempering knowledge of the inherent shortcomings of the technology.

Finally, IT managers have traditionally been put into situations of great responsibility but very little authority. Regardless of the background or experience level of an IT manager, there is little chance for other than marginal success without the fully visible commitment and support of corporate executives. Lack of top management commitment is the number one problem listed by the GAO and is generally the number one problem identified in the autopsy report of any failed IT project.

Top executive commitment can be demonstrated, if it is to be believed by IT managers who often must enforce unpopular or seemingly unnecessary systems or software development or QA and testing actions, only by requiring *consistent adherence* to the discipline of IT best practices and by supporting IT managers when they enforce such discipline. Executive action to implement the recommendations in this book would demonstrate such support and make possible the institutionalization of the lessons learned from the many audits of failed IT projects.

The most crucial improvements that can be made to support the management of IT are those that require and enforce forms of accountability. If anything is to be learned from the Y2K experience, it is that e-business, like any other aspect of the business, must be pursued within a framework of accountability. It became increasingly clear that, throughout the many months leading up the millennium turnover, the principal objective of IT vendors, service providers, and IT-intensive businesses was to disclaim responsibility for any adverse impacts resulting from data processing problems. Intriguingly, non-IT business in general, when given the opportunity to counter the IT industry's intense lobbying for increased protection from accountability for Y2K-related problems, chose to stand by and let "safe haven" legislation become law.

The latest movement of the IT industry to safe havens, and therefore lessened accountability, is the new initiative being spearheaded by the software industry, the Uniform Computer Information Transactions Act (UCITA). The UCITA is a proposed law for applying consistent rules to software licenses across all 50 states. The UCITA would amend the Uniform Commercial Code (UCC) and would essentially:

- Give vendors the right to repossess software by disabling it remotely
- Make the terms of off-the-shelf licenses more enforceable
- Prevent the transfer of licenses from one party to another without vendor permission
- Outlaw reverse engineering of software
- Allow vendors to *disclaim warranties*
- Allow vendors to not be held accountable for *known defects*

While the first four provisions may seem onerous to some, they are understandable attempts of an industry, besieged by piracy, to protect its intellectual property and revenue streams. The fifth and sixth provisions, however, are far more troubling from the perspective of an individual or corporate buyer of software. These provisions would seem to allow vendors to disclaim warranties for defective, buggy, or virus-infested software. According to Watts Humphrey, a fellow at the Software Engineering Institute at Carnegie-Mellon University, "the provisions say that software publishers are not liable for the poor quality of their products. Today, any feature that a vendor demonstrates at a trade show or writes about in a product manual must be a working part of the product. The proposed law would seem to change that."

The UCITA, it is feared, will cause a lowering of standards for software performance and will cost user companies more money because, having reduced faith in warranties, they will have to take extra testing precautions with software products to ensure that they are working as advertised.

Corporate executives of IT-intensive corporations should view the UCITA with great caution because it erases even the feeble accountability that now exists where software is concerned.

Require that a Formal Systems Development Process (SDP) Be Used to Construct E-Business Systems

Before experiencing Y2K and now the threats posed to e-business security, most buyers, users, or executives gave little thought to how IT systems and software products were constructed. The "quality movement" of the late 1980s never really changed the buying habits of IT consumers, and it has barely influenced how software and system products are actually built. Both software or systems supplier and consumer have stayed focused on "new" features and lower prices accompanied by appealing marketing promises that never fully materialize. Then there are the millions of consumers who have to go where the vendor leads them. Once a software vendor has a captive consumer, quality does not have to take a very high priority. Without any *real* competition, certain vendors can be nonchalant about customer desires for quality software. Depending on the terms used to describe quality, vendors can be very selective as to where they concentrate their attention and efforts. If, for example, consumers are more influenced by the creative use of screen icons and know or care little about the importance of having current and accurate software documentation, guess where the vendor will spend the effort.

In Exhibit 4.4 a list of quality specifications for software and systems are defined. Note that these are the same specifications depicted in Exhibit 2.6. Each quality attribute specified is important to the overall characteristics of a software product or system, whether off-the-shelf or custom-programmed. A quality software product or system cannot focus on just one or two quality attributes at the expense of others, since all attributes taken together describe a system that functions properly, is customer- or user-friendly, and can be modified and maintained easily and quickly by keepers of the code. *This, by the way, is the description of a stable and reliable system—one that can be secured.*

Quality software and systems are the product of a structured and formal system development process (SDP). There are several versions of SDPs, and they all focus on bringing engineering discipline to the business of software and systems development. Some of the more popular and time-proven approaches include:

Correctness The degree to which system outputs satisfy the accuracy requirements of the business activity being supported.

Availability/Reliability The degree to which the system is available and meets the business requirement for operational uptime.

Integrity A measure of completeness and soundness of design and construction. A system that has integrity can be trusted by the user.

Usability A measure of being "fit for use" by a representative employee in the actual workplace.

Confidentiality A measure of privacy or secrecy that is required by nature of the information involved or the sensitivity of the business process.

Testable Software that is designed to be easily tested when changes are made to functionality.

Maintainable Software that is designed to be easily main-tained, usually in modules that are completely documented to show all inputs, outputs, calculations, and quality metrics.

Exhibit 4.4   Definitions of E-Business Quality Specifications

- Structured Analysis and Systems Specification Method—DeMarco
- Structured Systems Analysis Method—Gane and Sarson
- Development of Real-Time Systems—Ward and Mellor
- Essential Systems Analysis Method—McMenamin and Palmer

Exhibit 4.5 Systems Development Review (SDR) Framework functions as a management review template covering the essential phases and control elements of a structured systems development process. Exhibit 4.5 is visited again in Chapter 6 as a major tool to be exercised by executive management in assuring that e-business systems are being constructed according to system development "best practices" and will therefore be more capable of being secured. Specific instructions for using the framework for this purpose are provided in Appendix B.

As is stressed in the remainder of this book, strict adherence to a formal SDP represents the single best available solution to the problem of developing and delivering high-quality and secured e-business software and systems. Unless a formal SDP for the definition, creation, and delivery of software and systems is adopted and enforced, the eventual lack of documented knowledge about "how an e-business system works" will plague the next generation of systems just as it did the "Y2K" generation of systems. The chaos many organizations endured during the Y2K episode will be experienced again and again whenever software or systems have to be modified to accommodate new requirements or whenever security controls must be adjusted to deal with new threats. Cost-effective and secured modifications to existing code are best accomplished on systems and software that are the products of the disciplined adherence to a structured SDP.

The emerging standard of "due diligence" will soon require proof of the use of structured systems development methodologies in countering charges of developmental negligence stemming from either a lack of system quality and reliability or a lack of security. Why is this so? Because once the *concept* of structured systems development and software engineering is clear in the mind of "judges and juries," any software or systems developer who cannot demonstrate their *use* will not be able to claim that "reasonableness" was exercised during development of the system or software in question. The power of the concept can be seen in the following example.

Using the example of building a custom home, use of an SDP would be akin to the disciplined process and procedure that an architect employs in defining client requirements, when designing a structure that satisfies those requirements, and when using design specifications to guide the work of construction workers. The architect adheres to an industry-accepted practice of requirements definition, design renderings, specifications development, materials acquisition, contracting for assembly, assembly, and final inspection with all those who have an interest in the final construction.

During the course of events, the architect develops "blueprints" to guide the effort of construction personnel who assemble the components of the house

MANAGEMENT REQUIREMENTS

Life Cycle Phases	Project Management Plan	Software or Systems Engineering Plan	Internal Controls Plan	Security Plan	Quality Assurance and Testing Plan	Configuration Management Plan	Documentation Plan	Technology Transfer Plan	Training Plan	Infrastructure Risk Monitoring		
										Hardware	Software	Network
Preparation												
Definition												
Design												
Development												
Deployment												
Maintenance												

Exhibit 4.5 Systems Development Review Framework

according to specification. Specifications include expressions of expected quality and can be traced back to the requirements and desires of the homeowner or to some "code" used to set standards for construction and safety.

It is the same with successful IT systems. The analogy is even valid to the extent of having to make major or minor modifications, such as changing access controls, to an e-business system after it has been completed and installed. Where the disciplined process and procedures of an SDP have not been followed, the engineered progression from requirements to a fully tested and documented, quality-inspected final system is haphazard at best and seriously deficient at worst. When modifications must be made to a deficiently constructed, tested, and documented system, chaos prevails, and usually an additional and costly effort is required to determine whether and/or how the modification can proceed without disrupting the business process. *It is like deciding to make a change, such as adding a picture window, to a nearly completed house but not knowing that the target wall happens to be load-bearing.* Why is this critically important piece of information missing? Because the discipline of following and updating the architect's drawings was not followed or enforced and critical information was not documented in the blueprints or in the building specifications.

Once it is recognized that software and systems development is not *magic*, but rather the result of an orderly and disciplined process of defining, designing, developing, and testing, all businesses will be forced to embrace and enforce an appropriately chosen SDP out of self-defense.

To be sure, some IT personnel will argue that the imposition of a structured development process will stifle their creativity. Or they will argue, and likely be supported by the software sales department, that the comprehensiveness of an SDP is overkill and will delay time-to-market expectations. But while corporations desire creativity during the design of a system, creativity during development (i.e., programming and the integration of software packages) is like allowing each construction worker to individually interpret directly from a blueprint and make unsupervised changes to "improve" the house.

Remember that the name of the IT game changes significantly once *accountability* enters the equation. To bring about this change, corporate executives must take action to ensure that all future IT projects and systems development initiatives are managed according to an industry-recognized SDP.

Best Practice #6: Establish a corporate policy that all e-business software and systems and integration efforts be guided by a structured systems development process (SDP) that incorporates the phases of requirements definition, design, development (i.e., programming and/or integration), testing, deployment, and maintenance. Monitor and enforce its use. As we have seen, Exhibit 4.5, Systems Development Review (SDR) Framework, portrays a review model whereby executives can visualize and grasp the many development phases and technical and management activities that constitute a best practice "due diligence" approach to e-business development and/or integration. Again, this framework and its use are discussed in Chapter 6, and detailed instructions for its application as a management review tool can be found in Appendix B.

Three Additional Uses of a Formal SDP—All of Which Contribute to Improved E-Business Security

Three additional uses of the SDP's engineering discipline should hold special interest for executive members of the corporate IT governing committee seeking to improve overall IT competence and value to the company.

First, a structured SDP can provide the controlling mechanism for guaranteeing the quality of all IT software, systems, and service products of a corporation whether for internal use or for delivery to a customer. Similar disciplined approaches guarantee the quality of other traditional corporate outputs—why not IT products and services?

Second, in preparing for the increased likelihood of systems-related litigation, executives must recognize that enforced use of an SDP provides a best practices proof of reasonableness when questions about due diligence in software and systems management are raised and when documenting evidence is requested to support actions taken and decisions made during the course of a development or integration effort (see Chapter 8).

Third, the SDP can be used as a tool to judge the maturity of a corporation's internal software and systems development capability or that of a business partner or support provider of IT products and services. A formal process for performing this type of evaluation has been developed by Carnegie-Mellon University's Software Engineering Institute (SEI) for the Department of Defense (DOD). The original purpose for development of an evaluation model was the desire of the DOD to improve its own software development capability and that of its contractors. The SEI Capability Maturity Model (CMM), as it is known, evaluates the current software practices of an organization, ranks its capability on a progressive scale of 1 to 5, and then, based on the evaluation, provides feedback on necessary improvements to raise the overall SEI-CMM rating. Each level is best described by the relative presence or lack of IT best practices governing the software and systems development and software integration environment of the organization.

Level 1 is noted for a lack of any standard best practice processes used during software development. With level 1 organizations, IT development personnel do their own thing based on their previous experience. According to SEI statistics, nearly 80 percent of all software development organizations are at level 1. In other words, they are essentially unmanaged and are not using any of the software engineering and project management techniques or tools that have been proven to deliver quality and cost-efficient systems.

Level 2 organizations have made attempts to adapt to some best practices techniques and the discipline of a structured SDP, but they are generally poor at enforcement and cannot replicate or repeat the use of techniques from one project to another. Employees in level 2 organizations are still essentially on their own but are a little more sophisticated in their use of tools. It is very much a project-by-project application of IT management practices dictated by the project management. Executives have not as yet required the institutionalization of a structured SDP, although they may have begun to gather some software metrics data.

Level 3 organizations, which may account for fewer than 10 percent of all software and systems developers, have adopted all aspects of a structured SDP and are now concentrating on improving their software engineering abilities and project management practices. There is considerable focus on training to improve individual skills and intergroup activities to facilitate coordination and knowledge exchanges.

Level 4 organizations have built a quality management and continuous improvement program mentality into the way they go about all aspects of the business of software and systems development.

Level 5, the "Holy Grail" of software improvement, is centered not only on efforts to improve development processes but also on applying techniques and tools to prevent defects from ever occurring. The ultimate benefits from efforts to gather software metrics data are now realized because organizations can be very effective in their resource estimating and project planning and also can use prior project data to better manage current workloads of a software maintenance nature.

Clearly, the higher an organization rates on the SEI-CMM scale, the better the chance that e-business security is achievable. Without doubt, there is a clear link between the ability of an organization to maturely manage their software and systems and their ability to secure their e-business.

Similar to the SEI-CMM is a model and appraisal method known as the Systems Security Engineering (SSE) Capability Maturity Model (CMM). The SSE-CMM is the result of a collaborative effort of members of the International Systems Security Engineering Association (ISSEA). The SSE-CMM describes the essential characteristics of an organization's system security engineering process that must exist to ensure good software or system security engineering. While the SSE-CMM does not prescribe a particular process, it does capture practices generally observed in industry. The model is becoming a standard metric for systems security engineering practices covering:

- The entire life cycle, including definition, development, testing, operation, maintenance, and system decommissioning activities
- The whole organization, including management, organizational, and engineering activities
- Concurrent interactions with other disciplines, such as system software, hardware, human factors, and test engineering; system management, operation, and maintenance
- Interactions with other organizations, including acquisition, system management, certification, accreditation, and evaluation.

Like the SEI-CMM, the SSE-CMM contains five levels depicting different degrees of maturity, which reflect the organization's capability to build and operate secured e-business systems.

An in-depth discussion of these five levels is conducted in Part Three of this chapter. For now, it is important that executive management recognize that the ability to develop and operate secured e-business systems depends on both the ability to build quality business systems that can be "trusted for use" and the ability to protect and secure those same systems through engineered confidentiality, integrity, and reliability and availability controls. Little progress can be made until this latter capability is assessed.

Best Practice #7: The Executive IT Management Committee should commission an evaluation of current corporate software development and maintenance capabilities using the SEI-CMM.

Best Practice #8: Once the present maturity level of software development and security engineering is determined, plans must be approved that will improve the ratings of the organization. An essential element of this plan should be the use of the Systems Development Review (SDR) Framework (Exhibit 4.5) to monitor systems and security activities during actual e-business development projects.

It has been a premise of this section that the SDP is the single most powerful tool available to managers and executives for getting a handle on the uses of IT and specifically the building of secured e-business systems. Use of the SDP brings to information technology an analytic integrity and developmental discipline that too often has been missing during the last three decades. During the last 10 years, methods to assess maturity in systems development and security engineering have evolved that can enable organizations to set forth "get well" plans to continuously improve their abilities even in the face of rapidly changing e-business technologies. Executive management must embrace these tools and methods if e-business security is to be achieved.

IT Software Vendor and Supplier Selection

The last 20 years of technological evolution have created a world of extensive, albeit not readily apparent, dependencies. Nowhere is this truer than with IT and the use of computers in e-business. Traditional management techniques have not kept pace with this evolution and will require attention over the next couple of decades to be more effective. One of the areas needing attention deals with the selection of future IT suppliers, service providers, and contractor support. Until rather recently, IT source selections were driven primarily by technical issues, evaluated by technical personnel on a purely technical basis, and cost. Great trust was placed in technicians to make the proper IT decisions and protect the interests of the company. Insufficient attention was given to examining business issues and the system management processes that competing vendors employed during construction of their products. There was a fundamental belief on the part of the buyer that IT vendors and the company's internal IT professional, as expert, knew what they were doing and that trust was necessary when entering into a contract. Besides, few people had any idea what to evaluate or how to conduct such an evaluation.

Over time, however, and in the wake of Y2K, many organizations have begun to feel as if their trust, at least in the IT vendor community, has been misplaced. And even though, to the layperson, it appeared that Y2K was a non-event, many of those internal IT professionals responsible for successfully negotiating the date rollover for corporate systems give no great credit to the IT vendors for their deliverance. Early assurances in 1997 and 1998 that software products and systems were compliant were generally proven to be untrue or only partially true. Many vendors couched their compliance claims in very strange language. Many products were not exactly compliant but were "ready." Other products were "compliant capable" or "compliant with exceptions." It has been reported that as many as 50 percent of software vendors made compliance claims that did not stand up to independent testing.

With hindsight, some may ask "so what?" Everything seemed to turn out all right; there was no meltdown, no catastrophes. Undoubtedly, the short- and long-term impacts of the Y2K episode on the future of IT will be debated for years to come. Appendix A identifies certain lessons learned from Y2K and discusses how these lessons impact the securing of IT systems. For our purpose here, the principal lesson learned from Y2K was the great lengths to which software and system vendors would go to absolve themselves from accountability (i.e., getting "safe haven" legislation passed) while still marketing consumers to continue to buy their "possibly compliant" products. *In such an environment, trust is very hard to maintain.* Many software vendors and service providers are suffering today because of the trust that was lost during Y2K and will have a difficult time recovering their reputation for quality software—if they ever had one.

Y2K finally forced business leaders to see the lack of confidence most IT professionals have had for many years in the claims of any software and system vendor. The annals of IT are full of exaggerated claims concerning the benefits and ease of use of a particular system while largely ignoring any downside or negative impact on a business.

So with trust of software vendors and system providers at a low point, how can business executives proceed to select the next generation of e-business system products and services? How can the "security" claims of software and system vendors be judged? What must an executive management committee do to better protect corporate interests and prevent being victimized by endless promises and unsubstantiated product claims?

There are several things that corporations can do in the absence of vendor trust to better protect their interests:

- Expect and require vendor adherence to an SDP that satisfies all the requirements of the SDR framework (Exhibit 4.5 and Appendix B).

- Require an SEI-CMM level of at least three of all vendors under consideration for software products or software support contracts.

- Negotiate meaningful penalties for nonperformance that reflect actual corporate losses incurred by the corporation. Do not just accept the standard clauses in most vendor-provided contracts. (Note: This action is primarily for custom-developed or customized software, not for packaged software.)

- As a businessperson, lobby against UCITA passage in your state, especially the provision that allows software publishers to disclaim warranties and the provision that holds publishers unaccountable for known defects. These favor only the software developer, with little benefit accruing to non-IT companies, and will only promote a lessening of software quality.

- Support user groups and use these affiliations to bring pressure on vendors to improve the quality of software products. As an example, IT managers recently decided to use their collective buying power to improve the usability of vendor-supplied software before they recommend purchase for their corporate clients. They are devising a standard way to measure software usability by working with industry software publishers and the National Institute of Standards and Technology (NIST). This is a good example of the power of organized buyers.

- Require not only marketing demonstrations of vendor products but also the execution of functional and performance benchmarks that reflect the workloads and unique characteristics of the company's e-business application. This technique is somewhat expensive and has usually been reserved for very large projects that include hardware purchases, but in an atmosphere of limited trust, this approach should be more liberally used than previously. Up-and-coming vendors wishing to establish themselves will cooperate with this technique and be thankful for the opportunity.

Best Practice #9: Establish IT criteria for selecting vendors and suppliers. Include the SEI-CMM method where appropriate, independent verification and testing of products, and functional and performance benchmarking. Establish selection evaluation committees with membership that represents all stakeholders to every e-business project.

Outsourcing for IT Support

Closely related to the issue of IT vendor and supplier selection is the increasingly popular practice of putting major portions or even the entire IT/computer processing activity under contract. Two rationales are usually offered: (1) it is more cost-effective than continuing to do IT in-house, and/or (2) the company simply *cannot* or *does not want* to perform the computing function, so "let's hire some professionals to do it for us."

Both rationales have appeal because there is an element of truth in each. At the same time, both rationales are very simple statements of a far more complex situation that requires extremely careful analysis that must now include the issue of security.

First, IT/computer processing support is not inexpensive no matter how the work is accomplished. If a comprehensive baseline economic analysis of the IT work to be performed has been completed (cost is not always the reason for an outsource decision), bidding contractors will find it harder to *appear* more cost-effective than in-house task performance, but only if a comprehensive analysis was performed using the cost categories of Exhibit 4.3. The more complete the cost model, the harder it becomes to bid substantially lower costs by being able to ignore expenses not evaluated by the model. A vendor-preferred scenario is to have unknown and unevaluated items of expense surface after contract award, when, for political reasons, there is little risk of losing the contract no matter what the cost.

A comprehensive cost model is constructed by paying careful attention to all foreseeable life cycle expenses identified during the economic and operational analysis of the feasibility study. For example, costs associated with maintaining and administering an operational system are wildly understated in most cost studies. Security administration is a vital part of ongoing systems administration and is subsequently ignored in many such studies.

With outsourcing arrangement, maintenance and system administrative expenses constitute the majority of costs, but since these costs are directly related to the quality, *security*, and production readiness of the system currently in operation, proposing contractors cannot intelligently bid unless they are allowed to conduct an evaluation of the existing conditions surrounding the system to be outsourced. This, however, is usually not allowed and is not practical since sufficient documentation does not generally exist to allow an examination by bidding contractors. Without such an analysis, outsource contractors are forced to keep lowering their bids through a negotiation process that blindly pits contractors against each other, with no one having a clear picture of the systems or the operational environment for which they are bidding. If contracting officials are not aware of the underlying technical difficulties associated with this approach, they will unwittingly force the bidding downward to the point where reputable contractors will bow out and the organization will be left with what is jokingly referred to as the lowest bidder. Seeking a low-cost bid is a worthy goal as long as there are few performance surprises later during the contract period and few preventable cost escalations due to the earlier lack of definition and blind bidding.

Due to the nature of competitive acquisition practices, the inherent difficulty in constructing realistic cost models, the even greater difficulty in attempting to develop value-added models (for such things as security), and the scarcity of IT-savvy contracting officials, IT managers dread the award of *any* contract to the lowest bidder, let alone an outsourcing deal.

Successful IT outsourcing results from intelligent bid preparation, measured proposal evaluation, and enforceable contracting. The success of these three activities depends on a clear and accurate understanding by all parties of the exact nature of the work to be accomplished, how performance will be measured, and a clear and concise knowledge of all aspects of the business and the IT environment within which the outsourcer will be expected to operate. Central to this understanding are the *baseline* inventories of business information, e-business systems, and other computing assets that constitute the information infrastructure of the company. These baselines, just recently updated because of Y2K, provide the essential foundation for any meaningful outsource undertaking. Ideally, these baselines, *if* they are being kept current using configuration management techniques, should make outsourcing less risky since all the information needed to bid, evaluate, and contract intelligently will be available. If, conversely, these baselines are not being kept up-to-date and accurate, outsourcing initiatives will remain high-risk since intelligent bidding, proposal evaluation, and contracting will not be possible and the lowest bidder phenomenon will continue to prevail.

The second rationale for outsourcing (i.e., we don't do IT very well, therefore . . .) must be approached carefully because this reasoning could result in several different situations, each with varying impacts on the company. First, depending on the nature of the work being considered for outsourcing, the idea can either provide a clear improvement or pose a threat to the very existence of the business. Before the Y2K experience, few organizations or senior executives thought about their IT applications using terms like "mission-critical" or "mission-sensitive." Unless the organization had experienced some type of computer-related business interruption, IT processing was just something that usually seemed to get done— if not today, then tomorrow. Unless the company's revenues were directly dependent on on-line transaction processing (as in e-business), the term *mission-critical* was not normally associated with IT. The term was reserved for such business activities as obtaining an increase in a line of credit or finalizing a merger.

Along came Y2K and corporations found that they were very closely tied to other companies and that other companies were highly dependent on them. And the source of the dependencies turned out to be the very IT systems that few executives gave a second thought to before then. Today, corporations find themselves in a maze of system dependencies and are discovering that many of these systems are not being managed with the same degree of rigor as other corporate systems and assets. Sounds exactly like the reason cited for outsourcing (i.e., we don't do IT very well, therefore . . .), except now the mission-critical nature of the systems is known and it is also known that no one is terribly confident about how they really work or how to keep them running. By the way, all those other corporate systems and assets that were thought to be well managed—we now know that they also depend on systems that no one is terribly confident about.

It may well be that the corporation does not do a very good job of IT management; but does the company *dare* to create an even greater dependency by contracting out mission-critical business systems when it does not understand how the systems really work? Remember, without the knowledge to conduct an intelligent outsourcing initiative, a company could end up in a lowest bidder situation and be worse off than before.

To be successful, outsourcing must originate from proper motivation and be influenced by the new sense of risk that Y2K and e-business dependencies have uncovered. Proper motivation for entering into an outsource arrangement will include a focus on making long-term improvements and efficiencies to corporate IT support activities through the establishment of stable and mature business relations with IT contract providers. Stable and mature relationships should revolve around two issues: fair and equitable treatment of existing corporate IT employees, and retaining the corporate ability and knowledge base to monitor systems management and performance of the outsource provider.

Fair and equitable treatment of corporate IT employees, subject to the consequences of an outsourcing, is not only morally right, but also necessary from a business survival perspective. In light of the poor system management conditions now known to exist in many IT support organizations, to invite the wrath of disgruntled employees who possess, in their heads, the process and practice knowledge of the business would be extremely foolhardy.

The Y2K experience has demonstrated the great dependency businesses have on the goodwill of their IT employees. Employee loyalty is certainly subject to change, perhaps for the worse, during times of upheaval brought on by a move to outsource. The company is at its most vulnerable during such times, and great efforts must be made to allay employees' fears and retain their support.

To be successful, outsourcing must be part of a much broader strategy for improving corporate capabilities to use business information and e-business processing systems for the long-term benefit of the company, shareholders, employees, and business partners. When embarking on discussions concerning the plausibility and benefits of outsourcing, care must be taken not to take a simplistic economic view but rather to balance short-term cost-cutting gains with the need to prevent *unacceptable* contractor dependencies and related vulnerabilities from developing.

The prevention of unacceptable dependencies developing in the working arrangement with the outsource contractor addresses the challenge of being able to monitor the contractor's technical, process, and performance management. If a company contemplating outsourcing cannot competently evaluate the technical performance of the provider, the contract should not be awarded. As Y2K illustrated, contract penalties and warranties provide insufficient protection when a corporation's livelihood is at stake and cannot be substituted for retaining sufficient system involvement and adequate "core" system employees to ensure continuity of e-business processes regardless of contractor performance.

To fully examine whether IT outsourcing is appropriate in a given situation, eight sets of questions must be answered.

1. Can the IT activity being considered for outsourcing be defined to a degree of precision that allows measurement of the work to be contracted? Can gradients of performance be determined?

2. Can the outsourced activities be adequately controlled by existing (or remaining) corporate technical managers, or does contract performance fall mainly to a contracting official?

3. Can IT tasks that extend into the future be delineated, or are there a great many *to be determined* (TBD) actions? Too many TBDs may indicate a lack of task understanding and not enough specificity to evaluate contractor performance.

4. If "information" products constitute a revenue-generating aspect of the business, who controls the information and makes decisions related to its generation, processing, storage, confidentiality, uses, and final disposition?

5. Is the corporation structured to permit the management of information as a corporate resource? Do data and information policy standards exist? Do quality standards exist, and are they measurable? Can these standards be contractually required of the outsource contractor, are they subject to audit, and how are they enforced?

6. Does executive management appreciate the need for sufficient funding to require a contractor to take necessary QA, contingent staffing, and maintenance task-related actions to ensure proper "best practices" management of the corporation's critical information and systems?

7. Can meaningful penalties for nonperformance be levied under the contract, or are allowed penalties merely token? Remember, the contractor will be dealing with mission-critical systems that support core revenue-generating business applications. The potential for lost revenues and the potential for collateral damage to business partners must be carefully considered (see Chapter 7).

8. Are all business principals comfortable with the degree of corporate dependency posed by outsourcing the proposed IT functions?

Best Practice #10: Commission a review of all existing and contemplated outsource arrangements to identify any risky dependencies of vulnerabilities that could threaten the viability of the business. For pending outsource contracts, require that a comprehensive feasibility analysis be conducted to allow for intelligent bidding, proposal evaluation, and enforceable contracting.

Best Practice #11: Review all existing and contemplated outsource arrangements to ensure the retention of adequate employee numbers and skills to effectively monitor and manage the outsource contractor.

IT Personnel Management

The dot-com meltdown notwithstanding, the IT labor market has been tight for at least a decade. According to a recent U.S. Commerce Department report, the growth rate for computer scientists, systems analysts, and computer engineers will have increased 100 percent for the decade ending 2006. That translates into 1.3 million new IT workers to fill new jobs and replace those leaving the industry or retiring. It is estimated that 12 percent of all IT jobs are unfilled and that of these open positions, 37 percent result from employee turnover. The labor shortage coupled with the high rate of turnover is bound to have a negative impact on e-business projects and ultimately on profits. It has been reported that 90 percent of projects are being delayed or were incomplete as a result of trained IT worker shortages.

Historically, there has always been a shortage of IT workers, primarily because technical breakthroughs always seem to stay ahead of attempts by universities, government, and businesses to train people in the myriad evolving computing techniques, computer languages, and vendor software packages. This has resulted in an employment scene where skilled, knowledgeable, and experienced personnel are very easily placed. This poses a threat to companies without effective human resource management programs, who can find themselves held hostage by a "key person" on whom an entire e-business system or systems may depend. *Faced with the reality that IT personnel are easily employable and hold special knowledge about "mission-critical" systems, special attention must be given to their management.*

Conventional practice has been to recruit IT personnel as needed for specific projects requiring specialized skills. Oftentimes, once the project is complete, the employee is let go. This scenario is the norm with both IT product and service companies and is becoming more commonplace among IT-intensive businesses. While viewed as desirable by some IT professionals who think of themselves as consultants, many others wish for more stability than the role of contract help offers them. The combined forces of technical specialization coupled with the movement to outsourcing have conspired to make difficult the creation and maintenance of a *steadfast* IT workforce. Yet the IT-dependent, and therefore vulnerable, corporation needs a steadfast group of IT professionals to support its goals and objectives, not hourly employees doing piecework with no sense of loyalty and then leaving.

During the last two decades, people in IT have tended toward three career paths. First are those who pursued the technical track of computer science, working to stay current with new manifestations of IT and being proficient with vendor product lines. Second were those who followed the IT management track, advancing through projects of increasing complexity and size. It has been within these first two tracks that the Peter Principle has been most often observed. It will be recalled that the Peter Principle states that people are advanced within an organization's bureaucracy until they reach their own individual level of incompetence. In the case of the IT technology track, promotion to management positions has often occurred to provide status and monetary rewards beyond those available in the technical track. Promoting people into management positions without adequate preparation usually has the undesirable effect of denying the business the services of a highly competent technician while saddling it with a new manager of questionable experience in a whole new set of skills.

The third career track, IT business development and corporate business management, was pursued by those desiring the rewards of sales commissions and corporate officer remuneration and standing.

These three career paths are frequently at cross-purposes when customer satisfaction, product quality, security, and project accountability are at stake. For example, an IT manager and technical specialists working directly for an IT-intensive corporation often find themselves at odds with an IT vendor or service provider producing or delivering poor-quality or unsecured software, systems, or services. Likewise, vendor managers responsible for product or services delivery may find themselves in conflict with their own business development and sales managers who are making unrealistic product and schedule promises.

These role distinctions and the problems that may exist between members of the same industry are important because they revolve around IT business philosophy, practice, and quality and ethical issues that many IT professionals find highly problematic. Executives in both IT and IT-intensive companies must recognize this dynamic, be aware of such distinctions, and not stereotype IT workers inappropriately.

Management of IT human resources will be critical in the next decade. All attention to process and practice management, risk identification and mitigation, QA, and vendor and supply chain management will amount to little without a *strategic* vision and plan on how to integrate the IT professional into the corporation such that all employees have a sense of shared purpose and belonging. However it is that IT human resource policies evolve over the next few years, they must assume the following employee-employment realities:

- Shortages of qualified IT personnel will continue, and this will increase pressure on traditional recruitment, hiring, and retention practices to be creative.

- Continue to expect a considerable amount of job-hopping from those professionals choosing the technical career path as the importance of résumé experience with new computing techniques and vendor products accelerates. Expect increasing difficulty in determining the truly experienced applicant from the resume inflator, and develop recruitment screening and hiring standards to assist with this difficult task.

- Expect an increase in disaffection among younger IT employees as the shortcomings of their elders' management styles continue to surface. This is the generation that just discovered they had been working for "worthless" stock options in lieu of salary for much of the dot-com era. This is also the generation that recently witnessed their parents being laid off after years of dedicated service, first in the name of reengineering and then during the merger mania of the 1990s. These experiences have left them with little sense of corporate loyalty. At a time when loyalty is essential to the corporation, it may be in very short supply.

In formulating new IT human resource management policies and practices, corporate executives should consider a number of things.

First, do not unconsciously blame today's IT worker for the acts and omissions of yesterday's IT and corporate management that led to the security problems now being experienced. Do begin to manage IT like any other aspect of the business and demand accountability of management, employees, contractors, and vendors. Recognize that while the current generation of workers may feel a general distrust of the corporation, they want to belong to something larger than themselves and to sense purpose in their employment. Their generation is as idealistic as any other and wants to labor for goals worthy of time and talents. Money may not always be their first objective. Challenge them with the importance of IT and their contribution to business, government, and society.

One extremely positive thing that corporate executives can do for IT workers is to jealously guard their time. This can be accomplished by demanding adherence to the chosen SDP. This will force system development decisions to be made in the prescribed analytic sequence, thus facilitating the productive use of human resources. Poorly managed IT projects are very wasteful of employee time as prior work products are constantly revisited to determine their appropriateness and validity.

Conclusion

This section has outlined those activities of IT systems management and systems development that need attention if overall e-business security is to be improved. The security of any IT system is based on the soundness of overall IT management. With poorly administered IT organizations and e-business processing environments the basic disciplines on which confidentiality, integrity, and system availability depend simply do not exist. Whereas, where strong IT management and systems discipline are the norm, a solid foundation does exist on which to build a viable and flexible e-business security program.

Part Three of Chapter 4 concentrates on the specific actions, above and beyond competent systems management, that will need to be taken to establish and maintain a program to manage, on a continuing basis, the security of e-business systems.

PART THREE: E-BUSINESS SECURITY PROGRAM MANAGEMENT
Introduction

The previous two parts of this chapter have described and discussed essential system management activities upon which an effective e-business security program must be built.

Security consultants are always amused when visiting prospective clients, usually with serious security problems, and observing how they operate their IT system organizations by the seat of their pants. When it is pointed out, prospective clients always claim to have neither the time nor the people to take a methodical approach to IT management. What they do not realize until later is that without the systems disciplines prescribed in the previous part of this chapter, *there can be no e-business security* and that the random introduction of security software, tools, and techniques only contributes to the unsecured nature of the operating environment by increasing the unmanaged "noise" level.

Building on Parts One and Two, this part addresses the organizational, methodological, and security management issues that must be considered when designing a corporate program to administer e-business security. It presents specific considerations concerning security of e-business systems as a supplement to each topical area of Part Two. In other words, each issue of systems management outlined in Part Two has a security component that completes the picture of total systems management necessary for establishing and sustaining a secured e-business system and operating environment. It is hoped that this approach will assist executive management to see the critical relationship between day-to-day system management improvements and the establishment and institutionalization of a security management program for all future e-business undertakings.

To visualize these relationships and their critical importance to achieving systems security, Exhibits 4.6 through 4.8 are provided. Each portrays one of the security objectives—*confidentiality, integrity,* and *availability/reliability* resting on a program of risk-based security and management controls, which are in turn supported by a foundation of system management "baseline" practices. Collectively, the "baseline" practices are essential for establishing an environment within which security can be achieved. The actual program of risk-based security and management controls will vary from system to system based upon the analyzed threats that are specific to each e-business application and its operational environment.

By understanding these relationships, it is easy to see that a successful e-business security program will be determined to a large extent by the sum total and the effectiveness of existing system management practices.

Before presenting considerations that are unique to the e-business security management program, the problem of nomenclature or naming conventions must be addressed.

Most information security tools and methodologies include a description and often a database of security vulnerabilities and exposures. However, there is significant variation among them and no easy way to determine when different descriptions are referring to the same problem. Since there is no common definitional language between tools, there exists the potential for gaps to develop in security coverage of an organization. This problem is being tackled by the independent, not-for-profit Mitre Corporation (www.mitre.org), with their Common Vulnerabilities and Exposures (CVE) project. The CVE is a dictionary that provides common names for publicly known information security vulnerabilities and exposures. Using a common name makes it easier to share security data across separate vendor databases and tools that until now were not easily integrated. This makes CVE the key to information sharing. If a report from one security vendor or tool incorporates CVE names, you may quickly and accurately

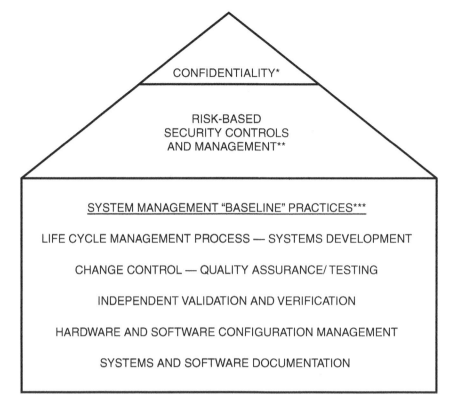

*This objective means that the privacy of customer data and the protection of other sensitive data can be assured.

**To be effective, security controls depend on the "best practice" management of the information system and the operational environment.

***These "practices" constitute a "due diligence" level of control needed to demonstrate an underlying ability to achieve and maintain confidentiality.

Exhibit 4.6   Security Objective: Confidentiality

access fix information in one or more separate CVE-compatible databases to remediate the problem.

The term *CVE-compatible* means that a tool, web site, database, or other security product uses CVE names in a manner that allows it to be cross-referenced with other products that employ CVE names. The term means:

- CVE searchable—the user can search using a CVE name to find related information.

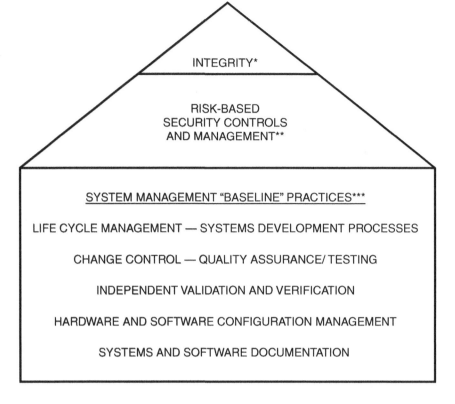

*This objective means that information systems and the output from those systems can be "trusted."

**To be effective, security controls depend on the "best practice" management of the information system and the operational environment.

***These "practices" constitute a "due diligence" level of control needed to demonstrate an underlying ability to achieve and maintain information and systems integrity.

Exhibit 4.7 Security Objective: Integrity

- CVE output—information is presented that includes the related CVE name(s).
- Accuracy—the provider has made a good faith effort to ensure that CVE names are used accurately in the product.

The CVE project is endorsed by leading representatives from the information security community. Its content results from the collaborative efforts of the CVE

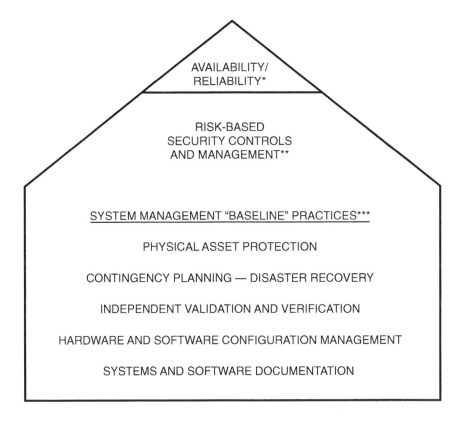

AVAILABILITY/
RELIABILITY*

RISK-BASED
SECURITY CONTROLS
AND MANAGEMENT**

SYSTEM MANAGEMENT "BASELINE" PRACTICES***

PHYSICAL ASSET PROTECTION

CONTINGENCY PLANNING — DISASTER RECOVERY

INDEPENDENT VALIDATION AND VERIFICATION

HARDWARE AND SOFTWARE CONFIGURATION MANAGEMENT

SYSTEMS AND SOFTWARE DOCUMENTATION

*This objective means that information and systems processing are dependable and ready for use as needed.

**To be effective, security controls that assure availability depend on the "best practice" management of the information system and the operational environment.

***These "practices" constitute a "due diligence" level of control needed to demonstrate an underlying ability to achieve and maintain availability.

Exhibit 4.8   Security Objective: Availability/Reliability

editorial board, which includes representatives from more than 15 information security-related organizations and associations.

Best Practice #12: As a matter of policy, adopt the CVE naming strategy and enforce its use in all aspects of the e-business security program management.

Establish Executive Security Ownership of All IT Systems, Computing Assets, and the Security Management Program

Historically, computer and communication security has been thought of as a technical problem to be solved by technicians in the data processing department. In the days of stand-alone mainframes, this thinking may have been sufficient, but not today when essential automated business processes permeate the entire company, are used interactively by employees of the company, and even extend to trusted business partners in a "supply chain."

According to surveys conducted by the System Administration and Networking Security (SANS) Institute, the top management errors that contribute and perpetuate the e-business security problem include:

* pretending the problem will go away
* failure to understand that information security is a business problem with substantial economic ramifications
* thinking "firewalls" secure the system
* taking reactive, short-term action so that problems quickly surface again
* failing to realize the "value" of their e-business information, processes, reputation, and supply chain responsibilities
* failure to have technical fixes integrated into the operational work-a-day business process
* assigning overworked and untrained people to establish and maintain security
* failure to enforce existing security rules and hold managers and staff accountable.

Today, e-business systems cross many organizational lines of authority, each with its own set of responsibilities and reward systems. Unless the challenge of "who speaks for the system" is resolved, systems ownership will be fragmented and security that should be seamless in its implementation will fall between the cracks.

Since contemporary e-business implementations must anticipate the collective requirements of cross-cutting business components, decisions concerning the *confidentiality, integrity,* and *availability/reliability* of those systems must be made with a single owner having responsibility for the whole. Without a high-level executive responsible for decisions and enforcement, e-business systems security will break down at the operational level. If the e-business system supports a supply chain comprised of different companies, the need for senior executive ownership by one of the companies is even more pronounced.

The first problem associated with system ownership stems from the fact that business unit and line managers tend to focus on that for which they are being rewarded. This is also true of their employees. Usually this focus is on production, sales, or service. In each case, numbers must be made and system security is often seen as an impediment to achieving those numbers. This means that to make a *glib* blanket statement that "security is everyone's job" is to effectively say that security is the job of no one. To be sure, at some point, employees will have responsibilities to take predetermined security actions for the state of security of their workplace environment; but overall security decisions and enforcement will always reside with the legally empowered leaders of the company.

Other problems that executive ownership solves are those of determining priorities and deciding when and where to allocate corporate resources to e-business security. Executive management is all about choosing between competing priorities and then allocating resources to those priorities. Only at the very pinnacle of the corporation can such decisions be made about the priority of securing e-business systems. Only near the top can resources be allocated to security initiatives or reallocated from a lower priority project to security, and then only if executives are *being evaluated* on how well they are supporting the security objectives of the organization. Business unit leaders, line managers, and staff directors must be given permission by those above them to secure their systems. As long as security is seen to be competing with "production" and senior executives have not provided the mechanisms to resolve the conflict, managers do not have permission to secure their systems. Until senior executive involvement signals the seriousness of the problem, e-business security will be an afterthought and the implementation of any security controls will be haphazard at best.

Best Practice 13: Establish a subordinate subcommittee for e-business security reporting to the executive IT management committee. For every e-business system (backroom and online), e-business application, and IT infrastructure support system, assign security responsibility to a member of the subcommittee. Members should be evaluated annually on how well they support the corporate goals of achieving adequate e-business security. This action will keep responsibility for e-business security, the burden of determining priorities, and the challenge of allocating resources to the securing of e-business systems at the executive level, where "due diligence" considerations are routinely examined.

Additionally, from the perspective of ownership, there is another aspect of the e-business security effort that senior executives must own, and that is the security program itself. The following discussion briefly identifies the "success criteria" that should be used in designing a corporate e-business security program that is both effective from a security perspective and responsive to changing technology and business needs.

Success Criteria #1: Adopt a Balanced Strategy. Traditionally, a strategy for computer systems and their operating environment has included three distinct elements: *prevention, detection,* and *response* or *reaction.* Security policies, controls, and procedures within each of these three areas are determined after conducting a technical vulnerability and threat assessment to uncover the risk that an organization is likely to encounter and the potential for suffering "quantifiable" and "nonquantifiable" losses.

Prevention includes the numerous proactive actions that are taken to protect information, processes, and computing assets against destruction, compromise, and unauthorized access, manipulation, or modification, whether deliberate or accidental. *Prevention* is "design in nature" and addresses such issues as the construction of systems to operate in a secure manner. This is accomplished through the effective use of many security tools and techniques, such as firewalls, passwords, encryption, virtual private networks (VPN), data integrity and processing checks, security testing, and the use of biometrics technologies in configuring computers and network elements to preclude accidental or deliberate events or actions that are deemed undesirable.

It is with the attempt to prevent security incidents that most of today's advertised security technology is employed. Despite the best-designed and implemented precautionary measures, however, attacks against an organization's information and information processing infrastructure will be attempted. Some will be successful. Furthermore, accidents and mistakes in daily e-business processing that threaten systems integrity, reliability, and data confidentiality will occur. It is important to know when such things happen.

Detection employs system network and host computer intrusion detection and audit techniques and tools, which perform functions from on-line scanning and transaction monitoring to trend analysis and attack prediction. *Detection* identifies attacks against the system as well as the unauthorized actions of "trusted" employees (remember the 70 percent figure from the FBI) as they are occurring, or shortly thereafter, and issues alerts to take protective and business response action.

Response, or *Reaction,* initiates damage containment, recovery plans, and corrective actions after an attack or unauthorized use has been detected. This includes actions to report security incidents to users throughout the organization so that corrective actions can be taken to execute predefined tasks that reconstitute systems, software, and information files to their full business functionality after the incident is detected.

A fundamental "success criteria" for the successful design of an e-business security program is the need to balance all three elements of the basic strategy by employing the concept of *defense in depth.* Defense in depth is defined as "not putting all your security eggs in one basket." Rather, create a number of complementary security, integrity, and system availability and reliability controls that will force an assailant to have to defeat multiple protective mechanisms and to do so undetected. The important factor to recognize is that the use of *preventive* security techniques alone will not provide foolproof protection for a business in today's on-line world. This means that an investment must be made in all three areas of *prevention, detection,* and *reaction or response* and a program to manage them.

Success Criteria #2: A Management Program Is Needed to Administer Security.
The nature of the e-business security challenge is that of dynamically changing vulnerabilities and threats based on ever-changing technology being used to evolve increasingly complex business applications and uses. This means that

organizations must build their e-business security initiative around a continuous improvement model of the type made popular by the total quality management movement. For purposes of quality improvement, this model was thought of as a *plan-do-check-improve* cycle. For e-business security, it can be thought of as a *plan-fix-monitor-assess* model.

An e-business security management program to execute the continuous improvement security model must be established, funded, and integrated into the day-to-day operations of the company. Integration into day-to-day management means that the security initiative does not stand alone as a "watch dog" or audit function. It is instead merged to ensure that the three "balanced" elements of security are integral to the SDP activities of requirements definition, systems design, programming, testing, systems documentation, training, and operations and maintenance. A security management program must be designed in such a way that the continuous improvement activities of *planning, fixing, monitoring,* and *assessing* are accomplished with e-business systems under development and on a continuing basis for those systems already in production. There are several commercial security program models available, and the federal government has a model that can be obtained from the National Institute of Standards and Technology (NIST), Department of Commerce, Special Publications 800 series.

Whichever model an organization chooses to adopt, the point to be emphasized is that executive level commitment and funding sufficient to sustain the program initially and in its continuous improvement mode must be made available and be considered as another operating expense. Chapter 7 discusses the challenge of justifying an e-business security program.

Success Criteria #3: Design to a "Due Diligence" Standard. The Y2K experience introduced business executives and IT managers to the concept of "due diligence" as applied to the uses of information technology. Because of the potential for legal fallout, it became necessary to view Y2K-related actions through the definitions of "due diligence" and "reasonable care." It became imperative to document all Y2K deliberations, decisions, and actions in order to be able to defend against possible charges of "laxity." The same focus now falls on e-business security and will influence all security deliberations and actions.

Due diligence: The degree of effort and care in carrying out an act or obligation that the average, sincere, energetic person would exhibit—conduct that is devoid of negligence or carelessness.

—*The Plain-Language Law Dictionary,*
Robert Rothenberg, Penguin, 1981

Reasonable care: That degree of care which a person of ordinary prudence would exercise in the same or similar circumstances—failure to exercise such care is ordinary negligence.

—Black's Law Dictionary

The significance of the concepts of "due diligence" and "reasonable care" is that they allow for an evolving metric against which any particular organization's e-business security deliberations, decisions, and actions can be compared. The comparison is usually against a like company in like circumstances of vulnerability and threat and with similar predictable adverse impacts on customers, business partners, shareholders, investors, and perhaps the public. For example, if one company does employ a "security or integrity control" and does not experience any security breaches that the control was intended to prevent, that fact could be used to establish a possible "control" baseline against which similar companies could be compared. The positive security actions of one or several companies can thus become a *de facto standard* for all companies in that industry. If enough similar companies employ the same technique, that "security or integrity control" may become categorized as a security "best practice" for that industry.

Now, if another company in that same industry were to not employ the "security or integrity control" and does experience a security breach of the type the technique was intended to prevent, it may be questioned whether that company exercised "due diligence" or demonstrated "reasonable care."

The standards of "due diligence" and "reasonable care," with regard to e-business security will continually evolve as the technology, vulnerabilities, threats, risks, and countermeasures change. This means that e-business security decisions and implementations are *not a one-time event,* but must be under a continuous process of risk evaluation and security program management. It is therefore important, in order to demonstrate the ability to exercise continual "due diligence," to establish a documented security risk management program and integrate it into the overall management processes of the business. Nothing less will demonstrate that a company is capable of assessing future e-business security threats and is acting in a "reasonable" manner. Documents that are presently seen to be "due diligence" guidelines include National Institute of Standards and Technology Guidelines and Special Publications, the Generally Accepted Systems Security Principles (GASSP)—International Information Security Foundation, and British Standard 7799—Code of Practice for Information Security Management.

In conclusion, an e-business security management program must be designed to satisfy these design criteria; to do so, ownership of the security program by executive management is necessary.

Best Practice #14: Establish a formal e-business security management program that satisfies the three success criteria prescribed. Pattern the program after national or international standards and guidelines that are CVE-compatible and appropriate to the business. This action will institutionalize the practice of e-business security for the corporation, establish a framework for managing security issues, and demonstrate "due diligence."

Determine Appropriateness of IT Projects (and Security Controls) Through Comprehensive Feasibility Studies

As stated earlier, feasibility studies of proposed IT systems are seldom conducted in their entirety, and when they have been performed, they are usually biased toward the technical and economic side of the equation and are usually light on analyzing operational issues. We have also seen that *e-business is nothing if not an operational issue.*

This thinking leads to retrofitting security controls into production systems and laminating security modifications onto the business process. No one is satisfied with the outcome, least of all the employees, who must still meet their "production" numbers.

Evaluating e-business security controls using the three tests of feasibility can proceed in two ways. First, and to be preferred, is the evaluation of an e-business *confidentiality, integrity, or availability/reliability* policy, control, or procedure as an integral part of a new systems proposal where the entire package is being subjected to all tests of feasibility. If the proposal does in fact include security controls as part of the design and if each control has at least been conceptually justified (see Chapter 7), then the most pragmatic combination of business productivity gains and security safeguards should result if all three tests of feasibility are conducted in an unbiased manner. Chapter 6 outlines how to manage the incorporation of designed security controls into an e-business system under development. This is the preferred way to ensure that future systems meet their business productivity as well as their security goals.

The second way in which the three tests of feasibility should be used in making security control decisions is on an "as required" basis. This approach recognizes that most organizations pursuing the e-business track will be forced, overtime, to retrofit policies, controls, and procedures in order to improve their security posture. This means that a baseline of the current e-business system and its security posture must be identified, security goals are then established that mitigate analyzed vulnerabilities in the system, its operating environment, and proposed technical and administrative safeguards are then subjected to the tests of feasibility. This strategy is much more difficult, but with many systems there is no choice. It is more difficult because any imposition of security controls is likely to fit awkwardly into the existing business process and have negative effects on workplace productivity.

With either method, the goal is to develop a new system or modify an existing system to gain as much security and stability as possible within the constraints of actual business processing. To do this, the proper sequence of feasibility tests must be followed—*technical* followed by *operational* followed by *economic.* This is how to achieve a pragmatic balance that achieves the goals of both security and productivity. The next section discusses the tests of feasibility within the context of a risk management review process for e-business systems.

Establish an Executive-Level E-Business Security
Risk Management Review Process

In Part Two of this chapter, it was stated that risk management, on the *rare* occasions when it has actually been performed, usually focused only on the assessment of computer and communications security vulnerabilities. Meanwhile, other long catalogues of threats to the success of an e-business system exist but are rarely addressed. These other threats originate from the use of technology itself, from the IT industry and how it conducts business, and from the poor system management practices that many organizations allow. Collectively, these categories of threats are regularly overlooked, unanalyzed, and unmitigated. These unattended threats put at risk the overall success of any system already in production or under development and therefore constitute a threat of systems security. The previous text then showed how to identify and manage these threats. Exhibit 4.5 provided a systems development review (SDR) framework for ensuring that security issues, as well as the commonly overlooked IT industry and system management threats, are addressed during the actual development of an e-business system. Additionally, Appendix D provided an additional review tool for monitoring other real world project risks that lie beyond the system in development and which can adversely affect the liability of the overall business as well.

But how should the special area of "computer and communications security" risk management of an e-business system be performed? How should the problems of *confidentiality, integrity, and availability/reliability* be analyzed and decided? What analytic processes exist to be followed in determining what needs protecting and how much time, effort, and money to spend on that protection? What is that "pound of security" worth?

Because of their inherent and extensive dependence on computer technology, e-business systems require a special form of analysis to uncover potential security vulnerabilities and to arrive at corrective actions. Whether this analysis is conducted during the formulation of a "new" system and its design or whether it is performed on an existing operational system, the process must be systematic, disciplined, and based on sound analytic principles. Exhibit 4.9, the Campbell and Sands Security Risk Management Model (RMM),[1] is representative of just such a process and is presented here in describing the specifics of performing an e-business risk management study.

The RMM was one of the first risk management models to recognize the importance of information security as opposed to just computer security. It was one of the first models to deal with the intangibles of information and business process valuation. This model acknowledges that e-business security is a corporate executive-level function and responsibility rather than a straight IT department or data center function. This is because if the information contained in any

---

[1]R.P. Campbell and G.A. Sands, "A Modular Approach to Computer Security Risk Assessment," *AFIPS Conference Proceedings,* Vol. 48 (NCC, 1979).

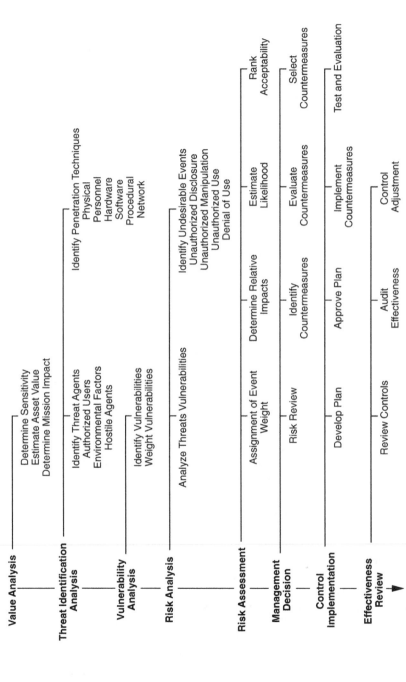

Exhibit 4.9 Campbell and Sands Security Risk Management Model

of the computer systems or networks were stolen, compromised, or unknowingly modified, the owners of the information absorb the loss, not the IT department. The same is true for an on-line e-business process. If the process is "hacked" or brought "down," the business owners, partners, and customers using the process sustain the loss, not the data center. The computer, network, and Internet folks, since they do not sustain a real dollar loss might be more inclined to accept the risk from a lack of e-business security rather than divert their resources to countering security weaknesses. This point of view, which may seem "reasonable" from their perspective, is still very prevalent today and explains why, at many corporations, computer and communications security is still weak even after all the recent publicity about cyber-security risks.

The Campbell and Sands model divides e-business systems risk management into eight steps: (1) value analysis, (2) threat identification and analysis, (3) vulnerability analysis, (4) risk analysis, (5) risk assessment, (6) management decision, (7) controlled implementation, and (8) effectiveness review.

Value analysis is conducted to determine the value of e-business processing to the corporation. It consists of three analytical steps that determine the sensitivity/weight/dollar value of the information being processed, potential losses in terms of identifiable dollars related to business process failures, and the hard asset value of the hardware, software, networks, and facilities and staff supporting the e-business system. Information sensitivity (i.e., value) is determined by identifying all direct and collateral uses of business information to include intellectual property, business data, customer data, and business partner data. The determination of dollar losses due to e-business process failures, for varying periods of time, extends to all uses both inside each specific e-business application system and to uses outside the organization where "supply chain" partners depend on information from our systems to conduct their business. An estimation of the hard dollar value of computer assets investigates the replacement or cost value of physical computing assets to include facilities, hardware and peripheral equipment and supplies, software, and/or any supporting communications assets.

Value analysis seeks to provide an economic foundation for the eventual justifications that will be required to budget for e-business security. A quantifiable *economic analysis*, however, is very difficult to develop with anywhere near the comprehensiveness needed to justify the substantial sums required for today's e-business security program. Chapter 7 addresses this problem in detail and explores several "nonquantifiable" arguments to supplement the rather weak dollar loss justifications that have been traditionally used.

Keeping in mind the extended treatment of "valuation" in Chapter 7, the next step in the RMM is the *identification and analysis of threats*. Threats are categorized into three general groups: environmental, authorized users, and hostile agents (e.g., hackers or terrorists). These threats can be further subdivided into actual documented threats and perceived threats (i.e., threats for which there is no hard evidence, but which seem extremely likely to occur under the right conditions). Once these threats are identified, an analysis is made of the different *penetration techniques* that might be used. These techniques include both deliberate and unintentional approaches. Penetration techniques are placed into one of six classes for further analysis. A penetration may be launched through any of the following avenues: physical, personnel, hardware, software, network, and procedural.

The third step in the RMM is to complete a *vulnerability analysis*, which identifies possible weaknesses in the defenses of the system, processing environment, and physical facilities. To facilitate the vulnerability analysis, two substeps are performed called vulnerability identification and vulnerability weighting. In the first substep, weaknesses or flaws in the design, implementation, or operation of the e-business system and its existing security controls are identified and then related to a specified threat. In the second substep, the vulnerabilities just identified are placed into an array that is ordered according to potential seriousness and the possibility of exploitation.

The fourth step in the RMM is the *risk analysis*, the purpose of which is to identify undesirable events through an analysis of the potential impacts of the threats and their possible exploitation of corresponding vulnerabilities just identified. The risk analysis has two major substeps. The first is an analysis of threat vulnerabilities. This means that the various ways a threat can exploit a vulnerability are fully analyzed and documented. Second comes an identification of undesirable events such as unauthorized disclosure of information, unauthorized manipulation of information, unauthorized use of information, and/or denial of service or use. These undesirable events and their relationship to a threat are then documented.

After the risk analysis is complete, a *risk assessment* is made. The primary objective of the risk assessment is to evaluate the severity of risks created by the combination of the threats, vulnerabilities, their potential for exploitation, and the likelihood of their exploitation occurring. Risk assessment is a four-step process, beginning with an assignment of a security event weight and/or dollar loss, the determination of its relative impact, an estimate of its likelihood of occurrence, and, finally, a ranking of the security event as being either acceptable or unacceptable. Until recently, estimating costs for security breaches has been more magic than science according to Bill Spernow, research director of information security strategies at Gartner Incorporated. After collaborating with some of the top information security experts in the industry, Gartner has developed a four-part model for estimating these losses. The model looks at how a security breach affects the IT organization, IT staffing, corporate profit, and clients. "Estimating Losses from an Infrastructure Compromise: A Generic Model for IT Security Staff" is available from Gartner Incorporated (www.gartner.com).

Once the risk assessment has been completed, a series of *management decisions* are required to determine how to proceed. First, a review of the risk assessment to this point is made to ensure that the risks deemed acceptable are indeed within tolerable limits. This is a decision that must be made by executive management. Also, at this time, any type of *risk coupling* must be reviewed and determined to be within tolerable limits of acceptable risk. Risk coupling describes a circumstance where two or more individual and lower impact risks combine to present a clear and present danger to the business. This determination should also be accomplished at the executive management level because in many cases only senior level officers are at the vantage point from which the impact of coupled risks can be perceived.

When complete, security countermeasures are identified, which can be effectively used against the identified threats and vulnerabilities.

Management decisions are next required to select appropriate and adequate safeguard *countermeasures* to those single and coupled risks threatening the e-business system and ultimately the organization. The act of safeguard countermeasure selection is accomplished against a backdrop of rapidly changing technology, quickly reconfigured systems, changes in business processes, and an ever-growing knowledge base of potential attacks. This means that countermeasures must pass all three tests of feasibility used to evaluate any systems proposal. To ensure that countermeasure decisions are adequate and appropriate, there must be an ongoing program of countermeasure identification and evaluation against e-business vulnerabilities, threats, and risks that are also being identified on a continuing basis.

It is important to realize that use of RMM, or any risk management model for that matter, is not a one-time event, but rather an essential element of continually evaluating any and all changes to the operations of the e-business portfolio of applications, systems, and workplace procedures. This means that an organization must dedicate sufficient resources to perform not only the risk assessment portion of the RMM but also the continuing countermeasure assessment task.

The seventh step of the RMM is to develop and execute a *controlled implementation plan* of selected security countermeasures. This requires an actual plan and schedule, a budget, and the necessary approvals of management and executive personnel. Whether security countermeasures are to be incorporated into the design of a new e-business system or are to be modifications to an existing system, the task of security test and evaluation takes on great significance. Security test and evaluations can be part of the existing QA program or they can be conducted as a separate independent validation, verification, and test (IVV&T) activity. If formal security certification and accreditation (C&A) of e-business systems is required by government regulation, then it is best to engage the services of an independent contractor to perform the test and evaluation function.

The last step of the RMM is an *effectiveness review*, which is a periodic review of the effectiveness of existing integrity and security controls, and system availability and reliability measures that have been implemented. Of concern are changes to the e-business system, both technical and workplace-related, changes to the supporting architecture and processing environment, and changes in vulnerability, threat, or risk exposure of the business system. This last phase of the RMM corresponds to the *planning, fixing, monitoring, and assessing* improvement cycle referred to earlier in this chapter in the discussion of security program success criteria.

During the actual performance of an e-business security risk management assessment, using RMM or a similar model, the latest technical information must always be brought to bear. An assessment performed in 2001 will not be the same as one performed in 1991 since technologies will have changed greatly. Likewise, an e-business system assessment performed today will not be the same as one performed in 2001, even though the technologies are essentially the same. This is because the process, configurations, vulnerabilities, threats, and risks are fluid, changing perhaps from minute to minute in response to evolving business demands. The best that can be done is to "approximate" the security posture of an e-business system at any point in time. Of course, the more accurate the approximation, the more likely existing security controls will be countering today's threats and not yesterdays. Chapter 5 presents a strategy for performing just-in-time security assessments using intrusion detection. This allows a system's security posture to be updated, analyzed, and changed as it operates its on-line activity.

Best Practice #15: Mandate the use of a risk management methodology with all e-business system developments or existing system modifications. When new systems are under design and development, the risk methodology should be incorporated into the systems development process (SDP) and should be monitored by corporate executives through use of the systems development review (SDR) framework (Appendix B).

Make Improvements to the Security Management of Information Technology

The most important steps to improving the security management of information technology and e-business systems has already taken place by directing senior management ownership of systems and by making them responsible and accountable for security. Without taking these steps, the organization may as well plan on periodically reliving the "crisis" of security and its accompanying hand-wringing while realizing that little will really change between episodes. Organizations that have been automated for two or three decades and yet have not made this level of commitment have had the "crisis" of security imposed on them several times by now. Each time, executive management is "shocked and dismayed" that incidents and breaches have occurred, and promises are made to improve security so that things will be different next time. But things cannot be different because the very people who can effectively balance security and production are not actively engaged and are not being held accountable to "make it happen."

But having made senior management accountable, an organization is well on its way to securing its e-business systems. Implementation of security goals and objectives now becomes the name of the game, and this requires the energies of a motivated workforce. This discussion is concerned with the creation of a workforce that is up to the task of securing today's complex processing systems.

It is a fact that the demand for computer security professionals is presently outstripping the supply and that this is resulting in bidding wars for qualified staff. Therefore, one of the first challenges in improving the security management of e-business systems must focus on recruiting and retaining a core of security experts. There are many industry resources that can be consulted concerning the staffing issues surrounding e-business security. Some of these resources include:

- The Information Systems Audit and Control Association and Foundation (*www.isaca.org*)
- International Information Systems Security Certification Consortium Inc. (*www.isc2.org*)
- The System Administration and Networking Security (SANS) Institute (*www.sans.org*)
- The Computer Security Institute (*www.csi.org*)

To aid in recruitment decisions, the following security certifications give a degree of independent assurance that candidates possessing the various certifications have some amount of proficiency with these specific security topics and products. For example, there are certified:

- Information Systems Security Professionals
- Intrusion Detection Analysts
- Firewall Analysts
- Unix Analysts
- NT Analysts
- Network Security Professionals
- Computer Forensic Technicians
- Computer Crime Investigators
- Computer Crime Prosecutors
- Computer Crime Attorneys

New certifications undoubtedly will emerge as business expands farther onto the Internet. These certifications probably will originate from groups such as the Internet Security Alliance (ISA) and others.

While helpful, certifications do have a downside. For example, certifications are only as good as their currency and the reputation of the conferring association. Also, certifications often highlight employees for headhunters, and this can make the security-staffing problem even worse.

What organizations must attempt to do is to create a work environment where e-business security analysts can progress professionally and where they feel they are contributing to the corporation as a whole. There is a certain pride in protecting something of value—especially if the "protectors" share in that value and if they sense they are appreciated for their efforts. Appreciation need not be only financial but may be demonstrated, for example, by the inclusion of security staff in the deliberations and decisions concerning the direction corporate e-business is taking and how security issues influence that contemplated direction. In other words, security professionals have knowledge and insights that should be tapped when making corporate e-business decisions. Loyalty is promoted by giving security professionals the opportunity to participate in decisions affecting the course of corporate e-business. They will be in a better psychological position to carry out their "protective" responsibilities if they are party to such security decisions—even if such decisions seem suboptimal from a security professional's point of view.

So much of e-business security rests on the "good will" of employees that extra special efforts are needed to get their "buy-in." The last section of this part, managing Security Professionals, addresses this special area.

Require That a Structured Process Be Used to Engineer the Securing of E-Business Systems

Just as e-business systems under development require the use of a structured SDP, so do the activities related to securing the e-business system. Whereas the SEI-CMM was previously used in Part Two of this chapter to evaluate the capability of an organization to construct soundly engineered software; the Systems Security Engineering Capability Maturity Model (SSE-CMM) from the International Systems Security Engineering Association (ISSEA—www.issea.org) is recommended here as a tool to assess, evaluate, and improve the security engineering capabilities of the business and support contractors.

Introduction to the SSE-CMM. The SSE-CMM describes the essential characteristics and operating processes of an organization that ensure good security engineering. The SSE-CMM does not promote a particular process or sequence of activities, but it is an attempt to capture and convey the "best security practices" observed in industry. The objective of the SSE-CMM is to advance the engineering of security as a defined and measurable discipline. The SSE-CMM model was developed to enable an organization to assess their security engineering maturity and plan necessary improvements.

The model for security engineering practices cover:

- The entire life cycle of the e-business system, including design, development, operation, maintenance, and decommissioning activities
- The whole organization, including management, organizational administration, and systems engineering activities
- The concurrent interaction with other IT management disciplines, such as software development, hardware, human factors, test engineering, configuration management, quality assurance, operations management, and system maintenance

- Interactions with other organizational elements including acquisition, business systems management, certification, accreditation, and audit or evaluation.

The SSE-CMM model and appraisal method was developed to enable:

- The focusing of investments in security engineering improvements
- Capability-based assurances of system "trustworthiness" based on confidence in the maturity of security practices and processes and the ability of systems developers and security professionals to engineer a secure system
- Selection of qualified providers of security products and services based on the SSE-CMM evaluation criteria.

According to the ISSEA description, "the SSE-CMM does not imply that any particular group or role within an organization must do any of the processes described in the model. Nor does it require that the latest and greatest security techniques or methodology be used. The model does require that an organization have a process in place that includes the basic security practices described in the model. The organization is free to create its own process and organizational structure in any way that meets its business objectives." (*Note: The history of computer security initiatives indicates that the need to formalize an organizational structure for security is very important. Consistency in purpose, policy, accountability, and enforcement is critical for e-business security to be effective.*)

The Basic SSE-CMM Model.   The basic model recognizes the importance of fundamental system and project management practices and their importance in providing the foundation for systems security. The model recognizes the relationship between systems management and the management of e-business security as spelled out in Part Two of this chapter.

The SSE-CMM identifies the following *project management process* areas (PA):

PA 1—Ensure Quality: define and measure systems quality

PA 2—Manage Configurations: control over work products and documents

PA 3—Manage Project Risk: identify, understand, and mitigate

PA 4—Plan Technical Effort: analyze, budget, and direct resources

PA 5—Monitor/Control Technical Effort: track progress and adjust

The SSE-CMM identifies the following *organizational process* areas:

PA 6—Define Security Engineering Process: require enforcement

PA 7—Improve Security Engineering Process: continuous improvement

PA 8—Manage Product Evolution: to ensure secure product and services

PA 9—Manage Engineering Support Environment: create an environment that will nurture success

PA 10—Provide Ongoing Skills and Knowledge: training and awareness

PA 11—Coordinate with Suppliers: secure the "supply chain"

Finally, the SSE-CMM identifies the following *security engineering* process areas:

PA 12—Administer Security Controls: unenforced controls are worthless

PA 13—Assess Impact: identify risks and impacts to the business

PA 14—Assess Security Risk: analyze impact and prioritize risks

PA 15—Assess Threats: identify threats and likelihood of occurrence

PA 16—Assess Vulnerability: understand system weaknesses

PA 17—Build Assurance Argument: devise strategy to meet security objectives of organization and systems, document the strategy

PA 18—Coordinate Security Efforts: control security engineering work and work products of project team

PA 19—Monitor Security Posture: detect, track, and respond to security incidents, revising policy as knowledge is gained

PA 20—Provide Security Input: to all system development decisions and security solution design efforts

PA 21—Specify Security Requirements and Reach Agreement: with all parties to the design and those with a stake in a secured system

PA 22—Verify and Validate Security: test and audit for security effectiveness—adjust as necessary to "real" operational conditions

Appraisal for Self-Improvement. An SSE-CMM appraisal performed for the purpose of self-improvement can provide an organization with valuable insights as to its own capability to practice security engineering. Typical goals for conducting an appraisal are:

- To gain an understanding of technical security-related issues affecting the business
- To determine the overall security engineering capability of an organization
- To plan the deployment of security practices within an organization
- To determine progress of security improvement initiatives

A self-appraisal must be closely tied to business activities the organization is undertaking. For example:

- Does the organization seek to practice security engineering in the course of developing new products and/or systems, integrating various off-the-shelf systems, or providing services?
- Does the organization want to improve its practice of security engineering to achieve repeatability, efficiency, continuity, or greater assurance?
- Does the organization seek to evaluate a specific process area or system under development?

The SSE-CMM appraisal identifies five capability levels to measure the security engineering maturity of an organization. The five levels are portrayed in Exhibit 4.10 and are defined as:

Capability Level 1—"Performed Informally" focuses on whether an organization or project performs a process that incorporates best practices. This level can be characterized by the statement "you have to do it before you can manage it."

Capability Level 2—"Planned and Tracked" focuses on project-level definition, planning, and performance issues. This level can be characterized by the statement, "understand what's happening on the project before defining organization-wide processes."

Capability Level 3—"Well Defined" focuses on disciplined tailoring from defined processes at the organizational level. This level can be characterized by the statement, "use the best of what you've learned from your projects to create organization-wide processes."

Capability Level 4—"Quantitatively Controlled" focuses on metrics being tied to the business goals of the organization. This level can be characterized by the statements, "you can't measure it until you know what *it* is" and "managing with measurement is only meaningful when you're measuring the right things."

Capability Level 5—"Continuously Improving" gains leverage from all the management practice improvements gained in the earlier levels, then emphasizes the cultural shifts that will sustain the gains made. This level can be characterized by the statement, "a culture of continuous improvement requires a foundation of sound management practice, defined and enforced processes, and measurable goals.

Best Practice #16: Require that internal system organizations responsible for e-business systems conduct a SSE-CMM appraisal to determine their current level of security engineering maturity. Use this information to plan capability improvements to internal organizations.

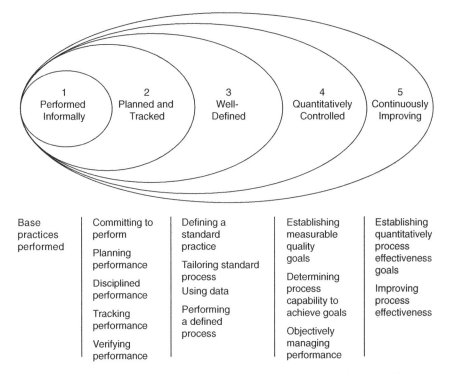

1 Performed Informally	2 Planned and Tracked	3 Well-Defined	4 Quantitatively Controlled	5 Continuously Improving
Base practices performed	Committing to perform Planning performance Disciplined performance Tracking performance Verifying performance	Defining a standard practice Tailoring standard process Using data Performing a defined process	Establishing measurable quality goals Determining process capability to achieve goals Objectively managing performance	Establishing quantitatively process effectiveness goals Improving process effectiveness

Exhibit 4.10 Capability Levels Represent the Maturity of the Security Engineering Organization

Selecting Security-Conscious IT Vendors and Supply Chain Partners

Earlier it was recommended to require a SEI-CMM evaluation of IT vendors and supply chain partners to determine their capability to develop quality software systems and provide "best practice" support services. Now it is advised that the capability of IT vendors and supply chain partners to engineer security into their e-business systems also be evaluated. The primary tool for this evaluation would be the SSE-CMM or a security assessment conducted by an independent third party, much like an International Standards Organization (ISO) audit determines the ability of an organization to produce quality products.

Supply chain management is becoming one of the most complex undertakings of the "new" e-business model. E-business economies are being sought in reduced inventories, streamlined order processing, and account receivables processing, and in generally speeding up the entire conduct of business to keep overhead low. This means that the various businesses making up your supply chain must work together quickly, smoothly, and securely. Much of this desired goal is to be found in the design of the systems that conduct business between companies, and these designs are predicated on the adoption of a standard way of expressing business transactions and function. From an automation perspective, standard data elements and codes, long a problem of data processing, are major keys to successful supply chain management. Equally important is the adoption of standard e-business software for the conduct of business between companies. Incompatible software packages can thwart the most elegant e-business design and throw business transactions into chaos.

As with all systems, integrated security controls, to be effective, must be considered from the very outset of the e-business undertaking—especially if more than one company is involved. To accomplish this, a collaborative effort must be initiated by the company at the top of the supply chain since they have the most to lose. For example, U.S. automobile manufacturers have initiated alliances for their suppliers to join as the many problems associated with reengineering the auto industry are tackled. In most cases, the cost of the alliance is being borne by the big three manufacturers.

Of critical importance to supply chain success will be the security of the "weakest" link in the chain. The nearer the top of the chain, the greater the adverse impacts of a security breach—especially system downtime or the lost productivity resulting from a successful denial of service attack coming from anywhere in the chain. It is therefore in the best interest of the "finished" product owner to be concerned about the security engineering maturity and the security posture of each supplier on whom they depend.

Best Practice #17: Require that members of the corporation's "supply chain" be subjected to a security evaluation using the SSE-CMM methodology or have an independent security assessment conducted to determine security risks that need attention. Be prepared to fund the evaluations.

Outsourcing for Managed Security Services (MSS)

Of course, the option for outsourcing e-business security services exists, but this decision requires careful examination to be executed successfully. Remembering that there are generally two reasons given for outsourcing: (1) it is more cost-effective than to continue performing the function in-house, and (2) a company simply *cannot* or *does not want* to perform the computing function to focus on meeting their "core" business responsibilities. Both reasons are valid, but neither should be used as justification for the outsourcing of e-business security activities in their entirety.

In the aftermath of Y2K, the concept of "due diligence" places the responsibility for vital information and computing assets directly on the desk of the chief executive. Y2K taught that any threat to the capability of an organization to process critical information posed a risk to the business and was not just a "glitch" to be fixed by the technical staff. This threat to business had to be analyzed with executive participation so that adverse impacts could be assessed, priorities set, and resources made available for corrective action.

E-business security threats posed by breaches of confidentiality, accidentally or deliberately triggered lapses in information and/or processing integrity, and interruptions in vital systems and services are clearly in the same category. It is against this background that the outsourcing of managed security services (MSS) must be considered.

There are many positive aspects to the MSS concept and it overcomes many problems likely to be encountered when attempting to build a complete e-business security capability in-house. For example, a provider of MSS can:

- Attract and retain personnel experienced in all the disciplines of systems security because a career path can be more easily provided
- Maintain all necessary vendor agreements and licenses
- Utilize their more experienced personnel in the design and continuous improvement of the e-business security controls of your organization
- "Time-share" experienced personnel, thus reducing overall cost to each of their customers
- Allow their personnel to concentrate on their chosen security specialty
- Maintain professional contact with all pertinent security associations and special interest groups
- Ensure an environment where security professionals learn from one another
- Provide "technology refreshments" as needed to maintain effectiveness
- Spread the expense of security research and development across their entire customer base, thus reducing total overall cost to each
- Assure the "trustworthiness" of assigned employees and confidentiality of each customer's security weaknesses, security controls, architectures, emergency response procedures, and incident record
- Take single source direction from client security officials in all matters pertaining to organizational security matters.

All things considered, MSS provide, for small to mid-sized companies, a focus on technical security matters that only the largest corporations can match with an internal security group. And implemented properly, MSS can prove cost-effective.

While it is understandable to want to keep overhead costs to a minimum and achieve cost-effective e-business security, such desires must be achieved in full recognition of evolving "due diligence" standards and the need to demonstrate corporate control in such matters. At a minimum, it is advised that organizations retain control over all system-related inventories and configuration management information, security policy, and enforcement authority. A company should retain sufficient business systems and e-business security expertise to exercise full oversight of MSS contractors, with an audit function capable of performing independent security verifications of the contractor's technical activities.

E-business security functions that lend themselves to outsourcing include the security analysis process whereby initial risk assessments are performed and kept current as the e-business environment changes. Contractors can also consult on the design of technical security and integrity controls and participate in their implementation. Contractors can recommend security policies but such policies will be effective only if closely aligned with actual business processes and kept under the direct control of corporate management. If not, system users will simply devise "workarounds," and the impractical policy will be thwarted with little or no enforcement.

Contractors can also perform security awareness and training, security administrator duties, and the staff system monitoring and incident response teams.

In selecting an MSS provider, the number one criteria must be the extent and quality of actual e-business security experience that can be substantiated through referencing checking and past performance.

For many years, the principal organizations addressing security have been those in the defense community. Because of this, the most experienced contractors will have worked on Department of Defense contracts, and, in a number of instances, this will have included intrusion detection and computer emergency response team (CERT) tasking. It so happens that intrusion detection and CERT work constitute the best possible experience for those needing e-business security support. This is because these contractors have been working at the operational end of the *security life cycle* where they must live with security recommendations made by themselves or someone else. The operative expression is "live with." They know the things that work and the things that do not and are sensitive to the "real-world" concerns of those in business who have to deliver the electronic service. Too many security consulting companies just do studies, make recommendations, and collect their money. They never implement their suggestions and they never have to "live with" them.

Contractors who work at the operational end of the *security life cycle* are "practicing" security under business processing conditions and pressures where security incidents must be detected and corrected within severe time constraints. (See Chapter 5 for a discussion of just-in-time security.) This requires a contractor staff possessing knowledge, skill, and confidence. Experience at the operational security level also results in excellent security assessments being performed on new or changing systems because such assessments are based on actual knowledge of the business system environment and this results in *pragmatic* recommendations that can be implemented.

Any reputable security support contractor should also be able to assemble a team of "certified" security professionals. At least some members of the team "working your contract" should possess certifications such as the Certified Information Systems Security Professional (CISSP).

Best Practice #18: When conducting the review of outsourcing contracts called for in Recommendation 11, include a special review of the risk exposure the corporation is taking by planning a move to managed security services.

Managing Security Professionals

Like most specialty areas in the IT industry, security professionals are in great demand, and being in demand means that, beyond money, most are looking for two things in an organization. First, security professionals are looking for enough IT competence in the organization they are joining to make their "security" efforts worthwhile. Second, they are hoping for an employment situation where they are taken seriously, as demonstrated by management's willingness to solicit their professional services and opinions before e-business projects are undertaken.

Information Technology security professionals believe that their contribution to an employing organization is of high value and will generally *not* put up with halfhearted attempts by management to address the security issue. For this reason, the problems of recruitment and retention are especially challenging when it comes to security personnel, but there are things an organization can do to impress the employment candidate and improve on the situation.

Since security professionals will critically judge whether a company seems serious about solving their e-business security problem, what must an organization do to pass muster?

A key indicator of a high level of commitment is whether by actions, and not just words, the organization is investing in such a way that reflects an understanding of the serious and long-term nature of the e-business security challenge. Security is not like Y2K, or most other IT challenges for that matter. It is not a one-time problem to be solved and forgotten before moving on to the next technology upgrade. As has been pointed out, security is central to the very nature of information processing and systems management and must be confronted on a daily basis. New threats are constantly materializing as business systems change, as new technologies are introduced into the corporation's processing mix, and as perpetrators become more and more sophisticated.

A visible long-term commitment, likely to impress an IT security professional, would minimally require the creation of an *internal* corporate environment where the quality and adequacy of e-business security efforts are closely monitored at the senior-most levels of the company. This degree of commitment would be reflected by an investment in the organization, people, tools, and continuing education. Evidence of such commitment could include the creation of a Cyber-Security Center (CSC) where staff resources can concentrate on the latest developments in analytic tools, methodologies, vulnerabilities, solutions, training, and system monitoring techniques. A CSC provides a managed knowledge base of current intrusion incidents and viruses for the organization and provides information on the appropriate technical solutions being employed by other members of the corporation's particular industry.

Structurally, a center may exist physically, be a collaborative "virtual" group using networks and the Internet to communicate, or be a combination of the two. A great advantage accrues from the synergy that is generated by a small cadre of security professionals who maintain state-of-the-art excellence while mentoring and providing technical quality assurance to the e-business security workforce of the larger organization. To the security professional, this degree of commitment indicates that their efforts and careers are viewed as integral to the overall success of the enterprise and are not just a momentary source of revenue or simply a response to the last negative audit report.

Of course, the organization gains immeasurably from such actions because in such an environment, the security professionals will be expected to apply and institutionalize their knowledge of e-business security as it relates to the business processes of the enterprise. The security professionals will feel secure and a working part of the greater company, not just an overpaid "techie for hire" laboring for an organization that views their efforts as a drain on productivity.

From a practical management perspective, certain precautions must be taken with those who control the controls. It is highly recommended that procedures be established such that no single security administrator is performing his or her duties without the participation of a backup individual. There have been too many cases where the security administrators, holding the security keys to the business system, have blackmailed their employer. Whether such individuals are ever apprehended and punished is little solace after the "news" has hit the street and the company appears to have suffered an e-business security incident.

For extremely sensitive positions, lifestyle background checks are advisable. As has been borne out in espionage cases of recent history, living beyond one's means, without benefit of an inheritance or having won the lottery, often indicates illegal activity with someone trafficking in information.

Pulling It Together: Justifying the Program

Before concluding with a discussion on pulling the e-business security management program together, it would be helpful to reflect on the potential success of any effort to solve the e-business security problem in light of a major *accusation* that surfaced in the aftermath of the successful resolution of the Y2K challenge.

Summarizing from Appendix A, the *accusation* was that Y2K was a relatively minor problem that had been created by consultants and that the whole thing had been greatly overhyped. Accusers held that the *accusation* was true simply because nothing much happened at the rollover and that *that* reality proved the validity of their *accusation*.

The origin of this accusation seems to have stemmed primarily from trying to justify non–revenue-generating expenditures to managers and casual observers who did not understand the true nature or potential adverse impacts of a problem that someone else was trying to prevent. It also stemmed from the fact that you cannot prove a negative. You could not prove to the uninvolved and ignorant observer that the time, money, and human capital spent on Y2K remediation was well spent simply because problems were averted. Such observers take the fact of problems not occurring as evidence that the problem never existed and that the threat was overstated—just to get funding.

With regard to e-business security, these same observers may be tempted to interpret the fact of security breaches not occurring, after an expenditure of time and effort on establishing a security program and controls, as evidence that such a threat never really existed, at least as far as their company is concerned.

In the cases of both Y2K and computer security, the money, time, and effort expended to prevent possible negative consequences to the business can be viewed with suspicion. Over the years, this same logic has stalked many of the efforts to improve software quality, testing, documentation, configuration management, and systems management. In fact, this type of thinking has stymied most efforts to manage IT with the same degree of discipline that is required of other business activities.

This "fact of life" must be anticipated by the sponsors of e-business security and defended against when justifying the expense of security controls and the program to manage them.

In pulling the security initiative together for presentation to executive management, the following systematic steps can provide just such a defense.

Step #1: Assemble the executive level e-business security decision team. Because of the importance of e-business security and the fact that funding will have to be diverted from revenue-generating activities to non–revenue-generating security activities, a senior team of business unit managers must be appointed to review and approve all security decisions.

Involvement by business unit managers ensures that possible negative impacts of security incidents are viewed from a "bottom line" as well as an "asset valuation" perspective. Because of their intimate involvement in security program and control deliberations, business unit managers can often become "champions" of security initiatives and thus ensure their success.

Step #2: Assure that the security initiatives being justified conform to the "criteria" for a successful program. This includes corporate adoption of the Common Vulnerabilities and Exposure (CVE) nomenclature for security information sharing. Before proceeding with security program development, the executive decision team should be assured that the overall design of the e-business security program meets the three criteria for program success.

If these criteria are not satisfied, there can be no confidence that individual and isolated security initiatives and tools will actually contribute to solving the security problem facing the business or be maintainable over time.

Step #3: Assure that national and/or international recognized guidelines for computer and communications security are being followed. To demonstrate "due diligence," nationally and/or internationally recognized guidelines for building and administering computer security programs should be adopted. Such guidelines ensure the rigorous and systematic approach promoted in this book. As a minimum, the following guidelines should be examined for appropriateness:

• The U.S. National Institute for Standards and Technology's (NIST) *Generally Accepted Systems Security Principles* (GSSPs) (*ftp.ru.xemacs.org/pub/security/csir/nist/nistpubs/gssp.pdf*).

• ISO 17799, the *Code of Practice for Information Security Management*, based on the British Standards Institute BS 7799 documents. The International Organization for Standardization (ISO) (*www.iso.ch/iso/en/ISOOnline.frontpage*) began the process of defining BS 7799 as an international standard; ISO 17799 was published in 1999.

• The COBIT™ (Control Objectives for Information and Related Technology), a business-oriented set of standards for guiding management in the sound use of information technology. COBIT was developed by volunteers working under the aegis of the IT Governance Institute® (*www.itgovernance.org/index2.htm*), which was itself founded by the Information System Audit and Control Association (ISACA).

• The *Common Criteria* (CC), a project that developed out of the 1985 *Trusted Computer System Evaluation Criteria* (TCSEC; also known as the *Orange Book*) developed by the National Computer Security Center of the National Security Agency of the United States. See *www.commoncriteria.org/faq/faq.html* for an overview of the CC, where one reads, "The Common Criteria for Information Technology Security Evaluation (CC) defines general concepts and principles of IT security evaluation and presents a general model of evaluation. It presents constructs for expressing IT security objectives, for selecting and defining IT security requirements, and for writing high-level specifications for products and systems."

Step # 4: Identify and Valuate "Quantifiable" Assets. This activity, addressed in more detail in Chapter 7, ensures that all "hard" assets such as hardware, software, communications equipment, and operational elements such as documentation and the facilities of the supporting infrastructure are identified and that associated "replacement" costs are calculated or estimated for each asset. This step provides an easy "quantifiable" dollar estimate needed for security program justification purposes.

Step #5: Identify and Valuate "Nonquantifiable" Assets, Processes, and Other Intangibles. Also addressed in Chapter 7, this activity seeks to ensure that the universe of corporate information assets, business processes, administrative systems, and "hard" computing assets are properly accounted for when e-business security decisions are made. The "value" imparted to many of these assets and processes may not be quantifiable in dollars and cents, but their intangible value and importance will constitute the major rationale of the benefits justification for increased security spending.

The following questions must be answered to place a "value" or "weight" on the information and computing assets of the corporation.

Question #1: Does the organization have a method for determining the value of information in the following categories?

• Intellectual property?
• Business proprietary?
• Client data?
• Customer data?
• Business partner data?

Question #2: Have each of these categories been "considered" in calculating an e-business security benefits justification? Has executive management been involved in assigning a dollar value or "weight" as a form of information valuation to each category?

Question #3: Have "critical business processes" been identified and has the value of those processes been determined? Has executive management been involved in assigning a dollar value or "weight" as a form of process valuation for each critical business process?

Question #4: Based on previously documented events, have "loss of revenue" figures been estimated for actual security attacks that resulted in the denial of business service to employees, customers, or business partners? Where empirical data are not available, has information from reputable sources such as the Gartner Group been used to estimate revenue loss based on different attack scenarios and varied time duration of system outage?

Question #5: Has the adverse impact of failures to "live up to" supply chain responsibilities been determined? If such failures "breach" contract agreements, has the liability potential been estimated and inputted to deliberations on security issues?

Question #6: Has an attempt been made to determine the "loss of business opportunity revenue" that could result should the organization fail to secure those systems on which future business activities are planned and future revenue estimates are based?

Question #7: Where future business "revenues" are dependent on the accuracy and reliability of consumer profiling data, has the assumed value of that data been independently confirmed in light of the tendency of many consumers to deliberately distort personal information?

Step #6: Identify "Reputation" Factors and Valuate. For many organizations, this category of valuation is the most critical since being perceived in a positive light is essential to conduct business and to raise money in the capital markets of the world. Even for government agencies, a favorable reputation is important to ensure continued "hassle-free" funding and to keep congressional interference to a minimum. In simplest terms, has the organization suffered from "security incidents" and have these received negative publicity? Of course, the adverse impact of a publicized security incident depends on the nature of the business and whether it would cause customers or business partners to question their continued relationship with your organization. In the case of investors, a "security incident" may undermine the market confidence so necessary for obtaining long- and short-term capital.

From a political perspective, an organization may be judged by their reputation for involvement and support to solve the Critical Infrastructure Protection (CIP) of the nation and their particular industry (see Chapter 9). Being a contributor to the larger national dialogue surrounding CIP can place a business in a favorable light and may even overcome the "adverse" publicity of isolated breaches of security.

Step #7: Summarize "Benefits" of Increased E-Business Security and Determine a "Due Diligence" Course of Action. Establishment of an e-business security management program will not necessarily be justified by "quantifiable" cost vs. loss calculations, or even "nonquantifiable" arguments; but may need to be determined, in today's litigious atmosphere, by imposing "due diligence" and "reasonable care" logic.

The minimal "due diligence" standard for determining the adequacy of an e-business security program and associated spending would be to implement those security controls and management practices that prevail within your industry.

A more rational and defensible "reasonable care" standard would be to implement those "proven" security techniques and "best practices" that facilitate continuous security monitoring and reduction of risk as technologies and e-business processing conditions change.

Conclusion

The purpose of this final part to Chapter 4 has been to provide pragmatic guidance and assistance to business executives and managers in the development of a viable e-business security management program. The key to success is to generate sufficient justification to establish an institutional program that is appropriately funded and staffed to continuously monitor security conditions within the e-business environment and make adjustments as technologies and threats evolve.

Chapter 5

A "Just-In-Time" Strategy for Securing the E-Business System: The Role for Security Monitoring and Incident Response

As explored in Chapter 1, the conceptual framework for e-business security results from three decades of evolution of computer security concerns. E-business security combines the need to protect the integrity and confidentiality of business information with the need to secure the underlying technologies that support the collection, processing, storage, and delivery of that information.

In other words, e-business security is concerned with protecting and maintaining the accurate portrayal of information so that it can be "trusted for use" and with ensuring its availability to legitimate users and customers when it is needed to perform an authorized business activity.

These concerns are addressed by concentrating on methods to ensure the integrity and confidentiality of information and processes, while at the same time assuring the ready availability of information, processes, and other system resources when required for use by legitimate users and customers. For example, "denials of service" attacks, such as those continually being mounted against the Internet, are now being viewed as the greatest single threat to our highly computerized and interconnected way of conducting business and executing the functions of government. This is because a successful "denial of service" attack not only prevents access to information and critical business processes but also destroys the ability of the "targeted" automated systems to function at all.

In response to these threats and because of increasing societal dependence on computers and the Internet, a number of significant efforts have recently been initiated by the federal government and the private sector to coordinate a national program aimed at protecting our critical information infrastructure.

Briefly, in 1998, the Clinton administration convened the Presidential Commission on Critical Infrastructure Protection (CIP). As a result of the commission's findings, the administration issued Presidential Decision Directive (PDD-63), which created the Critical Infrastructure Assurance Office (CIAO) within the Department of Commerce. The CIAO is tasked to work with the private sector to implement PDD-63. Presidential Decision Directive names five industry sectors as critical to the national infrastructure. They are energy, financial services, transportation, communications and information services, and vital human services. Member companies from these industry sectors have joined together as the Partnership for Critical Infrastructure Security (PCIS), which is jointly sponsored by the U.S. Chamber of Commerce and the CIAO for the purpose of implementing PDD-63. The communications and information technology (IT) industry's venue for addressing the CIP and for working with the PCIS is the Information Technology Association of America (ITAA). Information Technology Association of America is functioning as the IT industry sector focal point for coordination, cooperation, and information sharing across the IT sector and between the IT sector and the other critical sectors and government.

See Chapter 9 for additional information concerning the principal National Critical Infrastructure Protection initiatives and their importance to corporations conducting e-business.

Within each of these CIP initiatives, the function of Security Monitoring and Incident Response has been given a decisive role in the formulation of an effective information assurance program. The remainder of this chapter explores the criticality of security monitoring and incident response to an electronic-based business and explores implementation approaches.

THE CURRENT STATE OF E-BUSINESS SECURITY

In today's Internet economy, attacks on the nation's information processing infrastructure are becoming an increasingly serious problem. According to the national Computer Emergency Response Team (CERT) Coordination Center (CERT/CC) at Carnegie Mellon University, the number of reported security incidents handled by the CERT/CC has risen from over 2,000 in 1997 to well over 8,000 in 1999. This is an increase of over 200 percent in just two years. The year 2000 witnessed a similar increase and damage become more widespread. Whole systems and networks are being shut down for hours and even days, resulting in the loss of billions of dollars in revenues. Recent surveys place the average loss at over $250,000 per respondent's organization. Other surveys indicate that while internal breaches of security are still of greater concern, external attacks were increasing at an "alarming rate." Responding companies have experienced an increase in penetration attacks of from 12 percent in 1998 to 23 percent in 2000. This increase in the growth of incidents is reflecting the growth of the Internet, and the planned increase in e-commerce can only exacerbate this upward trend.

Sophistication of attacks is increasing and they are becoming more stealthy. According to Alan Paller, director of research for the SANS Institute, " *There is a steadily increasing number of these attacks. And there are more of these that have three characteristics that set them apart. The first of these is that attacks are coming simultaneously from multiple, coordinated sites. The second is that the*

attacks are coming with more stealth, escaping the detection of intrusion moni-
toring systems by limiting the number of 'pings,' or connections. These are com-
ing in just under the detection threshold, at one every hour, or every three days.
Third, they are coming from patient people, who are usually more professional
than children."

Additionally, there is evidence that hackers are banding together across the globe to mount low-visibility attacks in an effort to sneak under the radar of existing security controls. Coordinated attacks from up to 15 different locations on several continents have been detected.

Ease of attacks has been increasing as well, due largely to the widespread availability of intrusion tools and exploit scripts of known methods of attack that are shared by way of the Internet. Today, absolutely anyone can attack a network. Exhibit 5.1 illustrates that attackers require less knowledge as tool sophistication increases.

Incidents of computer crime are also increasing in record numbers. According to the School of Criminal Justice–Michigan State University, the percentage of 150 major corporations that reported computer crimes over the past five years are as follows:

• Credit card fraud (96 percent)
• Telecommunications fraud (96 percent)

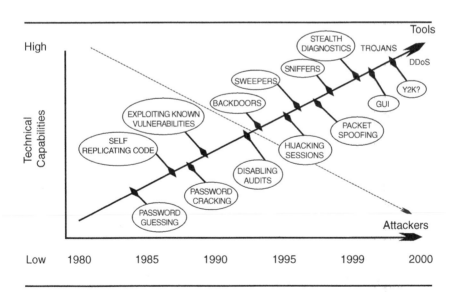

Recent hacks show just how vulnerable the national information
infrastructure is to relatively unsophisticated methods of attack

Exhibit 5.1   The Threat

- Unauthorized snooping of files (95 percent)
- Unlawful copying of software (91 percent)

At the same time, the FBI claims that over 70 percent of computer crimes originate with the "trusted" insider who has some degree of authorized access to corporate information and processing systems.

STANDARD REQUIREMENTS OF AN E-BUSINESS SECURITY STRATEGY

Summarizing from Chapter 3, computer and communications security strategies have been traditionally designed to satisfy three basic requirements—prevention, detection, and response or reaction. Most often these requirements have been thought of and graphically portrayed in a serial fashion similar to the "waterfall" model that has been used for years to depict the software and systems development life cycle. Commonly defined:

- *Prevention* includes the numerous proactive actions that are taken to protect information and system processing assets against destruction, compromise and unauthorized access, manipulation or modification whether deliberate or accidental. Prevention is "design in nature" and deals with such issues as the construction of software to be secure, testing of security features, and the effective use of security techniques, such as firewalls, in configuring computer and network elements to "prevent" accidental or deliberate events and actions that are deemed undesirable.

- *Detection* employs network management and audit techniques and tools, from on-line scanning and monitoring, to trend analysis and attack forecasting. Detection identifies attacks and unauthorized actions as they are occurring or shortly thereafter and issues alerts to take response actions.

- *Response* or *Reaction* initiates damage containment, recovery plans, and corrective actions after an attack or unauthorized use has been detected. This includes actions to report security incidents so that corrective actions can be taken to execute predefined tasks that reconstitute systems, software, and information files to their full business functionality after an incident is detected.

It is with attempts to prevent security incidents that most of today's advertised security technologies are employed. Technologies such as vulnerability assessments, firewalls, passwords and other access controls, encryption and public key infrastructure (PKI), virtual private networks (VPN), data integrity checks, security testing, biometrics, and personnel background checks all find their usefulness in attempting to prevent security incidents.

But despite the best-designed and implemented precautionary measures, attacks against an organization's information and information-processing assets will be attempted. Some will be successful. Furthermore, accidents and mistakes in daily processing that threaten systems integrity and data confidentiality will occur. An organization must be able to detect and respond to such attacks. Security monitoring and incident response tools and techniques combine to form the technology for the detection and response or reaction components of an e-business security strategy.

The remainder of this chapter addresses the use of security monitoring and incident response tools and techniques in satisfying the traditional detection and response or reaction requirements of an e-business security strategy. It introduces the reader to the emerging role for security monitoring and incident response as the principle means of assuring the continuous level of security required of today's distributed and Internet-based systems on which businesses and government operations depend.

A NEW SECURITY STRATEGY

A new security strategy has emerged over the last several years as industry and governments embrace the concept of conducting business within the context of Internet time. The building of just-in-time (JIT) systems that manage the ever-expanding aspect of e-business and e-government evidences the embodiment of this context. Whereas in the past, business systems were designed to complete a processing cycle in days or weeks, processes today complete their cycles in seconds, minutes, or hours. This means those reaction times for responding to any problem are becoming shorter and shorter.

Before having to deal within the accelerated pace and open context of the Internet, prevailing computer security models focused on performing a quantitative and lengthy risk analysis on which all subsequent security strategies, budgets, decisions, and actions were based. A risk analysis was supposed to be conducted at the time of system definition and design so that preventive security controls could be incorporated into the system. They would then be tested during application testing and put into operation as the system went into production. It did not always work that way, but at least the model was sufficient to the task and the technology of the times.

Today, however, with JIT e-business systems and networks operating and evolving at the pace of Internet time, we do not have the luxury of lengthy and quantitative risk studies for two reasons.

First, a large number of our operational e-business systems already exist—having been built over the last 3 or 4 years while everyone was busy solving the Y2K problem and had no resources available to conduct the necessary security studies.

Second, since the configurations supporting these systems change on a daily and often hourly basis, their design is never stable for a long enough period of time to do a "by the book" security analysis.

For these two reasons, a new security strategy has emerged that is based on the security monitoring and incident response function. This is because network and system monitoring activities occur within the framework of Internet time. By operating at the speed of the Internet, a business is afforded a 'frontline defense" against attacks launched through the Internet or through any other monitored communications medium that the business utilizes.

THE CRUCIAL ROLE OF SECURITY MONITORING AND INCIDENT RESPONSE TO THE SECURING OF E-BUSINESS SYSTEMS

To a great extent, most organizations are playing catch-up to the immense amount of technological innovation and growth of the last few years. Existing security strategies are mainframe-oriented while e-business applications are distributed processing and Internet-based. This means that the majority of existing computer security plans and implementations need to be reexamined. Organizations need to focus on designing a security strategy that is in sync with the speed of processing, the degree of network dependence, and risk exposure of the company. A strategy that will operate within the context of Internet time and provide a "frontline defense" against security attacks. A strategy that can respond in a JIT fashion using the same technologies on the systems the strategy is asked to secure. A strategy centered on security monitoring and incident response satisfies this challenge.

THE CURRENT STATE OF INTRUSION DETECTION SYSTEMS (IDS)

Since intrusion detection systems form the backbone component of a JIT security monitoring strategy, an examination of the present maturity and effectiveness of these systems is in order.

The following draws from a Technical Report from Carnegie-Mellon Software Engineering Institute (CMU/SEI-99-TR-028 ESC-99-028)—January 2000. The report is titled "State of the Practice of Intrusion Detection Technologies." The Air Force Research Laboratory and the Air Force Computer Resources Support Improvement Program sponsored the report.

Definition

"Intrusion Detection System—a combination of hardware and software that monitors and collects system and network information and analyzes it to determine if an attack or an intrusion has occurred. Some ID systems can automatically respond to an intrusion."

From the Management Summary

"Vendors make many claims for their products in the commercial marketplace, so separating hype from reality can be a major challenge."

"We are concerned that organizations are counting on these tools to solve a class of problems before they fully understand them. As a result, the solutions are likely to be inadequate or incorrect."

"Implementing intrusion detection systems on networks and hosts requires a broad understanding of computer security. The complexity of information technology infrastructures is increasing beyond any one person's ability to understand them, let alone administer them in a way that is operationally secure."

"Over-reliance on ID technologies can create a false sense of confidence about the degree to which tools are detecting intrusions against an organization's critical assets."

"Evaluating ID systems is non-trivial and there is a lack of credible, comprehensive product evaluation information."

"Hiring and retaining personnel to competently administer security in general and intrusion detection in particular are increasing challenges."

Even though the report is cautious in tone, it concludes that intrusion detection systems are seen by users of computer and networked systems as a viable tool to be included in their security strategy.

"After reviewing the surveys cited in this report, one could conclude that ID technologies are becoming an accepted part of many organizations' information security tool suite."

So, even if ID systems are less than mature in their present state, it appears that an increasing number of system managers see some innate benefit in their deployment and are including such systems in their overall security strategy. Because of this interest, ID systems will continue to improve and their use will become more commonplace in the years ahead.

Making IDS Work

As with any technology, it is important to set precise goals for the use of IDS in an e-business-processing environment. If the goal is to conduct network monitoring to keep informed of external attacks and unauthorized uses by internal personnel, then an organization will treat ID systems as limited tools for network security monitoring and heed the recommendation of the Carnegie-Mellon report that calls for the active involvement of experienced personnel in the diagnostic loop.

"While computers are capable of examining large quantities of low level data, they cannot match a human's analytic skills."

It seems clear that to expect IDS (given the current state of maturity) to realistically fulfill a preventive as well as a detection function, one must bring into the equation personnel experienced in network security monitoring and in the interpretation of monitored findings.

"Effective Security Monitoring Won't Be Cheap"

Projected IDS expenses will begin to rise and budget justifications may become more difficult once personnel are added to the equation.

Because of this, corporate executives must be convinced that a "clear and present danger" exists to the organization's information and e-business processing capabilities and that there is a requirement to know in near real-time when security incidents are being experienced.

To make this determination, executives must conduct a "high-level" adverse impact analysis or risk assessment to determine the appropriateness of pursuing the use of IDS within the larger framework of building an effective security monitoring and incident response capability. To do this, an organization must examine their business-processing methods to determine the potential seriousness of threats of undiscovered breaches of security.

Several questions must be answered in conducting this analysis:

- What information in our corporate systems could be of value to my competitors?
- Do we know that employees are not stealing corporate secrets?
- Do we know that systems are not being manipulated for illegal and fraudulent purposes?
- What is the adverse impact on our e-business processes should security breaches go undetected?
- Do security breaches need to be detected in real-time, near real-time, or is it acceptable to know about them days after their occurrence?
- What is our obligation to our employees, customers, and business partners?
- What are our regulatory responsibilities?
- What are our corporate responsibilities under applicable "privacy" laws? What are our moral obligations?
- Could officers and directors of the corporation be held liable for perpetuating (i.e., passing along a virus, etc.) a security incident by not employing an ID System and conducting system security monitoring activities? What is the rest of our industry doing? The "due diligence" question.
- What is our responsibility to the board of directors and stockholders?
- Knowing that we cannot ultimately delegate this responsibility, are we comfortable with these answers?

If the answers indicate a degree of risk or unease that should be mitigated, then justification for a security monitoring and incidence response capability exists.

The next section outlines issues to be considered when adopting a JIT systems monitoring security strategy and suggests implementation alternatives.

DEFINING A COST-EFFECTIVE SECURITY MONITORING AND INCIDENT RESPONSE CAPABILITY

To avoid wasted time and effort in the search for the right combination of intrusion detection systems, tools, intrusion knowledge base, and staffing models, it is advisable to first identify some criteria by which success of the effort can be determined. This exercise will help an organization "home in" on those aspects of a systems monitoring capability that are truly necessary and assist in "wade through" the advertising hype of the IDS marketplace.

Success criteria for the design, implementation, and operation of a security monitoring and incident response capability are many. Any acquisition strategy, whether to build and staff the capability from within or to obtain it through contractor support, should be analyzed to see how well the following requirements are met:

- Ability to detect internal misuse as well as external attacks or unauthorized access.

- Ability to develop, manage, and utilize an incident knowledge database in a proactive way to be used to design and implement preventive security measures.

- Ability to conduct the necessary exchange of incident data with industry sector, government, and IT industry special interest groups (SIGs) and appropriate information sharing and analysis centers (ISAC). Without this capability the company is isolated and not plugged into the world of intrusion detection.

- Adequacy of corporate policies and procedures for security incident information sharing between business units, business partners, and members of the corporate supply chain.

- Sufficient redundancy in the security monitoring and incident response architecture to assure reliability.

- Access to a "pool" of personnel experienced in security monitoring and incident response work. Such experience is commonly found with people who have performed computer emergency response team (CERT) duties.

- "Hard" securing of the monitoring and detection architecture. Such systems are targeted and must be secured to the highest level.

- If the capability is to be contractor-provided, the extent to which the contractor is focused on monitoring and incident reporting—is it considered a primary line of business or merely a sideline activity?

- If contractor-provided, the degree of trustworthiness that can be claimed for those consultants and technicians staffing the function.

- Sufficiency of funding to ensure adequate maintenance of the capability.
- Strategy for providing "technology refreshment" to maintain currency of tools and the ability to handle faster "response time" demands.
- Legal considerations that may need the general counsel's attention:
  - Security and privacy notification "banners"
  - Handling of alerts within the corporation and with business partners
  - Warnings back to perpetrator—"hack-back"
  - Guidance for law enforcement notification

By taking the time to define the criteria for success, an organization will be able to greatly increase their chance of fielding a functioning systems monitoring capability and reduce the false starts and project failures that are common to the IT industry.

ALTERNATIVES TO BUILDING "YOUR OWN" SECURITY MONITORING AND INCIDENT RESPONSE CAPABILITY

It is not within the scope of this chapter to suggest a specific technical solution for a security monitoring and incident response capability. But it has been possible to present for consideration information to guide an analysis whereby a design is defined that will meet specific organizational e-business requirements and be reliable and maintainable.

There is general agreement in the security community that there is a severe shortfall of knowledgeable and skilled personnel to undertake any security-related task, much less a task as complex and demanding as network security monitoring and incident response with the goal of proactively providing preventive recommendations

A review of the considerations, questions, and success criteria presented in this paper reveals this to be an area of great specialization and therefore an area of great competition for experienced personnel.

No doubt, some large corporations and government agencies may choose to build their own capability and make the necessary "continuing" investment to maintain the effectiveness of tools, techniques, and personnel. Others may choose to outsource this service. In most cases, small to mid-size businesses and local government organizations will be at a decided disadvantage because they will almost certainly be unable to compete in the ensuing bidding war for experienced and talented personnel.

So, how can the small to mid-sized company satisfy this need in a cost-effective and efficient manner? What alternatives exist to building your own security monitoring and incident response capability?

Keeping in mind the cautions outlined in Chapter 4 regarding outsourcing and unnecessary contractor dependence, the concept of contractor Managed Security Services (MSS) can provide a workable solution that satisfies the requirements of a Security Monitoring and Incident Response capability while overcoming the most common problems likely to be encountered in attempting to build a dedicated internal capability. Often MSS are offered on a "subscription" basis, which allows contractors to leverage security monitoring personnel.

SUMMARY

It is increasingly clear that the electronic interconnectedness of business, government, and society is threatened by breaches in information security and the proven inability of an information-processing infrastructure to function in a reliable fashion due to "denial of service" attacks.

Furthermore, it is clear that most previous attempts at securing information and the processing infrastructure are out of date, being mainframe-oriented and not network-focused.

Attacks against contemporary e-business systems are occurring within the context of Internet time. Therefore, security prevention, detection, and response actions should also strive to operate within a framework of Internet time.

When properly designed, configured, and staffed, a security monitoring and incident response capability forms a frontline defense against breaches of security because such systems operate within the framework of Internet time to provide the rapid response required by today's JIT processing and networked business environments.

Successful security monitoring and incident response capabilities require the combination of sophisticated electronic "sensing" and auditing tools and personnel experienced in the analysis of the outputs of those tools. Using tool outputs to diagnose security problems inherent to the systems under observation and making preventive recommendations requires yet another level of experience. When considering contractor support, only companies dedicated to providing security monitoring and incident response services as a primary line of business can create the career incentives necessary to recruit and retain the level of experienced personnel needed for success. As the frontline of defense, these functions are much too important to be delegated as a part-time or ancillary duty or to the lowest bidder.

Chapter 6

Designing and Delivering Secured E-Business Application Systems

Much in this book deals with the problems associated with playing "catch-up" and securing e-business systems already in operation and with the establishment of a security management program sufficiently robust to maintain a secured operating environment in the years to come.

This chapter concentrates on how to break the "catch-up" cycle by designing, developing, testing, and delivering e-business applications that have integrity, confidentiality, and availability as a principal design criterion. In other words, this chapter focuses on how to design security into future systems rather than just adding security on as an afterthought.

INTRODUCTION

The ability of an organization to define, design, develop, test, deliver, and operate e-business application systems possessing adequate and appropriate security controls has improved significantly during the last decade. Furthermore, the attention being focused on protection of the critical information infrastructure provides an unprecedented opportunity to build, for the first time, effective security and internal audit controls into the next generation of e-business applications.

For this chapter, an e-business application system and its relationship to the other technical systems making up the processing infrastructure are depicted in Exhibit 6.1. This figure was previously seen in Chapter 2 when the infrastructure and the vulnerabilities of the e-business architecture and operating environment were discussed. In this chapter also, the business applications system to carry out e-business activities are seen as central to Exhibit 6.1 and as the reason for the sum of hardware, software, data, communications, and other technologies to be working together to produce a product or service in direct fulfillment of an organization's business goals. The application is viewed as "nested" within other technical support systems since it will depend on their utility and rely on their security and integrity features to create an operating environment that allows the application's output products and services to be considered reliable and therefore trusted by the user.

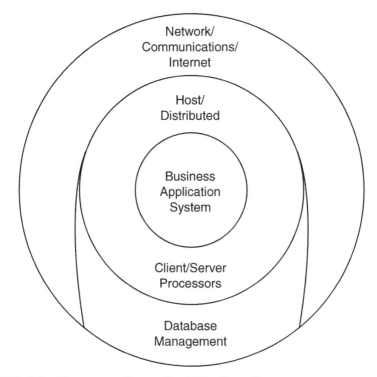

Exhibit 6.1   Component Parts of an E-Business System

A business application system carries out an e-business function by executing the predetermined logic of a design that best performs the function while satisfying certain predefined quality specifications usually expressed in terms of correctness, reliability, integrity, usability, and confidentiality. Defined quality specifications for an application system will vary, from one application to another, depending on the nature and criticality of the business function being performed and the sensitivity and privacy requirements of the information involved. The e-business application that performs a business function conforming to these defined quality specifications can be thought of as being "trusted for use" and therefore contributes value in meeting the business goals of the organization. Quality specifications are the "adjectives" that modify a data "noun" or the "adverb" that gives additional meaning to a compute "verb." Without quality being specified, a programmed function has no success criteria except to compile and "run." Without quality being specified, there is no formal way to determine the "correctness" of a programmed business function except that it "looks right." Exhibit 6.2 depicts the quality specifications commonly associated with a "trusted" application system.

Exhibit 6.3 lists those major categories of security and integrity control techniques, discussed in Chapter 3, that must be employed to foster "trust" in the

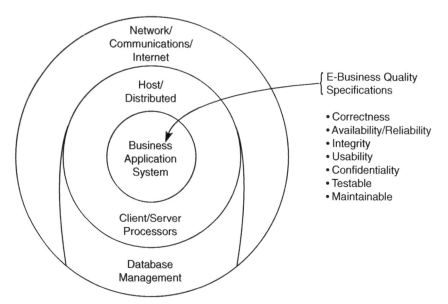

Exhibit 6.2   E-Business Quality Specifications

application system. This figure illustrates that the principal reason to employ security and integrity controls is to ensure that the application consistently produces quality output; output that can be "trusted" by customers, system users, and business partners as they carry out their business activity. Security and integrity controls are not employed to obstruct or slow down processing. They are not used to annoy users of the system. On the contrary, security and integrity controls are employed in the hope that customers and business partners will continue to use the system because they have "trust" in the outputs of the system and its processing. Exhibit 6.4 provides definitions for the quality specifications for e-business applications and the major categories of security and integrity and control techniques.

Exhibit 6.3 also depicts the business environment protections afforded by legal protections, physical security, personnel security, and procedural security.

The relationship between controls and the quality of system outputs (i.e., trust in the system) has not always been appreciated. But the high visibility of e-business systems with their "direct" link to the customer and business partners makes an understanding of the relationship between quality and controls easier to comprehend. An e-business does not have the luxury of the legacy "backroom" processing operation to make things right on the midnight to 8 A.M. shift; the e-business process, warts and all, is immediately judged by the user and "trust" is either established or undermined. Correctness, availability and reliability, integrity, usability, and confidentiality are judged, and the business either wins or loses the encounter with the customer. Security and integrity controls are imperative if the e-business wants to win.

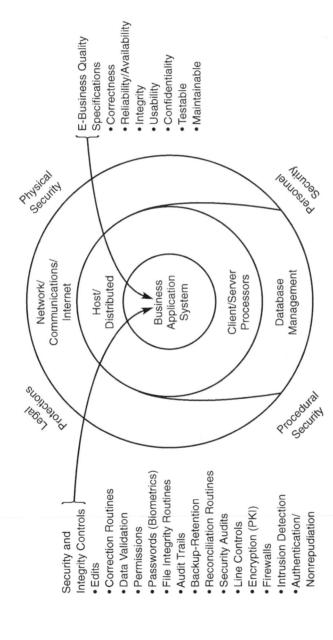

Exhibit 6.3 Security and Integrity Controls

Audit Trails Recording of three types of processing activities: (1) logs to aid in the reconstruction of transactions: (2) logs to meet the requirements of the audit staff; and (3) logs recording security accesses, activities, and suspected violations.

Authentication/Nonrepudiation The ability to verify the identity of a user and prove the validity of the transaction.

Availability/Reliability The degree to which the system is available and meets the business requirement for operational uptime.

Backup and Retention Policies and procedures for en-suring the ability to reconstruct files, software, and business transactions in the event of a processing interruption or to meet a legal requirement.

Confidentiality A measure of privacy or secrecy that is required by nature of the information involved or the sensi-tivity of the business process.

Correction Routines Software and/or manual routines invoked to correct errors and omissions discovered by an edit.

Correctness The degree to which system outputs satisfy the accuracy requirements of the business activity being supported.

Data Validation Software and/or manual routines to check the accuracy and appropriateness of data before entry into a system or database.

Edits Edits are defined checks and controls that ensure accuracy of input data. The sufficiency of edits and their use during the business process is based on the stringency of the quality attribute metrics. The more severe the metric, the more important the edits.

Encryption Encryption is a means of maintaining secure data in an unsecured environment. PKI is a contemporary implementation of encryption.

File Integrity Routines Software housekeeping routines for maintaining the trustworthiness of data in a database. The more severe the accuracy requirements, the more stringent these routines and the more often they should be run.

Firewalls A control technique to limit access to system resources; usually a combination of hardware and software.

Integrity A measure of completeness and soundness of design and construction. A system that has integrity can be trusted by the user.

Intrusion Detection Software that can detect unauthorized access and provide forensic data.

Line Control Physical location and/or placement of controls on communication lines to prevent unauthorized access to the line.

Maintainable Software that is designed to be easily main-tained, usually in modules that are completely documented to show all inputs, outputs, calculations, and quality metrics.

Exhibit 6.4 Definitions of E-Business Quality Specifications and Security and Integrity Controls

Passwords (biometrics) Access to systems, data, and the granting of permitted actions is based on recognition by the security software of a unique identification code. Passwords must be kept secure.

Permissions Actions that a user is permitted to take once access has been granted to a store of data. These per-missions may be to READ, WRITE, APPEND, DELETE, EXECUTE, or any combination based on job requirements.

Reconciliation Routines Procedures to bring about a settlement or adjustment between differing information sources, databases, or reports.

Security Audits Suspected violation or incident reports generated for the purpose of adjusting controls and managing system resources.

Testable Software that is designed to be easily tested when changes are made to functionality.

Usability A measure of being "fit for use" by a representative employee in the actual workplace.

Exhibit 6.4 *(Continued)*

PAST DEVELOPMENT REALITIES

Before discussing how secure e-business applications can be engineered with today's knowledge, methods, techniques, and tools, it may be instructive to briefly explore why the majority of "legacy" application systems now in operation do not possess adequate controls. "Legacy" is a term used to reference software and systems built during the last three decades of computing that were usually mainframe-based and where a single business function was addressed such as finance, personnel management, order entry, and so forth. These applications, usually written in COBOL, had minimal direct information transfer between "legacy" systems. Today's e-business applications are much more complex in their linked interdependencies and are much more likely to suffer data contamination or loss of integrity if even a single application in the linkage of systems is somehow compromised.

During the 1970s, 1980s, and 1990s a continuous flow of reports criticizing the lack of security and internal accounting controls in computerized application systems were issued by government organizations such as the General Accounting Office (GAO) and other audit groups and associations in the private sector. Repeatedly high on the list of criticisms were the following:

- Systems were not properly documented, making it extremely difficult to reconstruct processing or make necessary changes to an application
- Lack of software quality and insufficient testing
- Lack of access controls on computer processes and files
- Lack of internal accounting controls in application systems, making them subject to undetected manipulation.

These findings, while disturbing, were at least understandable given the realities of the times in which the systems were developed and the limitations under which most systems operated. During that period:

- The output products from most application systems were viewed as by-products of a business process (i.e., status information to management, reporting systems, record keeping, storage). As such, they merely substituted for long-established and familiar clerical operations and were generally viewed as rather straightforward in both design and operation.

- Limiting access through physical means and simple password schemes was seen as the principal control mechanism required for the mainframe and non-intelligent terminal environment.

- There existed limited knowledge of what constituted appropriate and adequate security controls for most business applications. Computer security at the time had grown out of the Department of Defense requirement to protect "classified" information and command and control and weapon systems. Audits and reviews had not yet documented the gradual loss of traditional accounting checks and balances, and consistency checks as business functions were reduced to computer code. Many cross-checking actions and supervisory reviews of business transactions, especially financial transactions, were "programmed out" as the computer absorbed more and more of the traditional processing. Preventive, detective, and corrective measures were slow in being devised and in being communicated to software developers. Testing techniques to ensure enforcement of proper design and programming techniques were even slower in development.

- Computers were physically limited in the amount of resources, especially memory, which could be dedicated to security and internal controls.

- Only preliminary work had been done on a risk management model that could assist in determining the adequacy and cost-effectiveness of system controls and formulate convincing justifications for their implementation.

- Since compelling business arguments for controls were difficult to make, top management was generally ambivalent to the subject. Controls sounded good, but they could not inconvenience anyone, slow anything down, or require significant funding.

- The system and software environment was not conducive to the close collaboration between the systems analyst and the business user that was necessary to design working applications possessing adequate controls.

- System and software development environments also were not conducive to the creation and maintenance of meaningful documentation for the application under construction.

- The number of systems analysts experienced enough in design to efficiently apply the concept of controls to application systems was extremely limited.

At the time, these conditions presented valid limitations on the comprehensiveness of all application systems being developed. These conditions had a major negative impact on the implementation of security and integrity controls that many businesses are still coping with today.

It is important to learn from past mistakes and to be familiar with examples of application system and software failures and the negative impacts they have had on organizations and individuals. Recently, these failures have been receiving increased publicity, resulting in three major trends in thinking about automated systems, their impact, and their management.

1. Due to the increasingly high negative impact when system failures adversely affect lives, investments, businesses, and even the natural order of things, there are those who suggest that we collectively rethink the use of computers, especially in those instances when the potential for damage seems to outweigh our limited capability to prevent or contain it.

2. Even if only economic loss is involved, the growing number of liability claims against software developers is expected to increase. According to computer law experts, increasing litigation, more and more of it successful, is raising the awareness of software developers and system service providers that contractual arrangements alone may no longer be a satisfactory means of avoiding responsibility for damages due to failure. Since the wholesale embrace of the Internet for B2C and B2B communications and the increasing use of commercial software packages to conduct business, the potential for harm has risen exponentially. All this potential for liability from an industry known to be woefully lacking in its ability to produce secure and reliable software and systems.

3. It has become clear that by focusing on the work processes whereby software and systems are developed, improvements can be made in the security and reliability of those resultant systems. This approach, compliments of *total quality management*, recognizes that work process discipline must be imposed on the development of e-business or any other application system, and with that discipline will come the resources needed to build and test the security and integrity controls required for tomorrow's systems to be "trusted."

It is this last evolutionary jump in thinking about systems and their management that provides some optimism that future e-business application systems can possess adequate and appropriate security and integrity controls before they are deployed to operation.

It is this new focus on the process of e-business system development with which we will spend the remainder of this chapter, for only during the development of a system can the "catch-up" cycle be broken.

CONTEMPORARY DEVELOPMENT REALITIES

During the late 1990s, many of the limiting factors affecting security and integrity controls and their inclusion in applications systems have been eliminated or greatly reduced. In today's reengineered e-business environment:

- Automated systems are no longer viewed as just delivering by-products of traditional business activity. With the advent of the World Wide Web and the ability to communicate directly with customers and business partners, some organizations are beginning to understand that the electronic system is increasingly becoming the business. E-business is expected to provide an advantage over competitors. Automation is supposed to help organizations work smarter, with e-business technology providing opportunities for new business and market share.

- Security and integrity controls are becoming seen as necessary for guaranteeing the full range of quality attributes and performance measures needed for e-business applications to be "trusted." Contemporary system engineering methodologies and techniques provide for quality and performance measures to be treated as integral to the application being developed. This focus on quality during the last few years makes the inclusion of security and integrity controls the next logical development step. (The model discussed later in this chapter illustrates how the inclusion of security and integrity controls into a new design can work)

- Government and some private sector industries are beginning to require *certifications* by appropriate officials which serve as explicit acceptance of their responsibility for the security and integrity of an application system.

- Rationales for a system reengineering effort increasingly look for justification to the business process being supported. These same justifications can now support the development, implementation, monitoring, and enforcement of e-business application controls.

- Risk management models used in formulating security and internal control determinations have matured and have recently been augmented by such practices as preventive thinking and error-free work techniques.

- Twenty-plus years of experience and research have provided the knowledge to adequately control and cost-effectively secure all but the most highly "classified" applications. *We know how to build adequate and appropriate security and integrity controls in the vast majority of instances.* Effective measures exist for prevention, detection, and recovery measures. They need only be designed into the e-business application and the technical support infrastructure. A lack of hardware capacity cannot be considered a valid limiting factor as in previous decades. Today's processors are inexpensive and fast, and any resultant "overhead" from controls is insignificant compared to the reliability gained.

- Modern e-business development environments promote and facilitate the necessary stakeholder partnerships required to arrive at a comprehensive set of system specifications. These include the security and internal controls deemed prudent by executive management and by independent audit groups required by law or by their organizational function to have a say in how the system must operate. The burden of capturing these specifications and of performing subsequent validation activities has been greatly lessened with the advent of software engineering methodologies and automated tools. Increasingly, security specification activities have become more practical and easier to perform through the use of automated testing tools that permit development of test plans, test criteria, test scenarios, and test execution concurrent with development of the e-business application.

While most of the realities of contemporary systems development are positive, there are three major negatives that must be factored into any strategy to improve security and integrity controls over e-business applications.

1. Severe shortages of adequately trained and sufficiently experienced systems analysts, security or otherwise, exist to meet demand, and it appears that the situation is getting worse as more and more computing systems are being dispersed throughout the enterprise. While many people are trained in the use of a specific programming language, software package, or network tool, far too few are educated and experienced in the analysis required to define, design, develop, test, and deliver an e-business application system for implementation in a client-server, web-based environment. Providing technologically sound solutions to business problems and creating opportunities is both an architectural challenge and a delivery challenge. The effort often required just making these new architectures function is reminiscent of the early mainframe days when the need to "get things working" eclipsed the requirement to "get things working properly" and pushed even the primitive security controls of those days into the background. There is a very real danger of the same thing occurring today.

2. The levels of potential complexity and uncertainty affecting the developers of application systems have grown exponentially in recent years. In government and industry, where large networked systems are becoming commonplace, the massive size and technological complexity of such projects have an explosive effect on the number and types of problems encountered in designing and delivering such systems. And almost every problem has a "security downside" associated with it. Despite the best efforts of managers, these complex projects, with their inherent uncertainties, often greatly exceed their original cost and schedule estimates, and, as every security officer knows, in an attempt to get back on schedule, systems application controls are given short shrift. This means that the security and integrity controls of Exhibit 6.3 do not

get built, and the quality, reliability, integrity, correctness, and confidentiality of the application is then opened to compromise.

3. Contemporary architectures for e-business systems plan to place many additional processing burdens on the desktop. Most of these applications are relying on the Internet, client-server, videoconferencing, imaging, and extensive internal networking to place the employee and customer at the center of the e-business process. Designing application security and integrity controls in this environment is certain to be difficult in the years ahead, and attention must be given now to how this development process should work. The next section of this chapter outlines the use of a development model that can guide the securing of tomorrow's e-business systems.

DEVELOPING SECURED E-BUSINESS SYSTEMS

"Business and government managers need basic tools and management techniques for use during systems development, and after the system has become operational, to provide reasonable assurances that the information processed by their systems is accurate, complete, timely, and authorized, and that the system itself is secure and auditable" (*Model Framework for Management Control over Automated Information Systems*—President's Council on Integrity and Efficiency (PCIE) Report, page iii, 1988). This statement is as true today as it was in 1988, even more so because the present complexity of e-business applications greatly exceeds that of the mainframe "legacy" era and the systems built during that period.

What are these basic tools and management techniques that could be used during systems development? How might *reasonable assurances* be achieved? How might a successful systems development environment be structured, a managed environment that would deliver secured e-business application systems? What methodologies would be involved, and who in the organization would participate in the process of development? What model could be followed in delivering systems worthy of the "trust" and confidence of the e-business user?

Exhibit 6.5 portrays the systems development review (SDR) framework whereby business executives can visualize and grasp the many development phases and technical and project management activities constituting a best-practice approach for an e-business development effort. The framework concentrates on the entire spectrum of development activities because to shortchange or overlook any one activity is to jeopardize the operational integrity and hence the security of the entire e-business system. *Remember, you can only secure that which is being managed*—and every activity in Exhibit 6.5 is required to develop, deliver, and maintain a manageable application system.

The (SDR) framework is laid out in columns and rows. The rows indicate the phases of a development and/or systems integration life cycle effort, and the columns are comprised of development management requirement categories with an infrastructure risk monitoring category for hardware, software, and network

MANAGEMENT REQUIREMENTS

Life Cycle Phases	Project Management Plan	Software or Systems Engineering Plan	Internal Controls Plan	Security Plan	Quality Assurance and Testing Plan	Configuration Management Plan	Documentation Plan	Technology Transfer Plan	Training Plan	Infrastructure Risk Monitoring		
										Hardware	Software	Network
Preparation												
Definition												
Design												
Development												
Deployment												
Maintenance												

Exhibit 6.5 Systems Development Review Framework

components of the operational support infrastructure that require continual risk assessments.

To increase the likelihood of success of an e-business development and/or integration project, development personnel must proceed down the rows, taking care to keep synchronized with the Management Requirement Plans and Infrastructure Risk Monitoring activities associated with each row. Each column represents a specialized project management view and a set of requirements to be imposed on the system as it is being defined, designed, developed, tested, and fielded.

Extend the lines separating each phase across the framework and you have a matrix. Within each box or cell formed by the intersection of lines, visualize a specific set of action statements describing what should be occurring within each management plan phase by phase.

Appendix B provides detailed definitions and a completed matrix for the whole of Exhibit 6.5. It describes in detail each column and row and provides executive management with an initial set of questions to use when conducting oversight project reviews for new e-business system development projects.

As an example, the columns labeled "Security Plan" and "Internal Controls Plan" refer to the project management action requiring that each of the phases of development be influenced by the task of securing a system and ensuring its processing integrity before it is put into operation. This means that from an oversight perspective, executives should expect that very specific action items exist in the security and internal control plans for the e-business system under construction and that these actions are actually taking place during each phase of the development. In other words, there are application specific security and integrity-related activities that must be accomplished during the preparation phase, the definition phase, the design phase, and so on, until a secured system with processing integrity is turned over to operational maintenance status. When using Appendix B, executive management can monitor an e-business development project from beginning to end by asking specific questions and by expecting specific answers with documentary proof for "due diligence" purposes.

Continuing the example, the "Security Plan" and "Internal Controls Plan" questions in Appendix B ensure that security and integrity requirements to be addressed during design and implementation activities are not lost in the totality of the development effort or overlooked because of unsubstantiated claims that "something is being done about security."

Use of the completed framework also forces attention on many of the other troubling areas of e-business systems development that tend to get lost in the generalized discussions about a project's progression through the phases of the life cycle. Such plan areas as documentation and configuration management (CM) are often given little attention during a development or integration project, and as a result, security and integrity of the operational business system are undermined.

Of these other plan areas, none is probably more critical, after security and internal controls, than the "Quality Assurance (QA) & Testing Plan." To be effective, QA and testing activities must progress phase for phase with the execution of the "Software Engineering Plan" for the e-business system being constructed. This means that QA and testing activities must be performed on the work products of the software engineering and/or software integration effort before the end of each phase of the Software Engineering Plan. If they are not performed at each phase, the risk of requirement errors and design and programming defects going undetected rises and the cost to fix problems later in the life cycle, as every QA proponent knows, increases dramatically. Also, undetected errors and defects lead to basic instabilities in an e-business system that can be exploited during its operation, thus contributing to the insecurity of the application and its processing.

Equally important is the need for project-level monitoring of the support infrastructure for risks that could adversely affect timely implementation of the e-business system (the last three columns of Exhibit 6.5). Each e-business systems project, and any other automation project for that matter, under development or resulting from the integration of off-the-shelf products, must continually monitor the planned support infrastructure on which the e-business system will eventually be based. Typically, this will mean anticipating support product upgrades, independently evaluating tested product reports, and monitoring support contractor viability for those hardware, software, network, and Internet elements on which the system will depend. At the conclusion of each major phase of the development, a status check of each of these areas must be conducted to affirm that basic infrastructure risk assumptions are not changing.

USING THE SDR FRAMEWORK

The SDR framework depicted in Exhibit 6.5 and further explained in Appendix B, is an amalgam of system development disciplines, usually treated separately, into a single holistic methodology for the expressed purpose of improving the security and integrity of tomorrow's e-business systems. This framework draws heavily on the PCIE model because that model was prepared by representatives of the computer security, the audit, and the inspector general communities for the expressed purpose of helping system developers build integrity and security controls into application systems. The PCIE model treated application security and integrity controls as an essential and integral subset of specifications that must be defined at the same time the business system functions are defined, not months later or after the system has gone operational. If "due diligence" and "security certifications" are required as corporate policy (see Chapter 4), then documentation to demonstrate "due diligence" is compiled throughout the development as a by-product of the process.

For realistic "security certifications" to take place, it is imperative that all security and integrity control requirements be identified during the preparation phase and be formally specified during the definition phase. Without this attention to controls during the first two phases of development, they are unlikely to be addressed at all during the latter phases of the development effort. But once defined and specified, control requirements should be processed through the remainder of development just as any other requirement. In fact, it is most help-ful to view e-business application security and integrity control requirements as just another expression of a complete business processing requirement needing to be satisfied before the system can be accepted for "trusted" operation. *It is one thing to build a system to "pay people" and quite another to "pay only the right people the correct amount mailed to their current address."* Many security and integrity controls are required to achieve the latter requirement, while none are required with the former.

The SDR framework also applies quality management principles that came out of the TQM movement of the late 1980s. One of those "key" principles is to spend a great deal of time on problem definition so that later misunderstandings during actual design and development will be kept to a minimum. Put into qual-ity management jargon, the adage to *measure twice and cut once* applies to secu-rity and integrity as well as to any other requirement of a system.

CHOOSING A SYSTEMS DEVELOPMENT METHODOLOGY THAT IS COMPATIBLE WITH THE SDR FRAMEWORK

As stated earlier, the SDR framework can be viewed as an overlay to the systems development methodology being used on the e-business project. But not all methodologies are up to the challenge of constructing systems that possess ade-quate security and integrity controls. In fact, most methodologies, due to their lack of quality management focus, allow critical controlling elements of a project (e.g., testing) to become subordinate to the task (e.g., programming) over which they are supposed to exert control. Predictably, the resultant system may not be adequately tested, and if security and integrity controls were to be included, they would not be tested either. This is a major caution pertaining to the extent to which the project management activities of the underlying systems development methodology support and enforce the *rigors* of constructing quality system. With-out the mechanisms to promote quality, the methodology is unlikely to produce secured e-business systems.

For example, does the underlying systems development methodology sup-port and enforce the discipline of structured systems engineering and promote sound project and quality management? Many methodologies do not. Many methodologies deal only with programming and are not comprehensive enough for an e-business systems effort.

In choosing a systems development methodology that is compatible with the SDR framework, the following considerations should score high.

PARTICIPANTS IN THE IDENTIFICATION OF SECURITY AND INTEGRITY CONTROLS

The greatest challenge to building adequate security and integrity into an e-busi-ness system is to get all of the necessary and desired control requirements on the table so they can be spelled out in the design and programming specifications. Exhibit 6.6 portrays the communities of interest that must be assembled during the definition and design phase of the development if all application, security, and integrity control requirements are to be identified and included as system design specifications. Each community of interest has a legitimate reason to participate, for they represent a constituency with economic or legal interest in what gets built. Each community of interest also brings knowledge concerning specific security and integrity controls and how they are best implemented so as to be auditable.

Business Managers and System Users.   Users bring operational knowledge of the business requirement, and business managers have the responsibility to ensure that the e-business application being designed accommodates all the corporate

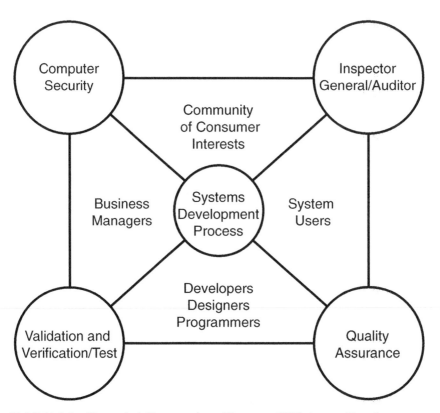

Exhibit 6.6   Expanded Community of Interests Will Assure Development of Secured Systems That Can Be Trusted

needs, as well as the customer and business partner needs. This is depicted in Exhibit 6.7, which illustrates all of the factors affecting the design of a system for the workplace. Exhibit 6.7 shows three aspects of any system designed for conducting business in a world of customers, business partners, and employees. In the left sector of the figure are the technical and computer specific portions of an e-business application. The sector to the right identifies three classes of system requirements for business partners, the customer expected to interface with the system in an on-line fashion, and the internal employee who uses the system to carry out a corporate function. In the center sector, we find interfaces between the automated system and the human element—the sector where automation must augment and supplement the human element if the system is to succeed. Audits have consistently shown that no matter how *elegant* the technical solution, if it does not integrate smoothly and complement the activities of customers, business partners, and employees executing the business process, the system will experience a breakdown in whatever security controls do exist. If the system is difficult to work with, people in the "real world" will endeavor to do their job, despite the system, by devising workarounds. Workarounds and security are incompatible.

It is within the context of the design of the total operation that systems are built that possess integrity of processing and can be secured. This means that the vast majority of issues affecting a successful and secure design will be human factor issues. While some of the technical challenges are formidable, the failure to design a system that interfaces smoothly and intuitively with its human operators is much more difficult. However important this challenge is to the ultimate security of an e-business system, it is not within the scope of this book to address the *sociotechnical design of systems.* For an excellent treatment of this subject, read *Information Technology and Organizational Change* by Ken Eason (London: Taylor & Francis, 1988).

Continuing, however, within the scope of this book, it is within the context of Exhibit 6.6 that overall security and integrity vulnerabilities must be assessed, risks weighed, and trade-offs made that will allow appropriate and adequate security and integrity controls to be determined, developed, implemented, tested, and monitored. Through the perspective of Exhibit 6.6, the total operational nature of the actual e-business system can be viewed.

Community of Consumer Interest.   Consumer interests represent the privacy, confidentiality, and public policy concerns of various special groups who will eventually use the e-business system or may be effected by it in some way. Depending on the nature of the information involved and the application being developed, these groups may be able to speed or hinder the systems implementation. It is important that the corporate legal staff monitor the leanings of such groups and their impact on such things as pending legislation and union negotiations.

E-business system applications that deal with customer data must be especially sensitive to the rapidly evolving issues of privacy notifications, opt-in or opt-out policies and practices, customer data challenging procedures, customer

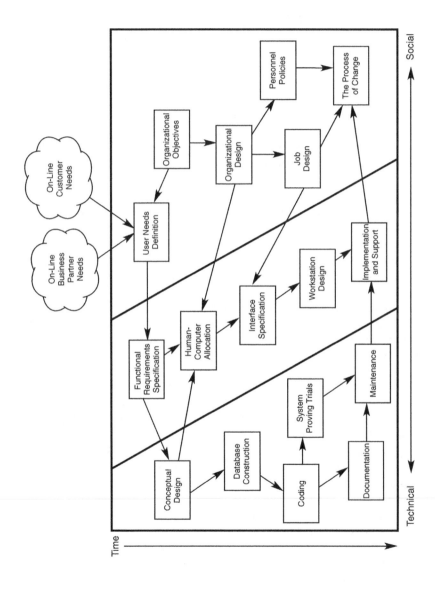

Exhibit 6.7 Elements Affecting the Design of a System for the Workplace

157

data correction procedures, shared data correction procedures, and what are considered to be "best practice" confidentiality controls.

Some organizations are creating the position of chief privacy officer (CPO) to fulfill this role on a full-time basis.

Developers, Designers, and Programmers. Developers are the participants in the construction of an e-business system who possess the knowledge and skills to convert business requirements, as modified by the interests of the other participants, into a tangible, functioning computerized system that will integrate smoothly into the workplace. This system will possess integrity and be secure.

Developers will be "professional" system analysts, programmers, and testers who understand the necessity for discipline in their actions and the need to follow a structured systems development methodology. They will document all work products so that the finished system will be manageable under a stable baseline that accurately reflects the software and system at any point in time.

The advantages of formally expanding the list of participants to the design and utilizing the SDR framework as a project management guide will not be lost on experienced developers. They will see the utility of both because for years conscientious analysts and programmers have been forced to deal with security and integrity controls in a vacuum. For years developers were put in the unenviable position of guessing what controls were adequate and then attempting to implement them in business applications without management's understanding or support.

Judicious application of this discussion regarding "participants to the design" to conducting oversight reviews of systems under development will prevent such problems in future e-business endeavors. Additional resources to supplement Appendix B can be found in Appendix E.

Auditor and Inspector General. These participants bring not only knowledge of where and when security and integrity controls are required but also an increased understanding of how to construct such controls within the entire work process environment. They have within their community of interest a growing body of knowledge of what works and what does not. They should be tasked to bring this knowledge to the e-business development project and assist as consultants to the designers and security officials. They should be allowed to take the position, as has happened in the past, that they cannot participate because it will compromise their later audits. If such a position is taken, outsider electronic data processing (EDP) auditor expertise should be obtained with internal audit concurrence.

Auditor participants generally bring a certain clout to the development project. They often have legal responsibilities and often are consulted by senior management before system deployment takes place. It is imperative that the specific controls the auditor needs to give their professional assurances to management be included in systems design so that these requirements will have been satisfied at the time of systems delivery.

Computer Security.   Participants from the specialty area of computer and communications security provide expertise on how to apply the security and integrity controls seen in Exhibit 6.3 and discussed in Chapter 3 to the e-business application under development. This includes securing host computer and distributed processing architectures, database management systems, networks, and interfaces to the Internet. Security experts may also be expected to provide input to physical security and personnel security decisions.

With regard to the specific controls depicted in Exhibit 6.3, computer security personnel would most likely provide expertise in system access controls and passwords, back up and retention, and audit security reporting, communication link controls, and encryption to include private key infrastructure (PKI) issues. Other controls would be the responsibility of other parties to the development since they deal with the application's business rules, data quality, internal accounting, customer or user acceptance, and auditability.

The role of the computer security community in the development of e-business applications is to advise developers on how and to what extent applications and supporting infrastructures can be secured given the hardware, software, and communications architecture chosen to host the system. They should be asked to advise on the weaknesses and risks that any envisioned processing environment would pose to the e-business application under development. They should be expected to be able to determine how different hardware components and security software packages can make improvements in security and reduce threats to the integrity and confidentiality of the application. They should also be expected to judge the potential survivability of a system's supporting architecture if it is subjected to denial of service attacks or natural disaster, and they should be expected to recommend "best practices" for developing disaster recovery plans and continuity of operations procedures.

Security experts cannot be expected to be the sole advisor on the best way to keep an e-business application free from being used for "fraudulent" processing and illegal activities. They should not be expected to substitute opinion for professional legal advice regarding the adequacy of privacy policies, privacy notifications, avenues of recourse, or other issues surrounding the use and/or correction of private data by the corporation.

Security experts must work closely with the next participant in systems design because the use of security and integrity controls is justified by the need to assure management and all other stakeholders that the e-business system will function as designed and will possess the quality specifications depicted in Exhibit 6.2.

Quality Assurance (QA).   Participants from this specialty area will contribute expertise at two levels. First, QA personnel assist users and the other participants in (1) identifying quality specifications, and (2) developing application-related metrics for each quality specification so they can be programmed and tested against meaningful and measurable criteria. Measurable quality specifications

(Exhibit 6.2) are the essential characteristics of a well-defined e-business application that allow it to be "trusted" in use. Quality specifications such as correctness, application reliability and availability, and confidentiality can be measured against specific requirements founded in the business process or in law, while integrity and usability are more subjective and are determined through customer use and acceptance of the system. If quality metrics such as numeric values, time limits, and range parameters are not specified, system developers cannot build or test the effectiveness of many of the security and integrity controls since no acceptable criteria have been established to measure against. Without establishing quality specifications, selecting and judging the effectiveness of security and integrity controls becomes a "guessing game," a game of "we'll know it when we see it." *In this type of specification vacuum, system developers will be forced to establish their own criteria in order to complete development and deliver "something." In short, developers will make "something" up just to get the "code" to work.*

The importance of the relationship between selecting and judging the effectiveness of security and integrity controls and the establishment of measurable quality specifications cannot be overstated. Security and integrity controls are implemented on a system for the purpose of ensuring that the quality specifications of Exhibit 6.2 are met and maintained. As discussed earlier, each security and integrity control seen in Exhibit 6.3 has a direct bearing on the e-business system's ability to meet and maintain each quality specification required of a system that can be "trusted" in use.

Reviewing the relationships between security and integrity controls and quality specifications found in Chapter 3:

Correctness is assured and maintained through the use of:

- Edits
- Correction routines
- Reconciliation routines
- Nonrepudiation
- Data validation
- File integrity routines
- Authentication/nonrepudiation
- Firewalls

Availability and Reliability are assured and maintained through the use of:

- data views
- passwords (biometrics)
- backup/retention
- intrusion detection
- permissions
- audit trails
- firewalls

Integrity is assured and maintained through the use of:

- permissions
- file integrity routines
- passwords (biometrics)
- reconciliation routines

- security audits
- encryption and PKI
- intrusion detection

- line controls
- firewalls
- authentication/nonrepudiation

Usability is assured and maintained through the use of:

- data views
- passwords (biometrics)
- authentication
- nonrepudiation

- permissions
- backup/retention
- audit trails

Confidentiality is assured and maintained through the use of:

- data views
- passwords (biometrics)
- encryption and PKI
- intrusion detection

- permissions
- security audits
- firewalls
- authentication/nonrepudiation

It can be seen from these relationships that close collaboration and support between security and QA participants is in order. The essence of a successful e-business system is found in merging these two distinct disciplines into one and proceeding on the conviction that they are absolutely necessary.

Quality assurance participation is also essential to ensure that quality versus operational performance trade-offs have not been overlooked during the early phases of the development. Quality, security, and operational performance form the three-legged stool that supports an e-business application system. Trade-offs are necessary but must be carefully balanced. The temptation to favor operational performance over quality and security is great and will usually result in a system that is not adequately secured.

Finally, the QA function is responsible for conducting the necessary reviews to uncover errors and omissions in requirements. The earlier such errors and defects can be identified, the easier they can be rectified. Later in the development, QA performs the task of identifying defects in intermediate work product from the development process. This includes an independent determination of whether security and integrity controls are actually being built into an application and its supporting infrastructure, and how effective the controls are in guaranteeing that specified quality criteria will be met. This latter phase activity of QA draws from the experience of the validation, verification, and test (VV&T) community and security experts.

Validation, Verification, and Test (VV&T). Construction of quality e-business systems possessing adequate security and integrity controls requires that time be taken to validate, verify, and test the work products of each development phase. Validation asks whether the *right system is being constructed,* whereas verification asks whether *the system is being built correctly.*

Validation deals with getting the *right* (i.e., correct) requirements from all participants and then reconfirming the validity of those requirements as the project progresses through the development phases.

Verification ensures, through a systematic procedures of reviews and analysis, that the work processes employed to develop the software and e-business system are being executed in a disciplined fashion and according to "proven" system development practices and standards.

Testing is the primary technique for validating and verifying that development work products *are being built correctly* and are satisfying the business requirement. The functional test design becomes the plan for validating and verifying the correctness of the business requirement. The structural test design becomes the plan for validating and verifying the design of the e-business process to include all interfaces to the customer and to the employee workplace. The unit test design becomes the plan for validating and verifying the executable software code, and the integration test design becomes the plan for validating and verifying the final operational business system. These are the plans referred to in Exhibit 6.5 as the QA & Testing Plan.

Additionally, verification imposes on the development the requirement that software and e-business systems are documented so they can be understood and evaluated by an independent third party. The objective is the delivery of software and systems that can be maintained without compromising security and integrity controls.

The extent of VV&T efforts will be determined by the criticality of the e-business system under development. How VV&T are to be performed is also dictated by the importance of the application. For a parking lot permit system, the VV&T actions of the actual programmer may be considered adequate. Perhaps for a financial support system, the peer review of a team of independent systems people from within the company will suffice. But for an air traffic control system, nothing but a completely independent review by an external testing group could be considered sufficient.

IMPORTANCE OF AUTOMATED TOOLS

To speed the process of developing systems, most IT organizations make judicious use of automated tools. Used in conjunction with the SDR framework, automated development tools are used to record the e-business application's security and integrity control requirements in the same way that all other business function and quality specifications are captured and recorded.

The basic capabilities of these tools include the graphic modeling of business data, work process flows, web page layouts, screens, report prototyping, code generation, and testing files. Collectively, these result in a well-documented system capable of being managed and secured. The power of automated development tools can be expressed in the adage "a picture is worth a thousand words." Used with the SDR framework, tools can illustrate for all participants in the effort exactly where e-business application security and integrity controls should be included in the design specification. Also of critical importance to subsequent systems *certification* is the ability to trace security requirements, and their implementation in design and programming, from initial definition to final systems delivery. This allows documented assurances to be given that nothing in the way of security and integrity requirements has "fallen through the cracks."

Adequate VV&T of systems is greatly enhanced through the use of automated testing tools. Using the speed of the computer to create and maintain software tests and results improves the comprehensiveness of the testing function and the subsequent quality and security of the system.

Like everything in the computer industry, compatibility between tools is essential for seamless use to result. Use of the generic tools listed in Exhibit 6.8 provides speed of development, with the graphic modeling and requirement traceability features necessary to create an application's comprehensive specification and implementation documentation for "due diligence" purposes. Such documentation is necessary to support security certification and to maintain security during the life of the application system.

Integrated with a well-managed structured systems development methodology, automated tools will satisfy three main security goals for a new e-business system.

First, improved requirement analysis and specification are achieved through broader user and stakeholder participation. Improvement occurs when modeling tools are used to gather not only functional business requirements but also quality, security, integrity, and audit needs. When done concurrently with the definition of business process functionality, such specifications present the defining parameters within which the application must be constructed and operated. *Without such controls being identified and specified, the e-business process design is incomplete and should not be developed. To do so is to put the business activity at risk.*

Second, the ability to trace requirements through design and development provides assurances to management that adequate e-business application controls have been identified, specified, designed, programmed, tested, and put into operation. Such traceability and supporting documentation constitute evidence needed for certifications.

Third, documentation describing how application security and integrity controls are met is needed to demonstrate a "due diligence" approach and to perform software maintenance that stays within defined specifications for adequate security.

	Initiation and Definition	System Design	Programming and Training	Evaluation and Acceptance	Installation and Operation
Documentation Generator	X	X	X	X	X
Data Modeling Facility	X				
Front-End Design Facility	X				
Requirements Traceability Facility	X	X	X	X	X
Code Generator			X	X	X
Cross-Referencer		X	X	X	X
Testing/Record/Playback		X	X	X	X
Test Data/Path Generator		X	X	X	X
Change Control/Tracking		X	X	X	X
Estimation	X	X	X		
Library Management and Control		X	X	X	X
Test Coverage Monitor		X	X	X	X
Data Analyzer	X	X			
Code Analyzer	X	X			
Data Normalizer	X	X			
Reusable Code Facility			X		
Optimizer			X	X	
Screen/Report Painter	X	X	X		

Exhibit 6.8 Automated Development Tools

A CAUTIONARY WORD ABOUT NEW TECHNOLOGIES

Those charged with the responsibility of ensuring the adequacy of e-business security and integrity controls must do so in an atmosphere that is increasingly charged with technological innovation and "marketing hype." During the five years preceding this book, the IT industry has provided the technology to move business from a predominantly mainframe (backroom) processing environment to an on-line worldwide distributed processing environment. And now, business is being told to prepare for a wireless world. A world in which all things will change—again.

While conceptually the technological and economic arguments for this rapid migration may have merit (see Chapter 2 for applicability to the e-business model), the *reality is that such architectures are actually a step backward when it comes to security.* Indeed, many of the system management functions, taken for granted in the mainframe world and necessary for effective security and integrity, are virtually nonexistent in the most publicized and marketed web-based versions being adopted by business for e-business processing. Or, the management, security, and integrity function is wholly under the control of a service provider, with only contract language acting as enforcer.

It is important that the lessons learned in the mainframe environment be brought to any e-business development to be implemented on a distributed and networked architecture. And, at the time of this writing, extra care must be taken when considering "wireless" in the e-business mix. Those charged with assuring adequacy of security and integrity controls may be required to exercise all their persuasive skills to convince management to forgo the latest technology until its security is proven.

The developmental risks of constant change will always be present, and since vendors and internal sponsors can be counted on to sing the praises of new architectures, management should be somewhat skeptical and exercise caution by demanding thorough analysis and testing before new technologies are considered for e-business adoption.

SUMMARY AND CONCLUSIONS

In closing, it can be said that the essential elements needed to build adequately controlled e-business systems are converging at this time.

- Management awareness is increasing.
- "Due diligence" is becoming a standard.
- Security, integrity, and systems availability techniques are known.
- Structured analysis, design, programming, and testing techniques have matured.
- Automated development tools provide improved design environments, traceability of requirements, more thorough testing, and much better documentation.

- The SDR framework and other models offer an easy blueprint for monitoring the implementation of controls in an e-business system.
- Auditors are more experienced with computers and want to help.
- System developers realize that the next level of improvements will come by opening up the requirements definition and acceptance process to all stakeholders.
- A more cooperative environment exists where organizations have adopted quality management principles.

It has taken over three decades for all aspects necessary for the construction of secured e-business systems to evolve.

Now, conscious actions must be taken to merge the required expertise and organizational elements into cohesive application development teams. The software developer can't do it alone! The user community can't do it alone! Security personnel can't do it alone! The audit community can't do it alone! Vendors can't do it alone! Just as the early PCIE model originated from the cooperative efforts of the developer, user, audit, and security communities, so must the actual development of tomorrow's e-business systems. There are number of reasons why this must be a collective effort:

- Systems analysts and users do not have the expertise to define and build adequate security and integrity controls into an e-business application and into the supporting infrastructure.
- As system "certification" becomes more commonplace, senior executives will look to the audit and security communities for the assurance that systems are being properly designed and developed.
- As computer liability litigation increases, senior executives will demand "certification" by audit and security personnel. To accomplish this, certain actions must be taken:
  - Auditors and system developers should be familiar with the SDR Framework and apply it to every development effort—especially critical e-business applications.
  - Managers, users, and security personnel must propose to senior management the active involvement of the auditor in the design of application controls to speed the "certification" process.
  - Auditors and system developers must reach out to each other and promote a sharing of information concerning the design of effective security and integrity controls.
  - Management must insist on the independent VV & T of critical e-business systems before going to production.

Chapter 7

Justifying E-Business Security and the Security Management Program

INTRODUCTION

The purpose of this chapter is to present a series of "arguments" to be employed by management personnel and corporate executives in developing a benefits justification for the increased spending necessary to secure those infrastructure technologies and applications that are essential to e-business operations.

Developing such justifications is a difficult task. But the time has come, in the evolution of awareness of business and societal dependence on information, computers, and networks, when difficult questions are beginning to be asked by "boards of directors" regarding the management of computer risks in general and the economics of e-business security solutions in particular.

Following concerns over potential Y2K liability, the continuing threat from computer viruses, and the increase in denial of service (DOS) attacks, most corporate executives and board members are aware, at least to some degree, that they may be at personal legal risk should an inadequately protected business system succumb to such attacks.

Such awareness, although incomplete, leads invariably to question what a "pound of security" is worth and how to justify security expenses? These are not new questions that are only now being raised by the Internet generation. These are questions that have been asked for at least 30 years, and to date, the answers have been less than satisfying. We know of this shortcoming because the first complaint usually registered by any computer security officer is the lack of adequate funding, while the complaint registered most often by funding officials is that the "cost-benefit analysis" required to accompany requests for capital expenditures is weak to nonexistent.

New "arguments" to guide the necessary studies that support rational security decisions have only recently developed to a point where meaningful analyses can be conducted. The central focus of these "arguments" is whether information, to include client data and intellectual property, computer systems, and the assets needed for communicating the transactions of business are viewed by the organization as valuable enough to be worthy of protection.

Since the early days of computing, this issue of information and computing value, while seeming to be intuitively obvious, has been difficult to articulate and even more difficult to present in the context of a cost-benefit analysis. Originally, data processing outputs from early automation were usually viewed as by-products of a speeded-up manual process. With the exception of manufacturing process control systems and the command and control systems of the military, most uses of computers merely captured, stored, and reported the results of an existing manual "paper" business process.

All this has changed during the last decade with the advent of the Internet and the revolutionary impact of data communications on how business is conducted. Today, in many cases, there is no predecessor "manual" paper-based process for the web-based e-business application, so dependence on the reliability and security of the computerized system is nearly total. For an increasing number of organizations, distributed computer processes, implemented via the World Wide Web and other networked environments, have become the mission-critical operating element of their business. In some cases, the system is the business.

When a networked environment does not function because of an electrical failure or because of a "DOS attack" instigated by a hacker, the business suffers. When proprietary business information or "intellectual property" data are compromised because of a breach of confidentiality and access controls in the processing environment, the business suffers. And when "private" customer data are compromised by a "breakdown in access controls," a company can expect to experience a potential "public relations" and "legal" nightmare.

Now, add to this increased internal corporate dependence on information technology, the resulting technical interdependencies between and among "supply chain" business partners, and the scope of a benefits justification, for increased security spending, expands well beyond the typical cost vs. loss analysis practiced by most organizations.

Due to this widening of scope, the development of comprehensive and useful justifications for obtaining increases for e-business security spending requires that some new nonquantifiable as well as the traditional quantifiable "arguments" be presented for consideration. The challenges of e-business security are far too numerous and complex to be effectively dealt with using only quantifiable terms.

The next section briefly reviews the principle quantifiable "argument" that has been used historically to justify increased computer security spending. Upon reflection, it will be seen that this traditional justification falls far short of what will most likely be needed to fund a realistic security initiative for e-business. Because of this justification inadequacy, most computer security efforts of the past have been undercapitalized, which has resulted in a piecemeal and ineffective application of security solutions. If efforts to improve the security posture of corporate e-business are to be successful, it is important solve this problem. Inadequate quantifiable "arguments" must be consciously augmented by some very important and relatively new nonquantifiable and often intangible "arguments." These additional rationales will help in presenting a more realistic understanding of what is at stake and result in benefits justifications requiring the "judgment" of senior corporate executives regarding the "value" of their business, the "value" of their information and processing capability, and their legal obligations and responsibilities to ensure secure e-business systems to others. It will also result in an analysis that is ready for consideration by the "board of directors."

THE "QUANTIFIABLE" ARGUMENT

Historically, the answer to the question about the worth of a "pound of security" has been that the cost to secure a computing asset should be less than the annualized replacement cost of that asset should it be destroyed, stolen, or lost. If an asset, say a personal computer, has an expected life of three years, can be replaced for $3,000, and it is determined that the probability of its being stolen sometime during the next three years is 50 percent because building security is so poor, then a case can probably be made for spending at least $15 on a cable and locking mechanism to "secure" the PC to the desktop.

Admittedly, this example is simplistic, but experience shows that with a scenario much more complex than this, the tendency to argue about any and all of the assumptions and probabilities underlying the scenario causes the analytic process to break down.

There are, of course, other factors about one example that everyone knows should be considered, but they have been very difficult to assess. For example, a major debate that should take place concerns the value of the information residing on the PC. Clearly, this question should be considered in any realistic discussion about how much money to spend protecting the PC that houses the information. But how is the loss of the information to be quantified?

Where there are information "classification" schemes, such as in the Department of Defense, there are associated security controls that are required to protect each different "classification" level. For example, certain safeguards and accounting procedures are mandatory for secret information, while a more stringent set of safeguards and accounting procedures are required for top secret information. But, outside of the government, there are few if any generally accepted "information classification" or "information valuation" schemes with which to associate security safeguards or their effectiveness. And unless an organization can agree on the value of their information and the "worth" of maintaining its integrity, confidentiality, and availability for useful processing, they are forever destined to argue about how many dollars to spend for a "pound of security."

Another important factor that should figure into our example centers on the use of the PC as part of a larger business process—perhaps a mission-critical process. As with information, there are no standard "process valuation" schemes to assist in the selection and implementation of appropriate security controls. In many cases, securing the process may be even more important than protecting the information. As already discussed, with many Internet-based businesses, the computerized process is the business. If the process fails, the business fails.

A reader may not fully agree with this assessment of the inadequacy of hard quantification for justifying e-business security spending, but any reader who has attempted to justify a computer security budget request to a corporate comptroller or a line manager seeking the same dollars for a revenue generating initiative knows that without "information and business process valuation" agreement, funding for adequate safeguards and their day-to-day administration will never be forthcoming.

The "replacement cost" approach is inadequate to the task at hand, and agreeing on "information and process valuation" is likely be stymied by endless debate. So the difficulty of developing a realistic benefits justification for increased e-business security spending cannot be fully resolved until some organizational metrics are devised to address the "valuation" problem.

For the present, most organizations will have to solve this challenge themselves by factoring in the potential impact of the following "nonquantifiable" discussion points.

EMERGING "NONQUANTIFIABLE" ARGUMENTS

First, it is recognized that some of the following "nonquantifiable" arguments may eventually become quantifiable. As more knowledge and experience are gained concerning the adverse impact of computer security failures on business, government, and society, the challenge of "information and process valuation" may be resolved. Also, as the collective database of security incidents builds, probability data will begin to emerge from actuarial analysis. As this happens, the ability to associate specific computer security safeguards with a desired level of protection and an acceptable level of risk will make benefit justifications much easier to formulate and defend.

For the time being, however, the following "nonquantifiable" arguments will need to be presented for the visceral reaction they elicit. If quantifiable "arguments" cannot get the e-business-funding job accomplished in an adequate manner, there is no recourse but to deal with the issue at an emotional level.

Security: A Necessary Cost of Conducting E-Business

The overarching nonquantifiable "argument" that supports attempts to justify increased spending on e-business security is the emerging realization that security is simply a cost of doing business in cyberspace. The greater a company's dependency on reliable and secure computer processing and communications, the more resources the company needs to spend to assure the confidentiality, integrity, and availability of its sensitive information, "intellectual property", and mission-critical business processes and support equipment. This "argument" begs the earlier perplexing question of "information and process valuation" and can be useful in overcoming the bureaucratic tendency to endless debate by providing a sense of urgency to do something now to correct a widely publicized problem of significant importance. This is especially true after a "security incident" or two has attracted the attention of the board of directors.

Revenue Loss Due to E-Business Security Breaches

"According to the 2001 annual Computer Crime and Security Survey conducted by the Computer Security Institute and the FBI, 85 percent of companies experienced cyber-attacks in the past year, up from 42 percent in 1996. Sixty-four percent acknowledged financial losses due to computer breaches. Nearly 200 companies reported losses of more than $377 million." In contrast, the losses from 250 respondents in 2000 totaled only $265 million. Such reported losses run the gamut from the theft of sensitive customer data and company proprietary "intellectual" property, to software piracy and losses endured because of systems downtime.

In fact, downtime due to security incidents such as a "virus" or a "DOS attack" can result in the most easily identifiable loss—revenue. The greater the dependency a company has on the Internet or other forms of communications to conduct business, the greater the potential for revenue loss should any part of the network be made unavailable for business use. Similarly, access control and hardware and/or software failures can lead to security compromises on host processing equipment, causing systems to "crash."

The following representative estimates of revenue losses will allow executives to estimate the potential for loss due to downtime that their business may face.

Industry	Application	Loss per Hour of Downtime
Financial	Brokerage operations	$6,500,000
Financial	Credit card sales	$2,600,000
Media	Pay-per-view	$150,000
Retail	Home shopping (TV)	$113,000
Retail	Catalog sales	$90,000
Transportation	Airline reservations	$89,500

Source: Gartner Group & Contingency Planning Research

Numbers like these from reputable sources are beginning to get the attention of corporate executives, and barring the "it can't happen here" syndrome, substantial progress can be made in obtaining their support without undue detailed quantification.

Responsibilities to the "Supply Chain" and Business Partners

This newly emerging nonquantifiable "argument" finds its origins in the Y2K experience, which focused attention on the responsibility of a company to their business partners and to anyone else in a "supply chain" who was dependent on the company's ability to continue conducting business.

As a result, reliable and secure systems and processes are now beginning to be mutually expected of all businesses that are members of a "supply chain." This "argument" recognizes the harsh reality that a lack of systems security with any one "link" company can adversely affect everyone else in the chain. No company wants to be known as a "weak link" in a "supply chain" and be threatened with possible breach of contract actions. While liability metrics for such "breach" actions may be years in the defining, and while this is an area that insurance companies are only beginning to explore, it is certainly an area where an "ounce of prevention" today will be worth a "pound of cure" tomorrow.

Secure the E-Business or Lose Revenue Opportunities

Information technology (IT) has been referred to as the "business enabler" of the twenty-first century, meaning that to survive and prosper in the "new" economy, a company must use IT successfully. If the previous "arguments" for increasing computer security are valid, then a corporation's ability to exploit and capitalize on future business opportunities may very well depend on whether their computer and communication systems are secure and perceived by the marketplace as being secure.

In the rapidly changing world of IT, it is difficult to know what "new" business opportunities lie ahead, but it is becoming increasingly clear that secure and reliable computing and communications will be required if such opportunities are to be exploited.

One area of particular concern that is likely to adversely impact certain "new" business opportunities is the area of consumer electronic "privacy and confidentiality." While electronic privacy is a "legal concept" to be worked out by the judicial and legislative branches of government, confidentiality at the systems level requires the application of system design approaches and security controls to enforce whatever privacy policies an organization deems appropriate.

Surveys show that most U.S. citizens, like their European counterparts, want companies to guarantee on-line privacy. According to CNN, a survey conducted by the Pew Internet and American Life Project indicates that "the majority of U.S. Internet users feel their rights are infringed upon by companies that track them online, and 86 percent prefer an 'opt in' policy that would require web sites to seek permission from users before they disclose personal information." This view challenges the preferred policy of many who would give web sites the right to track Internet users unless the user takes steps to "opt out" of being monitored. The Pew survey shows that "users want to be in control of what they share on-line and get retribution against any company that violates that trust". Ninety-four percent believe that corporations and top executives should be punished if they violate a user's on-line privacy.

It is becoming increasingly clear that if companies plan to take advantage of future consumer-based e-business opportunities, the many sensitive issues surrounding privacy and confidentiality must be addressed in a manner that establishes consumer "trust." It is also clear from the Pew survey that "untrusting" consumers can and do protect themselves from privacy intrusions in ways (i.e., deliberate data distortion) that can only be regarded as threatening the very foundations of an "information" and e-business economy.

Deliberate Data Distortion by "Untrusting" Consumers

E-businesses should be extremely concerned by the way increasing numbers of on-line consumers are responding because of their privacy concerns. Again, according to the Pew survey, it was "found that about a quarter of Net users have provided phony personal data to web sites: invented e-mail addresses, fake Social Security numbers, and alter egos complete with bogus incomes, genders, and hobbies.

The end result of "distorting the data collected on-line" must be especially worrisome to those corporate web sites that collect data for "personalized marketing" or sell the data to third parties. If one-quarter to one-third of the data collected on-line is bogus, what can be the value of the entire consumer profile database? And yet the purported value of much of the "new" economy is based on these collections of personal information and their use in "targeting" new customers.

If the critical customer relations problem of "trust" is not solved to the extent that consumers feel comfortable with the on-line collection and maintenance of personal data, in time, the future economic value of much consumer data must be questioned. What impact this will have on companies that traffic in information can only be surmised.

Dropping Off the Internet

While not directly attributed to privacy and confidentiality concerns, a recent *USA Today* news piece reported a troubling statistic: "as of the beginning of this year (2000), roughly 28.5 million "occasional" users have decided to stop using the Internet in the U.S. . . . ." If this statistic is valid and if consumer privacy and confidentiality concerns are one of the reasons for the defections, many e-businesses may be faced with a life-threatening phenomenon.

To avert the potential adverse impact of this emerging trend, companies that depend on increases in consumer Internet participation must take immediate action to secure their systems against actual as well as perceived threats to confidentiality.

While this area of consideration is far from "quantifiable," it clearly must be tracked and then factored into any "cost-benefit" justification for increased e-business security spending. The ability to take advantage of "new" consumer-related business opportunities demands it.

Obligations to National Critical Infrastructure Protection Efforts

In 1998, following recommendations of the President's Commission on Critical Infrastructure Protection (CIP), the Clinton administration promulgated a Presidential Decision Directive # 63. PDD-63 calls for a collaborative effort between industry and government to secure the United States' critical infrastructures against disruptive actions and natural disaster that could impair the ability of the nation to conduct business or defend itself.

To develop a national approach, 5 major industry sectors were identified as being "critical" to the nation: national defense, energy, financial services, transportation, communications and information services, health care, and vital government and human services. The Directive established the Critical Infrastructure Assurance Office (CIAO) to address risks to the nation's critical infrastructures and assure delivery of essential services. Each of the six industry sectors has a lead federal agency to coordinate efforts to develop a comprehensive approach and plan.

The Partnership for Critical Infrastructure Security (PCIS) is the industry association established to address implementation of PDD-63. Sponsored by the U.S. Chamber of Commerce, the goal of the PCIS is to collaborate with the CIAO in meeting the objectives of PDD-63. The PCIS will also coordinate industry inputs to a National Plan for Information Systems Protection. Version 1.0 of the plan focused on domestic efforts being undertaken by the federal government to protect the government's critical cyber-bases infrastructures. Version 2.0 and annual updates thereafter will address each critical infrastructure sector and the interplay among them.

To the extent that a corporation is involved or can be identified with any of the five "critical" industry sectors, they should become active with the national CIP efforts. No doubt this will involve some security-related expenses that are difficult to justify using traditional "quantifiable" rationales, but such involvement and participation may well be needed to be considered responsible and to demonstrate a "due diligence" approach to IT security matters.

For IT product and service providers companies, the need for involvement and participation in CIP efforts is highly important for the following reason. The vast majority of interdependent business relationships that have evolved within "critical" industry sectors and between sectors are finding that their "weak" link is something over which they have little influence and almost no control—the products and services provided by the communications and information services industry.

It is likely that sooner or later an information infrastructure failure in another critical industry sector will be attributed to a failure of the communications and information services industry to adequately address IT security and reliability issues. If an IT products or service provider company were participating with CIP efforts, their desire to be a "responsible" business partner to other industries would be noted. Likewise, a failure to participate may be perceived as "irresponsible" and will also be duly noted.

Loss of Corporate Reputation

Perhaps the most critical "nonquantifiable" argument that must be factored into a benefits justification is the potential for loss of corporate reputation. This is a loss that is virtually impossible to calculate precisely, but it is clear that a good reputation is essential for maintaining current customers and business partners, for exploiting future business opportunities, and for being able to obtain needed capital in the money markets of the world.

Damage to a corporation's reputation can result directly from security incidents that receive publicity through the news media or indirectly from audits published by independent organizations such as the U.S. General Accounting Office that may be authorized by Congress to critique security preparedness and practices of certain industries. Such reports are in the public domain and can prove damaging.

Much of the success in achieving Y2K compliance has been attributed to the filing of Security Exchange Commission (SEC) reports on Y2K status. It kept the issue on the front burner and got the board of directors involved.

There is, of course, no equivalent pressure on private sector companies regarding cyber-security, but executives should be reminded that the SEC does require that issues that could "materially" impact future performance be reported to stockholders. It may be that at some time in the future, cyber-security will be treated by the SEC as was Y2K and annual reports to stockholders will be required to address it. Corporate executives may want to ask themselves how they would fare under such a requirement.

BENEFITS JUSTIFICATIONS MUST COVER
SECURITY PROGRAM ADMINISTRATION

The following summarizes, from Chapter 4, the "success criteria" that should be used in designing an effective e-business security program that, from a security perspective, is responsive to changing technology and business needs.

It is especially important to note that a "benefits" justification must be convincing enough to support adequate funding to achieve and maintain not only e-business security for today, but also an ongoing program of security management. Anything less, and the e-business security effort will suffer from undercapitalization and be "compromised" from the very beginning.

Success Criteria #1: Adopt a Balanced Strategy

Traditionally, a computer security strategy has included three distinct elements: prevention, detection, and response or reaction.

Prevention includes the numerous proactive actions that are taken to protect information, processes, and computing assets against destruction, compromise, and unauthorized access, manipulation, or modification, whether deliberate or accidental.

Detection employs system network and host computer intrusion detection and audit techniques and tools, which perform functions from on-line scanning and transaction monitoring to trend analysis and attack forecasting.

Response or Reaction initiates damage containment, recovery plans, and corrective actions after an attack or unauthorized use has been detected.

A fundamental "success criteria" for the design of an e-business security program is the need to balance the three elements of the basic strategy by employing the concept of defense in depth.

Success Criteria #2: A Management Program Is Needed to Administer Security

The nature of the e-business security challenge is that of dynamically changing vulnerabilities and threats based on ever-changing technology being used to evolve increasingly complex business applications and uses. This means that organizations must build their e-business security initiatives around the idea of a continuous improvement model of the type made popular by the total quality movement.

For e-business security, it can be thought of as a plan-fix-monitor-assessment cycle. A security management program to execute this model must be established and integrated into the day-to-day operations of the business.

There are commercial security management program models available, and the federal government has one that can be obtained from the National Institute of Standards and Technology (NIST Special Publications 800-12, 800-14, and 800-18).

Whichever model an organization uses, the benefits justification must cover resources sufficient to sustain the continuous security monitoring demanded by today's computing environment and to administer security controls and their necessary improvement on a day-to-day basis.

Success Criteria #3: Design to a "Due Diligence" Standard

The Y2K experience introduced business executives and IT managers to the concept of "due diligence" as applied to the uses of IT. Because of the potential for legal fallout, it became necessary to view Y2K-related actions through the definitions of "due diligence" and "reasonable care."

The standards of "due diligence" and "reasonable care" with regard to e-business security will be continually evolving as the technology, vulnerabilities, threats, risks, and countermeasures change. This means that security decisions and implementations are not a one-time event but must be under a continuous process of "risk evaluation and management."

CONCLUSION

This chapter has endeavored to broaden the horizons of those responsible for developing funding justifications for e-business security safeguards and management programs to effectively administer security. Since "undercapitalization" has plagued most previous computer security initiatives, new "nonquantifiable" arguments must be developed so that sufficient funding can be made available to ensure e-business security success.

Chapter 8

Computers, Software, Security, and Issues of Liability

The purpose of this chapter is to briefly outline for executive management some of the legal issues that are emerging around the use of information technology (IT), especially those issues likely to arise from a lack of e-business security.

EVOLVING THEORIES OF RESPONSIBILITY

While contract and disclaimer language can reduce financial liability, it must be recognized that contracts and clauses work in some cases and are useless in others. Successful arguments have been made that contracts and disclaimer clauses can be ignored altogether in cases where a flawed computer or software system results in personal catastrophe. This argument falls under the category of negligence and is not based on any kind of contract. The question that is posed is simple: *"Did the company do anything or fail to do anything that caused harm to someone else?"* If so, the company can be held liable for that harm. This is based on the legal theory that companies owe customers a certain minimal "duty of care." But against what standard will duty of care be measured? For the individual programmer, the question of being held to a "professional standard" has been openly debated for years. It is clear today that programmers lack full recognition as professionals in the same sense as doctors, lawyers, and accountants, and therefore seem safe from malpractice suits. At the same time, others believe that the code of ethics to which some members of various IT associations and societies subscribe opens the individual member to potential lawsuits as a professional or at the very least a highly trained specialist. This evolution toward professional status is supported by the movement within the IT industry of requiring employees to possess third-party certifications in computer specialty areas (i.e., such as computer security) or specific vendor product lines. If so, computer professionals possessing certifications might find themselves in much the same position as accountants, for whom there are established precedents as to liability.

In some instances, the court may establish another standard of considering a computer program or system as an inherently dangerous instrument, as with air traffic control, nuclear plants, or medical devices and systems. Such labeling would demand the greatest possible degree of care in the construction and use of the system. The system's *integrity, confidentiality, and availability/reliability* characteristics would need to be of the highest possible order, demonstrating the use of "best practices" as a minimum and probably much more. The "much more" would be decided after a thorough analysis of risk had been performed and safeguards commensurate with the risk were selected and implemented. With such systems, safeguard determinations are on a "sliding scale" against a backdrop of acceptable risk, but never less than the "best practices" of the particular industry for which the system has been built.

There is also the legal catchall of strict liability. This is the foundation of the product liability suit. This rationale holds that if a company makes a product, it is in a better position than anyone else to anticipate and reduce hazards. Under strict liability, the company is expected to warn customers of any such remaining hazard. There is legal precedent for imposing liability for defective design, and a faulty program could be shown to be the result of a bad design. Note that the Uniform Computer Information Transactions Act (UCITA), now seeking ratification in each of the 50 states, allows vendors to not be held accountable for known defects (see Chapter 4).

Regardless of how the legal arguments are resolved, there will no doubt be an impact on organizations that design and develop software systems and those that use such systems in the pursuit of the e-business objectives. One of the impacts will center on the methods and practices used to determine appropriate computer security safeguards, implement, and administer those safeguards. It is not clear at this time how the courts will determine which methods, techniques, and practices should or should not have been used in the design and implementation of a program of security safeguards. The courts will probably hear testimony by computer security experts and decide whether the management team and assigned technical staff did what those of similar education, skill, and experience would have done with a similar set of business requirements and risks. And the courts undoubtedly will look at the issue of whether those responsible for security adequately tested the e-business system and warned users, customers, and supply chain partners of any known and/or suspected vulnerabilities remaining after testing. The court queries are aimed not only at the technical skill of those assigned to the task of securing the system but also at the organizational policies, procedures, and management controls governing corporate IT security.

LIKELY SCENARIOS

Corporate management and e-business system implementers may have to face any one of the following situations:

- Breaches in security or integrity controls cause e-business processes to fail, business cannot be conducted, and the company is sued.

- Confidential information is compromised because of a security breach and the company is sued.

- Denial of service attacks prevent business from being conducted and the company is sued.

- Breaches in security are *not the cause* of a failure but the company is sued anyway.

- Executives and managers are asked to give the board of directors assurances that the corporation is implementing secured e-business systems and could successfully defend against a lawsuit.

HOW MIGHT A LIABILITY CASE UNFOLD?

At the center of a plaintiff's strategy for winning a liability case will be the need to prove that the steps taken to secure the system in question did not meet accepted industry practices necessary to demonstrate that *reasonable care* was exercised. *Black's Law Dictionary* defines reasonable care as "that degree of care which a person of ordinary prudence would exercise in the same or similar circumstances." Put another way, those responsible for e-business security did not exercise due diligence, defined by the *Plain Language Law Dictionary* as "the degree of effort and care in carrying out an act or obligation that the average, sincere, energetic person would exhibit," also "conduct that is devoid of negligence or carelessness."

To satisfy these definitions, it must be shown that there exists a standard body of knowledge and practice concerning the securing of software and systems that is widely subscribed to by the industry, taught at the university, and used as a generally accepted method. Such guidelines and standards do exist, are taught at the university, and are recognized as the orderly, analytic way to achieve e-business security. First are the functional systems development process—the SDP of Chapters 4 and 6; second is the Systems Security Engineering Capability Maturity Model (SSE-CMM) from the Information Systems Security Engineering Association—also of Chapters 4 and 6. And third are the Generally Accepted Systems Security Principles (GASSP) from the International Information Security Foundation, the guidelines from the NIST, and standards from the ISO.

It may well be that a failure to demonstrate that each standard, or some variant thereof, was followed in both developing the e-business system and then securing it, would win a judgment for the plaintiff. In many of today's chaotic IT environments, the plaintiff will have the definite advantage. This is because while the SDP and the SSE-CMM impose discipline on the systems development process, in the rush to get something coded and to the customer, development methodologies tend to be ignored, circumvented, or applied haphazardly.

A classic cartoon says it best. A supervisor is pictured about to leave a room of computer programmers. His instructions, "You all begin programming. I'll go see what they want." In other words, start building a system before we have even defined the problem. An "insider" joke among systems people is the fact that they all admit to having some form of SDP to follow when doing their work, but they also will readily admit that they do not, for whatever reason, use or enforce use of the SDP. This is like a surgeon failing to follow standard operating procedures when performing an appendectomy.

However, SDPs and emerging standards such as the SSE-CMM are not definitive in terms of specifying exact security safeguard actions to take in a given situation. They are both thought processes to be used in analyzing and arriving at a reasonable course of action, and there will always be room for interpretation with their use. The importance of their use stems from the difficulty of proving that a measured approach to security was taken without their discipline. Developing and securing e-business systems requires order and discipline, and both the SDP and the SSE-CMM utilize engineering methods to construct computer-based systems.

Demonstrating *reasonable care* may be as simple, however, as applying the security controls determined by collective agreement of those in a supply chain or by the "top dog" of the chain. For example, *VISA* has published exacting security guidelines that all Internet-enabled business partners must follow if they wish to be part of the *VISA* family. These guidelines are very explicit and could act as a model for most finance-oriented e-business systems. As prescribed by *VISA*, we find the following:

- Install and maintain a working network firewall to protect data accessible via the Internet.
- Keep security patches up to date.
- Encrypt stored data.
- Encrypt data sent across networks.
- Use and regularly update antivirus software.
- Restrict access to "cardholder" data inside the business on a need-to-know basis.
- Assign a unique identifier to each person with computer access.
- Do not use vendor-supplied defaults for system passwords and other security parameters.
- Track access to data by unique identifier.
- Regularly test security systems and processes.
- Maintain a security policy for employees and contractors.
- Restrict physical access to "cardholder" information.
- Destroy data when no longer needed for business reasons.

Again, the question to be answered will be quite simple: *Did the company do anything or fail to do anything that caused harm?* If it failed to follow recognized industry practices for developing and securing software and systems, perhaps it did not provide the plaintiff with an adequate degree of care, given the potential for harm. And remember that the harm has already materialized or you would not have a liability suit on your hands.

QUESTIONS TO BE ASKED TO ENSURE THAT REASONABLE CARE HAS BEEN TAKEN IN DEVELOPING A SECURE E-BUSINESS SYSTEM

The rest of this discussion focuses on a series of questions that a project manager should be able to answer and show evidence of, as needed, to defend the company against a liability suit arising from a breach of security.

These questions follow the logical flow of the SDP phases and give special attention to those phases where security requirements are defined and where testing occurs. The questions and associated narrative focus on the types of documents needed to show evidence that an SDP activity actually occurred and that security issues were addressed during that activity. Required documentation must describe how the e-business system and software works, must be understandable and usable by other than the "creator" of the document, and must allow reconstruction of the SDP activities for audit purposes. These questions are easily answered if Appendix B, "Systems Development Review Framework for E-Business Development Projects," has been followed.

QUESTIONS: Who, from the customer/user's/supply chain organization, participated in the definition of the e-business security requirements? Were all parties to be "impacted" by the system represented?

Can it be proven?

DISCUSSION: Depending on the nature and complexity of the application, many "stakeholders" have an operational, legal, audit, security, management, customer, and public interest in the system being developed. They must participate or be represented in the definition of requirements and concur with those requirements if the developer is to know what to design, program, test, and deliver.

QUESTIONS: Were quality specifications defined describing the functional business requirements required of the software or system? Were *integrity, confidentiality, and availability/reliability* requirements included as specifications? Was it determined how satisfaction of each of these specifications would be judged?

Can it be proven?

DISCUSSION: Without a clear and concise understanding of how the business requirement and the security requirements are going to be measured, the e-business systems developer does not have the information necessary to design and program the system. Without this vital customer/user acceptance information, the developer has no realistic criteria against which to integrate and test the final system.

QUESTIONS: How was the feasibility of this project determined? Was a formal analysis required by the SDP that was used? Were the deliberations concerning technical, operational, and economic feasibility documented? Were security considerations included in the feasibility study?

Can documentation be produced that reflects this thought process?

DISCUSSION: A great number of "reasonable care" questions that can arise are answered by the analysis that was done to select the project's technical solution, the security solutions, and the strategy for managing the effort. Solutions that were not feasible were not by definition capable of being implemented successfully. Selection of a high-risk solution may cast doubts on the wisdom of proceeding with the project and on the competence of the management team running the project.

QUESTIONS: How were security and integrity safeguards and controls for e-business application/systems determined? Was a formal assessment conducted? Did experts or auditors consult on controls to prevent, detect, and recover from breaches of security and threats to systems integrity? Do these controls take into account the manual operations of the workplace?

Can documentation be produced that reflects this thought process?

DISCUSSION: It is important to show that security safeguard decisions were made after due consideration of risk. Here is where evidence of having utilized a risk management methodology (RMM) is required. Plaintiff would love to uncover that no structured analysis method was used and that safeguards, such as they are, were selected randomly.

QUESTIONS: How was the extent of testing for this project determined? Was the degree of testing rigor determined by an examination of application and security risks to the business or customer, or was it based on information sensitivity and privacy issues? Was the degree of testing considered reasonable by industry practice regarding similar systems?

Can documentation be produced that reflects this thought process?

DISCUSSION: Rigorous testing will be essential to demonstrate that "reasonable care" was exercised during systems development. To adequately test for security, a security risk assessment must be performed, safeguards should be selected, and security tests and success criteria formulated. These same tests also need to be updated regularly during the life of the system and used to retest all system changes.

QUESTIONS: Do company policies require the generation of a formal plan and budget for construction of the e-business system in question? Was security included in this plan? Were security controls budgeted for? Did this plan undergo formal executive review? Is there a process for modifying the plan and budget as needed?

Does a documented plan exist?

QUESTIONS: Did the SDP that provided guidance incorporate periodic progress and quality reviews where work on the system was validated against the requirements of the system? Were these reviews conducted? Did the customer/user/supply chain partner participate in the reviews? When omissions, errors, or necessary changes were discovered and corrective action was taken, were such actions reflected in security safeguard modifications and in updated systems documentation?

Can up-to-date systems documentation be found?

DISCUSSION: It is imperative to demonstrate that development of a secure e-business system was well supervised. An integral part of this demonstration are the review points where "progress against the plan" is examined to determine appropriateness and correctness of preceding work products. Evidence of having conducted these reviews is essential to claiming that reasonable care was taken during execution of the project.

QUESTIONS: How was the continuity of the software/systems development team maintained? How was knowledge of the design requirements, program status, and the testing criteria passed from one team member to another? On large projects, how were the many ongoing activities accounted for and kept in sync? Was configuration management (CM) formalized? Appendix B discusses CM within the context of the systems review framework.

Can it be proven?

DISCUSSION: Again, the need to demonstrate sufficient management control over the project is essential to claiming that reasonable care was exercised in the development of a secure e-business system. Configuration management is an essential element of any development if control over the project is to be demonstrable. Without CM, development projects quickly lose their integrity and chaos reigns.

QUESTIONS: Was there a quality assurance function operating during development of the e-business system? Was it active during the early phases of the project to ensure that all aspects of a quality product were addressed? What national or international standard (i.e., ISO 9000 series) constituted the benchmark for quality assurance? Did the people responsible for quality assurance work independently of the development team and the team's management?

Can documentary proof be provided that quality assurance was performed on this project?

QUESTIONS: As business and system requirements changed or were modified, how were they managed to ensure that unexpected adverse impacts did not creep into the software or system under development? What policies and management controls existed to prevent a programmer from making a change not analyzed for security implications?

DISCUSSION: Software and system projects are very difficult to manage. All formal SDPs provide project management techniques for assuring disciplined development of an e-business system. All too often, however, these techniques are not utilized, and programmers are given too much latitude to determine for themselves what they will and will not do while working on a project. To show that "reasonable care" was exercised, it must be clearly evident that system analysts and programmers were under management supervision and that their actions can be reconstructed.

Can documentation be produced that records all changes to the project as the work progressed?

QUESTIONS: Did the development schedule allot sufficient time for security testing? How was the testing strategy determined? For example, was the sensitivity of the e-business application analyzed? Was the degree of risk posed by improper functioning of the application determined? Was the extent and rigor of testing determined by these degrees of risk (i.e., little risk—less testing, great risk—a lot of testing)?

Can documentation be produced that links the test strategy to a determination of risk?

QUESTIONS: How was the testing effort for this project managed? What national or international standards guided the testing effort? Were any industry-unique or regulatory testing requirements used to direct the test effort? Were the testing methods employed consistent with those used by similar companies facing similar risk and testing similar systems?

Can evidence be produced that national or international testing standards and guidelines were followed?

DISCUSSION: Adequate and sufficiently robust testing will form the first line of defense against charges of liability for security breaches. Even though the existence of software "defects" and "bugs" are accepted by customers—what choice do they have?—a software products company may still be expected, as the "expert," to do whatever is necessary to deliver quality and secure systems using engineering and testing thoroughness geared to the criticality of the business function being supported by the software. This is why the criticality of systems being supported by the e-business software was examined. Mission- and life-critical software requires more stringent quality and security testing than do more mundane and less important applications. Developers must be able to show that the complexity of tests and the time allotted to testing was commensurate with the risk posed to company and individuals should the system fail or have security breached.

QUESTIONS: As testing progressed, how were defects and corrective changes managed? Does all subsequent software and systems documentation reflect such changes? Do test plans and test data reflect such changes? Were all changes made during testing analyzed for security, integrity, and audit implications?

Can it be proven?

QUESTIONS: Was all software and systems documentation kept current throughout the development efforts and not just fabricated at the end of the project? Were any corners cut either in testing or in documentation to "get the code out the door"?

Can it be proven that shortcuts were not taken?

QUESTION: What assurances can be given to the board of directors and to business owners that a liability challenge can be defended against?

The National Critical Infrastructure Protection (CIP) Initiative

THE PROBLEM OF DEPENDENCY

As we have seen, there has been a growing recognition in recent years that the "new economy" is very much dependent on information technology (IT) networks and systems, which are vulnerable to malicious disruption.

America's critical infrastructures are the foundation of our economy, national security, and quality of life. The functioning of critical parts of our economy, government, and national security now depend on computer-managed information systems and networks. This reality creates a new dimension of vulnerability that, when combined with an emerging array of threats, poses a new set of risks to the nation's security and economic poser. Potential adversaries—be they nation-states, cyber-terrorist groups, criminal organizations, or disgruntled employees—can easily develop attack capabilities to exploit this vulnerability. Also, there are the threats embodied in Pogo's famous observation, *"we have met the enemy and he is us"*—the threats caused by ignorance, incompetence, and mismanagement. An example still fresh in everyone's mind is Y2K.

Y2K was a computer security issue and a threat to the critical information infrastructure of the nation. At its core, Y2K posed a computer and communications security threat. It was primarily a threat to systems availability and data and processing integrity. Y2K had the potential to be the "mother" of all denial of service events and to put the continuity of business and government services at extreme risk.

The major challenge that was experienced with Y2K was not that a six-digit field needed to be changed to somehow accommodate an eight-digit date or even that the issue had been ignored until it became a crisis. No, the real problem with Y2K was that most organizations had such a very difficult time managing and accomplishing what was essentially a simple "code" change. Because of the mismanagement of fundamental software and system development and the failure to adhere to software maintenance principles, many projects had to first find and document the software that needed correction. This type of software and systems management information should have already been in existence. Because of the time wasted getting the code under control, many unnecessary expenses were incurred, which contributed to a collective price tag of over $100 billion in the United States alone.

Because of these conditions, so clearly demonstrated by Y2K and the fact that they still exist in a majority of organizations, a primary concern for corporate executives and e-business security officials must be the correction of these fundamental IT management defects or effective security can never be attained or maintained.

In other words, e-business security is first and foremost an exercise in the disciplined management of IT and the e-business system on which corporations and government agencies depend. *Simply put, you cannot secure what you are not managing; and you cannot manage what you cannot find.*

Y2K, as a business threat, was seen to be serious enough to force worldwide continuity of operations (COOP) planning. It was also serious enough to prompt the creation of the President's Commission on Critical Infrastructure Protection (CIP) to examine the growing issue of national infrastructure interdependencies and especially the growing dependencies of business and government on information technology.

Y2K was also seen as a computer security threat to the global infrastructure, creating high awareness in all industrialized nations of their great dependency on information and communications technology. In fact, the operational implications of Y2K are currently causing national and business leaders to inquire about other ways in which business and government is threatened because of the growing dependence on IT and other forms of technology.

This increasing awareness has created an opportunity for those tasked with e-business security that never existed before. Now, managers and security professional can capitalize on the infrastructure protection issue to take security out of the realm of the merely technical and establish it as a critical business issue. This places security squarely at the doorstep of the "board of directors."

CRITICAL INFRASTRUCTURE PROTECTION (CIP) PURPOSE, DIRECTIVES, ORGANIZATIONS, AND RELATIONSHIPS

In 1998, the Clinton administration convened the Presidential Commission on Critical Infrastructure Protection. As a result of the commission's findings, the administration issued Presidential Decision Directive (PDD-63), which created the Critical Infrastructure Assurance Office (CIAO) within the Department of Commerce. The CIAO is tasked to work with the private sector to implement PDD-63. PDD-63 names five industry sectors as critical to the national infrastructure. They are national defense, financial services, transporation, communications and information services, health care, and vital government and human services. Member companies from these industry sectors have joined together as the Partnership for Critical Infrastructure Security (PCIS), which is jointly sponsored by the U.S. Chamber of Commerce and the CIAO for the purpose of implementing PDD-63. Each sector has also taken steps to create industry-unique

Information Sharing and Analysis Centers (ISAC) for the purpose of sharing vulnerability and corrective action information about threats to their mission-critical business or governmental processes.

The goals of the PCIS and the sector ISACs are to collaborate with each other and the CIAO in addressing risks to the nation's critical infrastructure and thereby assure delivery of essential services. The PCIS also coordinates industry sector inputs to the National Plan for Information Systems Protection. Version 1 of the plan, published in 2000, focused on domestic efforts being undertaken by the federal government to protect their critical information processing infrastructure. *All members of a critical industry sector should join their industry ISAC and consider participating in PCIS activities.*

Before creation of the Information Technology (IT) Information Sharing and Analysis Center (ISAC) in January of 2001 (next section), the IT and communications industry's principle avenue for addressing their CIP responsibilities and for working with the PCIS was the Information Technology Association of America (ITAA). The ITAA, an IT industry association, functions as the IT industry sector focal point for coordination, cooperation, and information sharing between the IT industry and the other critical sectors.

Any IT company would be well advised to participate in the ITAA's efforts at representing the IT industry to each of the other critical industry sectors. This is especially true if an IT organization is supporting any of the other "critical" sectors either "in-house" or through contract arrangements. The principle reason for this involvement is going to be one of self-preservation, for it is now appreciated by all industry sectors that the major, nonnatural vulnerability threatening them comes from their dependence on information and communications technology. Consequently, it will not be long before a failure in another "critical" sector industry is laid at the doorstep of the IT industry.

It is therefore important that IT product and services companies and in-house support organizations become active in the CIP's search for solutions. It has become essential to be perceived as being part of the CIP solution—not part of the security problem.

At a personal level, computer security professionals must be well versed in the activities of the CIAO, PCIS, and the industry ISAC and should lobby for their corporation's participation in the PCIS and ISAC programs.

THE IT INFORMATION SHARING and ANALYSIS CENTER (ISAC)——IT-ISAC

WASHINGTON—"Some of the biggest names in technology, including bitter rivals Microsoft Corp. and Oracle Corp., are forming a private alliance to share sensitive information about cyber-attacks and vulnerabilities in their software and hardware products, which are used by much of the world's businesses and governments. 'The overriding goal is to protect ourselves from cyber-hazards, whether they be deliberate attempts or accidental events,' said Guy Copeland of Computer Sciences Corp., a board member of the new center, . . . 'We've known that each of us have a little bit of the picture. By sharing the information, we can be that much smarter.'"

—Wall Street Journal

FREQUENTLY ASKED QUESTIONS ABOUT THE IT-ISAC

What is the IT-ISAC?

The IT-ISAC is a not-for-profit corporation serving the IT industry and established to report and exchange information concerning electronic incidents, threats, attacks, vulnerabilities, solutions and countermeasures, best security practices, and other protective measures. The IT-ISAC will collect, synthesize, and disseminate information about threats and coordinate the IT industry's response to such threats.

Originally comprised of 19 founding member[1] companies, the IT-ISAC welcomes general corporate membership from the entire IT industry representing hardware, software, services, communications, and security service providers. The technical operations of the IT-ISAC will be conducted through contracts with firms specializing in intrusion detection, analysis, and information sharing.

Why was the IT-ISAC created?

While hackers often collaborate on the best intrusion techniques, private sector companies and organizations—the victims of such attacks—often have no outlets for sharing information, gauging vulnerabilities, and collectively responding to threats. Attacks can be critical industry sector–specific; as a result, great leverage can be gained through cross-sector collaboration. If an attack is against the information infrastructure of a critical industry, say the financial industry, then a coordinated and collaborative response by the IT industry is absolutely necessary if the financial industry is to be able to respond in an effective and timely manner.

As a result, major information technology companies have joined together to make the information infrastructure and the Internet more secure. The IT-ISAC enables the high-tech industry to:

- share state-of-the-art information technology security measures
- spot potential threats to the information infrastructure quicker
- respond rapidly when security incidents occur

---

[1]Founding members include: AT&T, Cisco Systems, Computer Associates, CSC, EDS, Entrust Technologies, Hewlett-Packard, IBM, Intel, KPMG Consulting, Microsoft, Nortel Networks, Oracle, RSA Security, Securify Inc., Symantec Corp., Titan Systems, Veridan, and VeriSign.

The IT-ISAC shares the latest and best IT infrastructure security data, almost like a "poison control center" hotline. Nothing can completely prevent threats to the infrastructure, but the IT-ISAC effectively anticipates and responds to such threats.

How will the IT-ISAC operate?

Information is provided to the IT-ISAC contractor on a voluntary basis by the members of the IT-ISAC and will be shared with members and the general public. There are confidentiality agreements in place to protect sources, but the information is to receive the widest possible distribution to all users of IT, especially critical industry sector users. Physically, the IT-ISAC will operate on a 24-hour-a-day, 7-day-a-week schedule.

Why has it taken the IT industry this long to respond to the information infrastructure threat?

The great strength of the Internet is that no one organization controls it and it is available to everyone. But that also means that almost anyone can try to disrupt it, use it to gain unlawful access to other systems, or use it to carry out fraudulent activity. Assuring the security of the Internet is enormously complex and potentially very expensive. Of course, the IT industry has been working to solve security problems long before the ISAC was established—each corporation within its own sphere of computing influence. The ISAC is a collaborative effort of companies that normally compete with each other. It has taken some time, a great deal of effort, and much goodwill to develop a plan that is cost-effective and has broad industry support. The ISAC is now in its second year of operation, and as membership grows and successes are experienced, the potential effectiveness of the ISAC will be realized.

If there were another Internet-launched denial of service attack today against the infrastructure, would the IT industry response be different because of the ISAC?

Yes, all members of the IT-ISAC would collaborate in identifying the scope and severity of such an attack and would simultaneously take actions to alert and protect their customers. This would occur in a standardized and timely fashion across the subscribing IT community and would have a direct and positive impact on the other critical industry sectors.

But the real substantive difference brought by the ISAC to the challenge of critical infrastructure protection will be the collaborative research into the potential significance of what appear to be isolated incidents or suspicious activities across elements of the heterogeneous infrastructure. It is this *research* capability that truly sets the IT-ISAC apart from other incident-reporting and alert organizations.

The ultimate benefit of the ISAC's organizational structure and extended membership is the ability to correlate many seemingly separate and benign incidents into potential "attack" scenarios that no one member would see by focusing on the products alone. The ISAC will function as an intelligence-gathering, analysis, and solutions-generating body for the IT industry, not merely an alert mechanism.

What difference will an IT-ISAC make when there is an Internet security incident and how will it affect my business?

The high-tech industry will have a "quarterback" in place who knows all the members of the team, what plays to call in a particular situation, and how the plays are supposed to be executed. The IT industry will have a system, will be prepared, can save time, and can quickly apply new security knowledge as it is developed through membership collaboration.

Can the IT-ISAC prevent denial of service attacks or Internet security breaches?

No. There is no way to eliminate the human instinct to make mischief. The IT industry can, however, understand what types of mischief are likely to be made and how best to head off trouble. The IT industry can then use such knowledge to build better-secured products.

How does an IT company become a member of the IT-ISAC and what is the cost?

Membership information can be attained by accessing *www.it-ISAC.org* and clicking on Join. An Annual membership is $5,000.

CRITICAL INFORMATION INFRASTRUCTURE PROTECTION ISSUES THAT NEED RESOLUTION

From the broadest perspective of the nation's critical infrastructure, there are several issues that need resolution before the full promise of the IT-ISAC and its relationship with other critical industry ISACs can be realized.

Issue #1: The determination of a critical industry's IT interdependencies, initially identified during the Y2K effort, must be reverified in the post-Y2K era and then continuously evaluated for changes and additions. Protection of the information and technical IT infrastructures supporting these interdependencies is one of the goals of the CIP movement, but it cannot be effective unless mechanisms are devised to monitor changes to these infrastructures within and between critical industry sectors.

Issue #2: Mechanisms for the effective "sharing" of security incident information must be refined and expanded. Currently, there are several Information Sharing and Analysis Centers (ISACs) for the collection, distillation, analysis, and dissemination of data about computer security vulnerabilities and system attacks such as those from "hackers" and "viruses." Some of these are government-sponsored and some are commercial. The various ISACs, functioning as separate entities, must be integrated so that the interdependent nature of business and government is reflected. It is planned for the PCIS to perform this function, but there are issue #3 inhibitors that must be resolved before that can occur.

Issue #3: For the IT-ISAC mechanism to work, there must be legislative relief, for security incident data, from the Freedom of Information Act (FOIA), and from Anti-Trust Laws. At present, any security incident information made available to a government agency or government-sponsored ISAC can be obtained from that agency or ISAC through a Freedom of Information Act (FOIA) request. Because of this, IT vendors and service providers may be hesitant to make important information about a security incident available to government agencies, since it is possible for competitors to obtain it through a FOIA action.

Also, without relief from antitrust laws, vendors working together to solve a joint security problem could be accused of working in a manner that will give them a future competitive advantage.

These are issues of great importance to the "players" in the information security arena and must be solved for "effective" information sharing to take place between and among interdependent industries.

Y2K Lessons Learned and Their Importance for E-Business Security

LOOKING BACK

The most important lesson that architects of successful computer security programs can draw from the year 2000 (Y2K) problem may well be that they will find themselves accused of fraudulent misrepresentation.

Put simply, because there was no Y2K disaster, it has been alleged that the possibility of a disaster never really existed.

Readers will recall that the use of two digits to represent dates, originally designed as a memory-saving measure when both live memory and mass storage were relatively expensive, led to a flurry of remediation in the 1990s, with a peak of public alarm in the months before the end of 1999. There were however, few reports of catastrophic failures and certainly no widespread breakdown of infrastructure or of law and order anywhere in the world due to date errors. In the aftermath of this nonevent, voices arose accusing the entire information technology (IT) industry, and Y2K remediation experts in particular, of having whipped up hysteria as a mechanism for tricking management into spending billions of dollars on unnecessary modifications to computer programs.

The fundamental problem underlying this kind of allegation is the difficulty of justifying non-revenue–generating Y2K activities after the fact to observers who never understood the nature and seriousness of a problem that someone else was trying to prevent. The difficulty also stems from the impossibility of proving a negative. For example, one cannot prove to the uninvolved or unimpressed observer that the time, money, and human resources spent on Y2K remediation were well spent simply because a disaster was averted. Such an observer will take the fact that a disaster did not occur as evidence that the possibility of disaster never really existed or that the problem was exaggerated in the media. In the same way, a skeptical observer may take the absence of security breaches as evidence that no such threat existed or that it was never as bad as claimed. The problem is exacerbated after spending time and effort on establishing security policies, security controls, and enforcement mechanisms.

In both cases, the money, time, and effort expended to prevent adverse computing consequences from harming an organization are viewed with suspicion. But such suspicions are not new in the world of information processing. Throughout the history of IT, this attitude has existed regarding problem-prevention activities such as quality assurance, quality control testing, documentation, configuration management, and other system-management controls designed to improve quality, reliability, and system maintainability.

Y2K: THE ACCUSATION AND A DETAILED REBUTTAL

The following analysis is based in part on material from *Y2K Lessons Learned: A Guide to Better Information Technology Management.*

First, it is accused that Y2K was a scam foisted on the unsuspecting community of information-technology users. It has been suggested that unscrupulous IT vendors and consultants created a hypothetical problem and hyped it beyond its true importance in order to create work and wealth for themselves. To give credence to such accusations is to, by inference, accuse sophisticated executive management at such corporations as Citibank and AT&T of incompetence, or worse. No corporation spends $900 million (Citibank) and $500 million (AT&T) on a hyped hypothetical problem. To be sure, some of the monies associated with Y2K were probably misdirected, exaggerated, wasted, or even spent on non-Y2K activities, but not $100 billion.

An early argument advanced to support the accusation of scam centered on the apparent fact that countries and businesses that spent little or nothing of Y2K appear to be doing as well as those that spent heavily and were experiencing no greater number of date-related problems. To assist in making some sense of this seemingly powerful proof, four categories of IT systems and related business settings likely to be operating in any given country or company need to be identified. The following system categories, based on their intrinsic technical vulnerability to the Y2K problem, were catalogued by the Institute of Electrical and Electronics Engineers (IEEE):

1. *Physical Control Systems* are those that control physical things and processes, such as poser generation and distribution, water treatment and distribution, phones, airplanes, elevators, traffic lights, etc. These are the systems where the dreaded embedded chip failures were most anticipated. These systems, however, are well engineered and better understood, better tested under stress, and often designed with redundancy built-in. Such systems have always had a good degree of management attention and investment because in many cases these systems actually constitute the business.

2. *Primary Production Systems of an On-Line Transaction Processing (OLAP) System* such as ATM and e-commerce processing systems were on the vulnerability list because of the highly integrated and frequently customized

nature of hardware and software components and their convergence. Also, OLTP systems are often not engineered with sufficient redundancy and are not adequately tested.

3. *Support Systems* are those that monitor and detect faults, schedule maintenance, automatically order parts, etc., and to some extent manage primary production systems (OLTP) for efficiency and safety. Such systems are not overly complex and are generally well understood. They are not as well engineered as OLTP systems, are not stress tested, and have limited redundancy. Note that Y2K problems with Support Systems would not appear immediately but would surface only after a preprogrammed time interval has elapsed. In other words, these categories of systems can be deemed safe only after all time intervals with 1999-initiated start times have been successfully compared to a post-2000 stop time and all computations and resulting programmed actions have been carried out. Also note that a combination of category 1,2, and 3 systems, operating at different companies, constitute and support the just-in-time (JIT) business model on which many corporations depend.

4. *Administrative and Accounting (A&A) Systems* are heavily date dependent and support the general economic activities of organizations such as purchasing, order processing, invoicing, accounting, human resources, payroll, benefit calculations, tax reporting, etc. These systems are virtually all software and after years of modifications and extensions are extremely complex. A&A systems run on daily, weekly, monthly, quarterly, semi-annual, and annual cycles; meaning that an entire software portfolio may not execute under actual year 2000 conditions until next December. These systems typically provide the data against which "what IF" queries are run and are also used for "data warehousing" activities. A&A systems are oftentimes very large, highly interconnected with many shared data sources, and are often composed of heterogeneous technologies of diverse vendors, models, and age. As a whole, such systems are not generally well understood due to a lack of documentation. These systems present virtually the worst-case scenario for all Y2K-related risk factors and, because they have historically been reviewed as a cost center, they have received relatively little management attention and investment.

   But A&A problems due to Y2K may cause great, unexpected internal turmoil as systems progress through their calendar year 2000 processing cycles. Only the readers of this book will know whether such conditions have occurred in their organization. Although failures with A&A systems may be difficult to link to Y2K date-processing problems, this does not lessen the impact. An increase in problems over last year will be a telltale sign.

The existence of these four categories of systems, with their intrinsic Y2K vulnerabilities, provide a partial answer to the accusation that non-spenders are faring as well as heavy spenders. It seems likely that there are two possibilities with regard to Physical Control Systems, Primary Production Systems, and their Support Systems. First, since these are highly visible and liability-prone systems providing the basic infrastructures of a nation and corporations, they were in fact rigorously remediated and tested. Due diligence would have demanded nothing less. Secondly, such systems in developing nations and less IT-intensive businesses do not even exist, at least to the degree of sophistication that they do in developed nations and large corporations. In which case, there were no reported problems simply because there was nothing to fail that could not be handled manually. Only in more advanced and sophisticated systems has the progressive elimination of the human override element become a desired cost-cutting design goal. Such systems had to be fixed, whereas less sophisticated systems in developing nations or less IT-intensive businesses retained the luxury of the human override and workaround.

There has also been an accusation that those addressing their perceived vulnerabilities spent too much money on Y2K. In response, it can only be pointed out that "reasonable" men and women, upon analysis, practiced responsible risk management and perhaps erred on the side of caution. Again, it is a fact that developed nations and highly IT-intensive businesses had more at risk because of their great dependence on systems built to reduce the labor-intensive (ie. potential human override) nature of the work processes.

The Accusation and the Human Element

In a January 10, 2000 editorial by Tim Wilson of *Internet Week,* appears the following: "Sometimes I wonder why anybody works in the IT Department. If computers fail, you get yelled at. If Internet or dial-up connections fail you get yelled at. *And now, if everything works well, you really get yelled at.*"

It is clear, looking at this *not uncommon reaction* to Y2K related by Tim Wilson, that dealing successfully with future IT problems—perhaps an Internet security crisis—will become a complex *social* as well as technical undertaking. The apparent fact that many users of IT perceive the IT industry and IT workers with such suspicion and antipathy means that much IT industry/user mutual respect work lies ahead.

This essential work can begin by identifying and exploring the IT management lessons to be learned from the Y2K experience. This is because Y2K, as a discrete event in the history of IT, presents a unique opportunity to examine past practices and then use what we have learned to positively influence the future evolutionary path of IT. At the same time, if the poor IT management practices of the past, which contributed to the Y2K problem and the extreme expense of its resolution, are allowed to continue, Y2K can be viewed as just a minor "harbinger" of things to come.

This self-examination is absolutely essential for *anyone striving to improve the state of e-business security.* Now is the time to challenge and change those systems development and IT management practices that led to Y2K. For if the same inadequate practices are left unchanged in the face of increasing security threats, they will only continue contributing to the insecure systems of *tomorrow* just as they contributed to the insecure systems of *today.*

Looking Ahead

The major problem associated with Y2K was not that a 6-digit date field needed to be changed to somehow accommodate an 8-digit date or even that the issue had been ignored until it became a crisis. *No, the real problem was that most organizations had such a very difficult time managing and executing what was essentially a simple "code" change.* Because of the general lack of basic IT organizational discipline and adherence to fundamental software/system development and maintenance principles, most remediation efforts became fiascoes with a collective price tag of over $100 billion in the United States alone.

Because of this reality, which was so clearly demonstrated by Y2K, the primary concern for the e-business security practitioner must be the correction of these same basic and fundamental IT system management defects or else *effective security can never be attained or maintained.*

Simply put, you can't secure what you aren't managing; and you can't manage what you can't find.

Y2K Was Really a Computer Security Issue

At its' core, the threat posed by Y2K made it a computer and communications security issue. It was primarily a threat to systems availability and data integrity. It had the potential to be the "mother" of all denial of service events and put at extreme risk the continuity of business and government services.

For many in the security community, Y2K was seen as a "dress rehearsal" which would *hopefully* prepare an IT dependent society to address the technology and business management practices that had put us all in such peril. It would also hopefully begin a meaningful dialogue about the public policy issues surrounding computer security, privacy, and confidentiality.

Y2K, as a business threat, was seen to be serious enough to force worldwide Continuity of Operations (COOP) planning. It was also serious enough to prompt the creation of the *President's Commission on Critical Infrastructure Protection (CIP)* to examine the growing issue of national infrastructure interdependencies and especially the growing dependencies of business and government on information technology.

(Chapter 9 has a detailed discussion of the CIP initiatives that are shaping the future of information and e-business systems processing.)

Y2K, seen as a computer security threat to the global infrastructure, created high awareness, in all industrialized nations, of their great dependency on information and communications technology. In fact, the Y2K experience is presently leading many leaders to inquire about other ways in which business and government is threatened because of a growing dependence on IT and other forms of technology.

This increased awareness has creating for the computer security practitioner an opportunity that never existed before Y2K. And that is that each security professional can capitalize on the infrastructure protection movement to take computer security out of the merely technical realm and establish it as a business issue. This then will place computer security squarely on the doorstep of the "Board of Directors".

Y2K Lessons Learned and Their Benefit for E-Business/CIP Security Initiatives

An overarching lesson learned from the recent Y2K experience is that "no organization is an island." Computers and communications have linked organizations together at a technological level and globalization has linked them at a business and economic level. Those who feared a downside to such linkage were vindicated when the potential impacts of an uncorrected Y2K problem were uncovered. And, it is now clear that the same linkages and interdependencies are at risk from cyber attacks against the computer and communications infrastructure of any country.

So what lessons from Y2K can the computer security practitioner use to further their efforts to establish effective e-business/CIP security initiatives?

Lesson #1: Information and Process Integrity Are Now **Known** *to Be Important to the Business.*   Before Y2K, executive management of most organizations gave little thought to the importance of the integrity of their corporate information assets and their computer processing capabilities. These were issues for the Chief Information Officer and the technical people who ran the computers and networks.

Awareness has grown gradually since the early days of computing and Y2K brought it to full maturity. In the early days, the information from computerized operations was generally seen as by-products of a manual paper-driven business process and was historic in nature. Such information, it was felt, could always be recreated by going back to the original manual transaction and business would go on as usual. People conducted business and computers were merely used as recording, storage, and reporting tools.

All this changed during the last decade with the advent of the Internet and the revolutionary impact of data communications on the way business is conducted. Today, in many cases, there is no predecessor "manual" paper-based process for the web-based e-business and so dependence on the reliability and security of the automated system is nearly total. For an increasing number of organizations, distributed information processes, implemented via the world-wide-web and other networked environments, have become the critical operating element of their business. In some cases, *the information processing system is the business*! Not only must the processing system work when needed, but the information processed must retain its integrity so it can be "trusted" for use.

Because of the impact assessments that were done for Y2K, it is now *fully understood*, if not fully appreciated, that when a networked environment doesn't function because of a software defect, electrical failure, a "denial of service" attack instigated by a hacker or any other interruptive activity, the business suffers.

And, because Y2K threatened to destroy the integrity of date related processing and many data bases, it is now *better appreciated* that breaches of security controls resulting in unauthorized or accidental modification or compromise of corporate or private information can lead to a "public relations" and "legal" nightmare.

Lesson #2: The Importance of "Supply Chain" Teamwork in Achieving Mutually Assured E-Business Integrity Is Now Sppreciated. Y2K demonstrated to private sector companies how really *interdependent* they had become, cross-sector in their day-to-day operations, and how this dependency was based in computer and communications technology. This new awareness has focusing attention on the responsibility of companies to their *business partners* and to others in a "supply chain" who are dependent on reliable systems for their capability to conducting business without interruption.

As a result, reliable and secure systems and processes are now beginning to be *mutually expected* of all businesses that are members of a "supply chain." For example, Visa recently published exacting security guidelines for their Internet-enabled business partners Computerworld 10/2/00. Visa partners must:

- Install and maintain a working network firewall to protect data accessible via the Internet.
- Keep security patches up to date.
- Encrypt stored data.
- Encrypt data sent across networks.
- Use and regularly update antivirus software.
- Restrict access to "cardholder" data inside the business on a need-to-know basis.
- Assign a unique identifier to each person with computer access.
- Do not use vendor-supplied defaults for system passwords and other security parameters.
- Track access to data by unique identifier.
- Regularly test security systems and processes.
- Maintain a security policy for employees and contractors.
- Restrict physical access to "cardholder" information.
- Destroy data when no longer needed for business reasons.

These requirements recognize the harsh reality that a *lack of systems security with any "link" company can adversely affect everyone else in the chain.* No company wants to become known as a "weak link" in a supply chain and be threatened with possible breach of contract actions and the related loss of reputation.

Lesson #3: Information and Computer Processes Are Important Corporate Assets That Need to Be as Rigorously Managed as Other Corporate Assets. Y2K demonstrated that information and the supporting information and communications technology assets are the "glue" that holds the modern enterprise together. In other words, they are critically important.

Yet, historically, no other corporate asset is as poorly managed as these. This fact has been documented time and again by independent audit groups not the least of which is the U.S. General Accounting Office (GAO). The GAO reviews not only government agencies but, at the request of congress, private sector companies doing business with the federal government or receiving federal funding. In other words, reading GAO IT Management Audit Reports presents a pretty fair picture of IT management across both the government and the private sector.

From a high-level IT management perspective, the GAO and others have consistently identified the following problems as fundamentally contributing to IT project and management failures:

- Lack of top management commitment
- Inadequate IT planning and execution
- Abandonment of the project plan
- Inexperienced project managers
- Flawed technical approach
- Failure to anticipate advances in technology
- Failure to satisfy user needs
- Inadequate documentation of systems decisions
- Acquisition problems

While each of these appear to be separate areas of difficulty, they all concentrate their impact and directly affect the IT manager and the security officer, who must somehow orchestrate these, and myriad other issues, to establish and maintain a secured system and processing environment.

Unless and until these overall management problems are corrected it will be virtually impossible to adequately secure the e-business systems that support the enterprise.

It must be recognized that many computer security problems are merely symptoms of poorly managed applications of IT to the business. Unless the underlying systems management problems are solved, treating symptoms will at best be a "hit and miss" proposition.

Lesson #4: In Most Instances, Y2K Demonstrated That Existing Technical Infrastructure Management Was Poor. For most organizations, Y2K, a simple technical problem to fix, became a far too expensive nightmare because it was discovered that most software and systems, at the technical level, were generally not being managed according to the known "best practices" of the industry.

Y2K was a wake-up call for improved management of systems and software. Major improvements in quality assurance, configuration management, software development and testing, documentation, intrusion detection, and continuity planning activities will be required *or computer security can never be fully achieved.*

Lesson #5: Risk Management Must Become a Way of Life. Unlike Y2K, the computer security challenge will always be with us and will continually take on "new" forms as technologies and business processes evolve. While Y2K was a one-time event, computer security is "forever" and the only way to manage it effectively is to integrate the practice of assessing security risks into each and every systems decision.

The type of risk assessment that is needed goes far beyond the "replacement cost" analysis of the superficial risk analysis model. Summarizing Chapter 8, the degree of dependence that most organizations now place on automation requires a much broader scoping of potential damages than just estimating the cost of "replacing" hardware and software assets.

Effective risk management, for the contemporary risk faced by most organizations, must begin by placing a value on some or all of the following information categories:

- the value of corporate proprietary information
- the value of "intellectual" property
- the value of client and customer data
- the value of business partner information

Additionally, "critical business processes" must have a value associated with them and the adverse consequences of an inability to process need to be determined. From this analysis, revenue losses due to system outages can be estimated based upon appropriate threat scenarios.

Further extension of the risk assessment thought process should also take into account such things as:

- potential for liability exposure if business partners are harmed due to your system's insecurity or unavailability
- loss of business opportunity revenue because system insecurities don't allow exploitation of new business opportunities

- potential for liability exposure should confidentiality of sensitive information be compromised
- loss of reputation with consumers and with the capital markets of the world due to publicized security exposures

And finally, there is the important perception of stepping up to responsibility. Whether or not a company measures up to that challenge will likely be determined by their participation in national critical infrastructure protection and computer security initiatives.

Lesson #6: Automated Business Environments Must Be Continually Monitored for "New" Vulnerabilities and Their Protection Improved. Unlike Y2K, the nature of the computer security challenge is that of dynamically changing vulnerabilities and threats based on rapidly changing technologies being used to evolve increasingly complex business applications. This means that organizations need to build their computer security programs around the idea of a continuous improvement model of the type made popular by the total quality movement. For purposes of quality improvement this model was viewed as a plan-do-check-act cycle.

For computer security it can be thought of as a plan-fix-monitor-assess cycle. A Security Management Program (Chapter 4) to execute this model must be established and integrated into the day-to-day operations of the business. Integration into day-to-day management means that the computer security initiative does not stand alone as a "watch dog" or merely an audit function. It is considered integral to all other systems development and management activities to include requirements definition, systems design, programming and package integration, testing, systems documentation, training, configuration management, and operations and maintenance.

The Security Management Program must be designed in such a way that the activities of planning, fixing, monitoring, and assessing are accomplished in an iterative fashion for systems under definition, design, and implementation and for system that are executing the existing production applications of the business.

While many organizations were being diverted by the Y2K problem, today's networked business environments were being built with little or no attention being given to security concerns. Subsequently, many of these e-commerce and Internet based businesses are now in full operation and the only way to *realistically identify and assess their security risks* is to begin aggressively monitoring for intrusions and then design and implement countering security policies and controls. The effective sequence then for the continuous improvement model will be to begin by monitoring current operations, assess suspicious system activity, plan a corrective policy or technology control, implement the fix on the system, and then monitor for continuing effectiveness.

*Lesson #7: Y2K Became a "Due Diligence" Issue for the "Board" and So Will
E-Business Security.*   To effectively address the computer security issue, it must
become an issue for the "Board of Directors" just as Y2K demanded "board"
attention.

The Y2K experience introduced business executives and IT managers to the
concept of "due diligence" as applied to the uses of information technology.
Because of the potential for legal fallout, it became necessary to view Y2K-
related actions through the definitions of "due diligence" and "reasonable care."
It became imperative to document all Y2K deliberations, decisions, and actions in
order to be able to defend against possible charges of "lax Y2K preparations."
This same focus now influences computer security deliberations, decisions, and
actions.

The significance of the concepts of "due diligence" and "reasonable care" is
that they allow for an evolving metric against which an organization's computer
security deliberations, decisions, and actions can be compared. The comparison
is usually against *a like company in like circumstances* of vulnerability and threat
and with similar predictable adverse impacts on customers, partners, shareholders, employees, and the public.

For example, if one company *does employ* a security control and *does not*
experience any "security breaches" which the technique was supposed to prevent,
that could establish a possible baseline against which other similar companies
could be compared. If enough similar companies employ the same technique, the
security control may become categorized as a "best practice" for that industry.

Now, if another company in that same industry *were to not employ* the security control and *does experience "security breaches"* of the type the technique
was supposed to prevent, it may be questioned whether that company exercised
"due diligence" or demonstrated "reasonable care."

This means that e-business security decisions and implementations are not a
one-time event, but need to be under a continuous process of "risk" evaluation,
management, and improvement.

It is therefore imperative, in order to demonstrate the ability to exercise continual "due diligence" to the "Board" to establish a documented computer security risk management program and integrate it into the overall management
processes of the business. Nothing less will demonstrate that a company, and
therefore the "Board," is capable of assessing future computer security threats and
is acting in a "reasonable" manner.

Due diligence guidelines include:

- The U.S. National Institute for Standards and Technology's (NIST) *Generally
  Accepted Systems Security Principles* (GSSPs) (*ftp.ru.xemacs.org/pub/secu-
  rity/csir/nist/nistpubs/gssp.pdf*).
- ISO 17799, the *Code of Practice for Information Security Management*, based
  on the British Standards Institute BS 7799 documents. The International
  Organization for Standardization (ISO) (*www.iso.ch/iso/en/ISOOnline.*

frontpage) began the process of defining BS 7799 as an international standard; ISO 17799 was published in 1999.

- The COBIT™ (Control Objectives for Information and Related Technology), a business-oriented set of standards for guiding management in the sound use of information technology. COBIT was developed by volunteers working under the aegis of the IT Governance Institute® (*www.itgovernance.org/index2.htm*), which was itself founded by the Information System Audit and Control Association (ISACA).

- The *Common Criteria* (CC), a project that developed out of the 1985 *Trusted Computer System Evaluation Criteria* (TCSEC; also known as the *Orange Book*) developed by the National Computer Security Center of the National Security Agency of the United States. See *www.commoncriteria.org/faq/faq. html* for an overview of the CC, where one reads, "The Common Criteria for Information Technology Security Evaluation (CC) defines general concepts and principles of IT security evaluation and presents a general model of evaluation. It presents constructs for expressing IT security objectives, for selecting and defining IT security requirements, and for writing high-level specifications for products and systems."

In the post-Y2K analysis, it was generally agreed that the involvement of the "Board of Directors" was essential to solving the problem. Success in solving the computer challenge will also eventually require intervention by the "Board." Presenting the security challenge and possible solutions to a "Board" will require considerable preparation. The next section will outline those essential steps.

BRINGING E-BUSINESS SECURITY TO THE BOARD OF DIRECTORS

To successfully present the issue of computer security to a Board of Directors, the following activities need to be undertaken. It is important that this task be accomplished using the various staff disciplines of the corporation, to include the CEO, CFO, CIO, HR Department, the affected Business Unit Managers, General Counsel, Public Relations, and the corporate Risk Management Office.

A guiding principle for such an undertaking should be an emphasis on the non-quantifiable elements of the benefits equation which members of a "Board" should be able to identify with. Another principle to impress upon the "Board" is the need for continuous support and funding to counter the reality of a continuously evolving threat.

The Steps:

Step #1: Conduct a thorough inventory of all information technology "hard" assets and identify replacement costs.

Step #2:   Identify information assets to include intellectual property, business proprietary, client data, customer data, and business partner data.

Determine a *dollar value* or *weight* as a form of information valuation for each category.

Step #3:   Identify "critical business processes" and determine a value for each process by estimating loss revenues should the process be disrupted. Do this also for each process in which a "business partner" has a direct business interest.

Step #4:   Perform a security vulnerability and threat assessment of the cyber environment in which your business is operating. This may include attempts, by an independent third party, to penetrate the system defenses currently in place. For each confirmed vulnerability, estimate a probability of occurrence based upon various threat scenarios and identify potential losses both quantitative (ie. replacement costs) and non-quantitative (i.e. loss of business, corporate reputation, competitive edge, standing in financial markets, liability exposure, etc.). *Note: Since a hard quantification will be difficult to calculate and defend, concentrate on the non-quantifiable but highly visceral issues of loss of reputation and trust with customers, business partners, the business community in general, and with investors.*

Step #5:   Examine your dependence vulnerabilities that exist with regard to business partners and ask for assurances of their commitment to security. In certain critical instances, your company may want to issue security guidelines for business partners as part of contract renewal requirements.

Step #6:   Join your industry sector's Critical Infrastructure Protection (CIP) Group.

Step #7:   Determine your corporation's legal exposure to customers, business partners, shareholders, other investors, employees, and third parties. Include the General Counsel in all security deliberations.

Step #8:   Based on a program of continuous technology and business risk assessments fund, design, implement, test, manage, and monitor computer and business process security controls and business recovery plans. Just do it.

Step #9:   Formulate a Business "Crisis" Communications Plan for computer security incidents.

Step #10: Monitor the computer and business process security practices of your business partners and competitors in your industry sector. This is important to stay current with industry "best practices" so that "due diligence" can be demonstrated.

Step #11: Stay active—make computer security a periodic agenda item for the "Board." Practice "due diligence" and create a documentation trail of computer security actions, deliberations, and decisions.

Step #12: Maximize legal defenses remembering the *Business Judgement Rule*.

Step #13: Review corporate indemnification and investigate the purchase of specialized insurance.

Challenges to Be Overcome

Any organization's long-term ability to contain and manage the computer security problem will depend on several *premeditated changes in the way IT systems and computer security is managed*. Until senior executives and the Board of Directors demand the following, little true progress will be made.

Challenge #1: Executives must require that system activities be managed according to "best practices" of the IT industry with special emphasis on those practices that insure the integrity, availability, and confidentiality of information, processing assets, and business processes. This is imperative to form a "due diligence" defense and establishes the minimum foundation for the practice of computer security.

One final time, you can't secure what you aren't managing.

Challenge #2: Convincing business unit managers and the Board of Directors that computer security requires a program of continuous measurement and investment to counter a continuing evolving threat of increased sophistication.

Challenge #3: Organizations must demand better security in the products they buy or lease from IT vendors. This is best accomplished by bringing pressure to bear through the Special Interest Groups (SIGs) that represent the users of vendor products and by making security an agenda item of great importance in all enterprise acquisitions of hardware, software, and services.

CONCLUSION

Those who cannot remember the past are condemned to repeat it.

—George Santayana

The Y2K episode offered many lessons concerning the effectiveness and efficiency of IT management as it had been practiced in the years leading up to the year 2000. Organizations were generally found wanting and as a result, a relatively minor problem became huge and cost the United States in excess of $100 billion.

And once again, it is extremely important for the corporate executive manager to understand that the same IT management deficiencies, left unchanged, will continue to sabotage efforts to establish and sustain effectively e-business security programs.

Systems Development Review Framework for E-Business Development Projects

This systems development review framework presents for executive management an easy-to-use guide for exercising oversight of an e-business development project. It is comprised of two parts: the generic life-cycle phases of a systems development effort and the several management plans that ensure project success. It is a theme of this book that the most secure system is one that has been defined, designed, developed, tested, and delivered to be secure. While security and integrity controls and system availability/reliability measures are essential to e-business security, it is the overall *integrity* of the entire system determined by how it was developed that is the lasting measure of security. A system is only as secure as the degree to which it adheres to proven structured techniques, has been robustly tested, and is comprehensively documented. All the "firewalls" in the world will not secure a system that is poorly designed, inadequately tested, and incompletely documented.

The ability to give confidentiality, integrity, and system availability/reliability assurances to management is a direct result of the discipline applied during development of the e-business system and the enforcement of maintenance discipline after the system has become operational. The layout of the Systems Development Review Framework (Exhibits 6.5 and B.1) is explained in Chapter 6 and expanded upon here.

The framework can be viewed as a matrix of cells by extending the horizontal lines separating the phases across the form. Executives should know that distinct actions must be accomplished in each cell for each management requirement at each phase of the development if the effort is to deliver a secured system. The framework presents those development life cycle phases and management requirement plans that are generally thought of as "best practice" in the IT industry. Progression down the phases should be uniform, with no one management requirement plan getting too far ahead or behind the execution of the other plans. Since the management plans influence each other, it is important that they be exercised concurrently.

To aid executive management in their role as overseers, this appendix provides a short description of each life cycle phase and each management plan. It also provides key questions to ask concerning each management plan to determine project progress and integrity.

LIFE CYCLE PHASES

These phases (i.e., the rows of the framework) identify the discrete steps to be followed in engineering e-business systems. Each phase produces specific work products resulting from analysis and work performed during that phase. A project should not progress from one phase to the next until all work products are completed or waived by senior management.

Preparation Phase

The preparation phase requires that overall project definition and scope be determined to the extent that initial budgets, time, and personnel resources estimates can be made. Each management requirement plan category should be examined for applicability to the project being considered and initial plan outlines should be developed. Each management requirement must have a high-level plan generated or be waived with justification. If known, the hardware, software, and network infrastructure needed to operate the contemplated system should be documented. The project's concept should be formally documented and submitted for feasibility analysis and an initial risk assessment.

Definition Phase

The definition phase proceeds with the detailed definition of the e-business requirement and associated technology support needs. A determination is made concerning the most feasible solution from among the alternatives surviving the feasibility study. Each management plan determined to be appropriate for the project defines its unique set of requirements dictated by the business function and the selected technical solution to be developed or integrated over the remaining phases. Each management plan, by the end of this phase, will have a documented list of requirements that will need to be satisfied before the overall development can be considered complete. Some of the plan requirements deal with business aspects of the system such as auditing, some deal with ensuring that quality specifications are met, while other address confidentiality, integrity, and systems availability needs. For the majority of e-business systems, all management requirement plans should be invoked.

Design Phase

The design phase is involved with designing a technical and a human factor solution to the business problem or opportunity while satisfying the requirements imposed by the applicable management requirement plans. For virtually all systems, the design will have to comply with security, internal controls, and documentation requirements. Software or (systems) engineering plans ensure that the design and subsequent development adhere to proven structured software engineering techniques.

To ensure a quality system and one that can be maintained over its projected life, other management requirement plans are used to guide the development and/or integration activities of quality assurance (QA) and testing, technology transfer of the system to users and customers, and training. All plans conform to standards prescribed in the project management plan as enforced by the project manager. Participants to the design (Exhibit 6.6) should review and concur on all design and project plans.

Development Phase

The development phase converts the business and technology systems design into an e-business system that meets the requirements for confidentiality, integrity, and systems availability as well as satisfying other quality requirements. Development may require original software programming and database development or, more commonly, the integration of various commercially available products into an operational system that performs the e-business function. It is likely that many separate e-business applications will have to be integrated into a complete system that performs an e-business function. And these systems will have to be integrated across supply lines with other companies.

During development, the QA and testing plan and the configuration management (CM) plan take on great importance as those plans that oversee development to ensure e-business/system/product/service completeness and integrity.

Deployment Phase

Upon completion of development and following customer or user acceptance of the system or integration, the deployment phase addresses the *fielding* of the system for operational business use or, if it is a product, sale. For a deployment to be successful, all applicable management requirement plans must have been completed through the end of the development phase. Planned actions not completed means the e-business system or product or service is not yet ready for introduction to the workplace or marketplace.

Phased deployments are common with large distributed systems of great hardware and network complexity. Phased software deployments where incomplete functionality is released for use should be considered incomplete and highly risky projects. At the end of deployment, all business, technical, and management requirements need to have been completed, fully tested, and well documented.

Maintenance Phase

This final phase requires the accurate completion and constant currency of all systems and software documentation, complete inventories of vendor products and network components, and complete descriptions of security and integrity controls placed on the system. This information must be kept up to date in order to modify, enhance, or correct system defects and/or suspected security weaknesses in a timely fashion. If maintenance is not given full attention, organizations using e-business systems will, over time, experience the same loss of systems knowledge that hampered Y2K remediation efforts, and this will prove disastrous from a security perspective.

MANAGEMENT REQUIREMENT PLANS

The following management requirement plans (i.e., columns) of Exhibits 6.5 and B.1 can be briefly described as follows.

Project Management Plan

This game plan for project and subproject managers ensures that the entire development effort will satisfy the e-business requirement by delivering a quality and secured product within budget and time estimates. Budgets and time estimates are the product of analyses performed during the first two phases of the life cycle and are then modified as needed as the project progresses. In executing the plan, traditional project management tools would be employed to monitor progress and reallocate resources as required. The project manager (PM) should insist on having written management requirement plans for each area affecting the project. This will give the PM an effective method of obtaining project feedback and protecting against *surprises* later in the project schedule.

Software or System Engineering Plan

This plan lays out the work tasks to build the technical e-business solution for the stated business requirement in a disciplined and structured engineering fashion. This is accomplished by using one of many methodologies such that each phase of the project builds on the work products of the previous phase. In other words, working backward from the final system under maintenance, the ease and speed with which maintenance changes can be made is predicated on the deployment (installation) of an e-business system that not only executes its code efficiently but also was delivered having satisfied all elements of each management requirement plan. A system delivered in this condition meets all aspects of what the IT industry would generally judge to be a project conforming to "best practices."

Furthermore, the successful deployment of an e-business system depends not only on the successful completion of this *software or systems engineering plan,* but also on the successful completion of each management requirement plan through the end of the development phase. If, for example, the project is late according to the documentation plan, then the system is not ready for deployment unless executive management is willing to accept certain risks. The risk of confused employees projecting a less than professional image to the customer and a business partner. The risk of confused potential customers losing patience with your portal interface and "surfing" elsewhere. The risk of confused system operators ill-prepared to run the system. Or the risk of confused help-desk personnel ill-prepared to talk users through routine deployment questions that are sure to be raised.

To ensure the readiness of an e-business system to progress to the next phase of the life cycle, all planned activities of each management requirement plan must be complete, and any potential changes to the assumed hardware, software, or network infrastructure must be considered. This process can be monitored efficiently by the IT executive committee once the management requirement plans have been formulated and agreed to.

There will be conflicts. Marketing and sales, business development, and many other corporate centers of power will balk at this approach to managing IT the first time they must adjust their expectations rather than deliver a system before it is ready. This is why top management support for IT management discipline is so important. Improved systems (and hence a better security posture) will not happen without such support because no CIO alone can withstand the pressures to please the revenue-generating managers of the company by cutting corners and making compromises in security, training, and other important system management and maintenance activities.

It is likely that even the CEO cannot create, with a single edict, such fundamental change; that is why continuous involvement and oversight will be necessary until cultures change and the positive fruits of this approach begin to become evident. Remember, the opposite has already been proven. Lack of management direction creates influence in the opposite direction. In other words, management can prevent the use of best IT practices by not dictating their use.

Internal Controls Plan

This plan sets forth the requirements for auditability and identifies specific internal application software controls operating within the e-business system to ensure accounting rule consistency and data integrity. This plan is essential to meeting the "integrity" requirements of an e-business security program. This plan contains actions that call for close coordination with the corporation's audit group to identify both internal and external audit requirements and reporting needs. Internal controls represent an area beyond the expertise of most IT professionals, which is why the auditor is named a "key" participant to the design in Exhibit 6.6. Qualified computer audit personnel must be intimately involved whenever it is necessary to develop an internal control plan.

As with any business requirement that is being reduced to computer code, the construction of internal controls must progress in sync with the overall development of the software engineering plan or the controls will be "slapped on" late in the development, if at all, and be ineffectual.

Security Plan

Because of the critical importance of this issue, the framework includes it as a separate plan to encourage high-visibility monitoring. The security plan takes form after a security risk analysis of e-business proposal has been performed and the environment in which it will operate has been assessed. While the computing infrastructure's security measures provide a certain degree of access control, virus scanning, and backup or recovery services, it is the application-specific controls, based on the unique sensitivity characteristics of the business process being developed, that offer the most effective and efficient security. Thus, the security controls to be placed on a company-sensitive research and development application will be different from the controls placed over accounts receivable processing and different still from those controls placed on the parking lot permit system.

When it comes to an e-business system, security controls built into each application will have to serve as the last line of defense in a world of increasing Internet vulnerability.

This management requirement plan allows the unique security needs of each e-business application and the system under development to be defined, designed, developed, tested, and deployed as an integral yet separately tracked set of specifications.

Quality Assurance and Testing Plan

This plan ensures that those quality characteristics that can be quantified or otherwise meaningfully specified are present in the project's final work products, whether code, database, screens, reports, or systems documentation. This plan also outlines the use of standard QA techniques and tools to ensure that "best practices" were properly employed during code development and during all testing. Using a best practice approach, initial QA activities and tests are accomplished by the developers themselves as they work through design and coding issues. Later, independent QA reviews and final prerelease testing should be performed by a totally different group from the original development team. The greater the risk posed by the release of flawed software or systems, the greater the necessary rigor required of the QA and testing plan.

Quality assurance and testing are areas where automated tools can be of great help. Tools, however, require a sizable investment in time and money and should be carefully selected to augment standardized QA and testing procedures required of the development group and any contractors supporting the project.

Substantial improvements in systems security and integrity can be realized by the rigorous enforcement of a comprehensive QA and testing plan because the overall reliability of the e-business system will be greatly improved and the occurrences when defective code trigger security and security-like incidents will be reduced significantly.

Configuration Management (CM) Plan

This plan is one of the most important in the framework. It prescribes how each of the individual "work products" from the many activities of an e-business development or integration project are to be controlled and accounted for. This process of managing the many configurations of developmental products as they progress from phase to phase to be consolidated into a finished system is critical to both completing the e-business system and securing the system. For a system to be under proper CM means that at any moment in time and at any point of the life cycle, all system products, final or intermediate, can be identified and located in their most recent version. In a small to medium-size development or integration effort, system products and items requiring CM easily number in the hundreds. On large projects, a CM database may have thousands of entries all reflecting the current status of a development product and where it is in the development cycle.

Without CM, projects spin out of control and the ability to judge actual progress becomes next to impossible because interdependent development activities do not necessarily proceed in unison. Products, system components, and other items such as security test plans that, in the finished system, must work together may take many paths to final assembly. One module of an e-business application may skate through testing while a sister module runs into test difficulties and is forced to revisit previous phases of the life cycle in order to solve the problem. Configuration management is needed to maintain consistency and agreement among the system or software requirements, design, code, and test cases. When all of these elements are consistent, the developer has a "baseline" (i.e., the last known instance when all elements agreed with each other) of the system under construction at a particular point in time. As a project nears completion, all baselines merge into one final tested and documented system for user acceptance and deployment.

Automated tools may be of benefit to configuration management. As with QA and testing tools, the payback dividends are well documented in that systems maintenance, and hence security, becomes far easier during e-business operation. Because all system documentation, software versions, and hardware configurations are known, changes and security modifications can be made in a confident and timely fashion.

The major enforcement mechanism of configuration management is change control, a procedure whereby routine and emergency modifications to e-business systems are brought under a controlling process. Change control requires that all changes to the baseline of a system be analyzed for risk and for any adverse impact on other aspects of the operational e-business system. This type of procedure, when enforced, prevents unknown, and therefore uncontrolled, changes to a system's baseline by any one individual without a review and an impact study being accomplished.

Change control is absolutely essential for maintaining the integrity and security of software and databases and the stability and availability of the hardware and network infrastructure.

Documentation Plan

This plan specifies the documents that are to be generated during the course of the project. Documentation is often thought of as the "glue" that holds a project together during times of staff turnover and ensures that replacement personnel do not make unnecessary interpretations of work that has gone on before their arrival. The more that unnecessary interpretations can be kept to a minimum, the easier it will be to stay consistent with original design and with work products already completed. Without adequate and accurate documentation, progress between phases may be delayed, as documents describing previous work products have to be researched for meaning and accuracy. It would be like handing incomplete blueprints and work order instructions to a subcontractor and expecting a task to be completed on time and according to original design intent. Time and effort would be wasted as the subcontractor researched the intent of the original design. Of course, the worst case would be if the incomplete blueprints or the inaccurate and/or inadequate systems documentation were actually followed as if they were accurate. In such cases, the effects of the miscommunication between workers may not be discovered until very late in construction, when only major and expensive retrofitting can meet the original intent—all because the discipline of documenting and reviewing work products was not enforced.

Technology Transfer Plan

From a security perspective, this plan is one of the most important since it and the training plan are the plans that control the introduction of the e-business system into the workplace and onto the Internet for customer use. This plan must take into account the knowledge and skills gap between what the workforce and customers are capable of and what effective, efficient, and secured operation of the new system demands. Too often, software and systems are programmed and delivered on the misassumption that the employee and/or customer possess the same basic technical experience as the developer.

If a certain level of increased technical sophistication is required of the employee or customer, the technology transfer plan should identify the means by which the less sophisticated employee or customer can become proficient. This is more than just training, and it applies more often to custom-developed solutions than to commercial off-the-shelf packages. Technology transfer also applies to preparing the operational workplace to receive the new e-business system. Often the hardware, operating system, support software, and network elements of the infrastructure must be in place and operating successfully before newly developed e-business software can be installed and turned on for production work. This requirement posed a huge challenge to solving the Y2K problem, and it is a problem when attempting to field a secured e-business system. When a secured application needs to be delivered, it must be deployed on secured desktop computers and secured servers communicating over a secured network with interfaces to an unsecured Internet. All of these security-ensuring activities are going on concurrently and must be integrated into a secured operational e-business system simultaneously. This calls for a great deal of sophisticated planning, and the technology transfer plan ensures delivery of the planned results.

To be sure, not every e-business undertaking requires a technology transfer plan, but such plans are essential for any medium-size to large project and are especially useful where a number of vendors and/or contractors are involved.

Training Plan

This plan is required to ensure that employees and business partners are properly educated and equipped to use the e-business system successfully and efficiently in performance of their job duties. This plan must reflect not only technical aspects of the new system but also any workplace procedural changes. Attention should be focused once again on Exhibit 6.7, which illustrates all aspects of job training that may need modification for the inclusion of security actions because of the new e-business system and its processing.

Infrastructure and Risk Monitoring

This is a critical element of the framework since unknown changes to any of the supporting system elements on which deployment depends could have adverse effects on timely fielding of the e-business system. The infrastructure elements being monitored (i.e., hardware, operating systems, software, and networks) were also included as items monitored by the "Risk Management Review Model" in Appendix D. These three technology elements plus business system–unique and business partner–specific items represent areas of constant and rapid fluctuation. Assumptions concerning the operational environment must be revisited frequently and reassessed for continued validity or new e-business system deployments may experience delays, have operational problems, or be open to unacceptable security risks.

Instructions for Use

Executives may use the review framework in an active or passive manner. Active is recommended if significant improvement in the security of future e-business systems is desired. First, it may be necessary to impose the framework on the system developers and support contractors of an organization if they do not employ one of their own choosing. If this is the case, the problems facing the IT group probably are far greater than can be solved just by requiring the use of this model. If the IT group is not using some formal methodology in the development of e-business systems, a significant overhaul of IT management is called for.

It is hoped that senior executives have some form of IT organizational structure to work through; in such case, a less direct approach will suffice. A more passive implementation would be simply to use the framework and questions in each of the management requirement plan areas as a "crib sheet" to guide progress reviews. Much depends on management style.

MANAGEMENT REQUIREMENTS

Life Cycle Phases	Project Management Plan	Software or Systems Engineering Plan	Internal Controls Plan	Security Plan	Quality Assurance and Testing Plan	Configuration Management Plan	Documentation Plan	Technology Transfer Plan	Training Plan	Infrastructure Risk Monitoring		
										Hardware	Software	Network
Preparation												
Definition												
Design												
Development												
Deployment												
Maintenance												

Exhibit B.1 Systems Development Review Framework

Life Cycle Phases	MANAGEMENT REQUIREMENTS		
	PROJECT MANAGEMENT PLAN: This plan is the control point for project planning, budgeting, resource management, risk management, and technical reviews. This plan should adhere to a corporate standard for project management. A business unit executive should be named sponsor for the project before work begins.		
Preparation	• Have all actions to make this an approved corporate work project been completed? • Have initial draft budgets been prepared with input from business units and other stakeholders? • Has a full feasibility study been performed? If not, why not? has an initially feasible solution been determined? • Has an initial security and project risk assessment been conducted?		
Definition	• Have all business units and stakeholders defined their respective requirements for this system? • Are all requirements associated with an approved business function or corporate management need? • Does the completed definition of requirements have the approval of the security, legal, and audit staffs?		
Design	• Have all requirements been accepted and approved by the appropriate business unit before detailed design begins? • Is a structured design methodology being followed? If not, why not? • Has the initial risk assessment been updated? Is the solution in design still feasible?		
Development	• Has the system's design been approved by the appropriate business unit? Have workplace issues been included? • Are quality assurance procedures being followed during programming? Are structured tests being conducted? • Are all necessary hardware, software, and network acquisitions under way and on schedule?		
Deployment	• Have all systems, including packaged software, completed integration testing before deployment? • Have all supported hardware, software, and network modifications been installed and checked out? • Have systems passed user acceptance testing? • Are all documentation and training materials complete? Have all user acceptance signatures been obtained?		
Maintenance	• Is staffing sufficient and prepared to conduct maintenance on the system? • Is change control in place and being enforced? • Are security and internal controls being monitored according to security policy? Is intrusion detection in place?		

Exhibit B.2 Project Management Plan

Life Cycle Phases	MANAGEMENT REQUIREMENTS
	SOFTWARE ENGINEERING PLAN: This plan concentrates on the structured software engineering methods to be followed when creating the software system or integrating off-the-shelf packages and system components. This plan enforces structured methods throughout the development as an IT best practice.
Preparation	• Has a structured software development and/or integration methodology been selected? Is it sufficient to the task? • From a staffing perspective, can the IT organization support the methodology, or will contractors be required? • Do automated tools, software packages, or additional hardware need to be acquired to support the project?
Definition	• Are users and other stakeholders prepared to interface with the development team in use of the methodology? • Does the engineering methodology capture and document all requirements needed for this development? • Have all business requirements and management plan requirements been captured according to the methodology? • Have all requirements been approved by appropriate managers? Have risk assessments been updated?
Design	• Are "logical" models of the system being developed to record the design? Are all data elements standardized and recorded? Are "logical" models updated as changes in design occur? • Do quality assurance reviews occur periodically? Is the design under configuration management? • Have all system requirements been satisfied by the design? Do all stakeholders concur?
Development	• Do programming and/or integration specifications exist? Do they reflect the design? Have they been reviewed for quality? • Are code inspections being conducted? Are technology transfer and training materials being prepared? • Has unit, system, and integration testing been completed? Have all tests and materials been documented? • Are all code, data, tests, and test materials under configuration management?
Deployment	• Are documentation requirements satisfied? • Are supporting hardware, software packages, and networks ready for deployment? • Have end-to-end system tests with business partners been completed? Have users accepted the system?
Maintenance	• Are requests for system modification submitted for impact analysis? • Are approved changes under change control and configuration management? • Is all systems documentation up-to-date?

Exhibit B.3   Software Engineering Plan

Life Cycle Phases	MANAGEMENT REQUIREMENTS
	INTERNAL CONTROLS PLAN: This plan focuses attention on the need for the system under development to satisfy the legal, accounting, and data consistency requirements of the corporation, the corporation's industry, and regulators. The American Institute of Certified Public Accountants (AICPA) prescribes such rules as does the company's auditor.
Preparation	• Have pertinent legal, accounting, audit, and internal control requirements been identified? Have stakeholders to these requirements been alerted to the need for their assistance in determining those requirements? • Are all regulatory reporting requirements known? Does this effort require a special legal review?
Definition	• Have accountant and auditor stakeholders participated in defining comprehensive system requirements? If not, why not? • Have specific internal controls and audit trails been proposed that are adequate to identified risks and to meet regulatory requirements? • Are specific tests and test data for internal controls being defined? Are system success criteria known?
Design	• Do "logical" design models of the system reflect the presence of internal controls and audit trails? Are specific data and processing "consistency" checks designed into the system? • Have the design of internal controls been reviewed, and are they deemed adequate by an external auditor? • Have test materials for internal controls been independently reviewed and verified as sufficient to verify the controls?
Development	• Have internal control and consistency checks been included in programming specifications before coding begins? • Are internal control and consistency checks under configuration management? • Are all controls and consistency checks being included in program and systems testing?
Deployment	• Have accounting and auditor stakeholders approved the code implementation of specified internal controls and checks? • Are programmed controls adequately documented to facilitate efficient use by auditors during systems operations? • Are user documents and training clear about internal controls and user interface during the systems operation?
Maintenance	• Are routine system modifications reviewed for impact on internal controls and consistency checks? • Are controls periodically tested to ensure continued reliability and to uncover possible tampering with the controls? • Are all controls documented and kept current under CM?

Exhibit B.4 Internal Controls Plan

Life Cycle Phases	MANAGEMENT REQUIREMENTS
	SECURITY PLAN: This plan ensures that security, confidentiality, integrity, and system availability/reliability features are designed into the system under development and are integral to its operation. This is opposed to the piecemeal approach of adding security features onto a system, with little or no analysis, as it nears completion.
Preparation	• Have all pertinent security and data confidentiality requirements been identified? Is a security risk analysis required by statute, regulation, or industry standard practice? What availability/reliability levels are needed to support the business? • Are security stakeholders involved in this development or integration project? If not, why not? Is legal reviewing for security issues? Have any security models or standards been identified that should guide this effort?
Definition	• Has a formal threat assessment been performed to uncover technical and business risks associated with this system? • Has security been included in the project's budget? Are business continuity plans being developed for the system? • Are security control specifications included in the approved statement of a system requirement? Do stakeholders concur?
Design	• Do "logical" design models include security features? Are database controls being designed? • Are design reviews examining security features? Is an independent group reviewing the design for security adequacy? • Are security feature tests being prepared? Are success criteria for these tests known?
Development	• Are security controls being integrated into system's program code and documentation? • Are security controls and security documentation under configuration management? • Are third-party software packages being researched and/or tested for security features and reliability?
Deployment	• Have all security test results been reviewed and approved by security stakeholders? • Are security features still accurately documented? • Do operating instructions reflect security? Is training in security controls complete?
Maintenance	• Are all system changes reviewed for their impact on security and system availability/reliability? • Are all system modifications tested for security rule adherence and for negative security impact? • Are all security documents up-to-date and under configuration management?

Exhibit B.5 Security Plan

Life Cycle Phases	MANAGEMENT REQUIREMENTS		
	QUALITY ASSURANCE (QA) AND TESTING PLAN: This plan prescribes the quality certifications required of the finished software or system. The International Standards Organization (ISO-9000) and American National Standards Institute (ANSI) series guides quality efforts and are required by many customers. System criticality and information sensitivity determine the degree of testing that is appropriate and demonstrates that "reasonable care" was exercised in the development of the system.		
Preparation	• Have quality standards for this development been determined? • Have ISO-9000, ANSI, and/or industry-specific standards been selected to guide the project's quality assurance effort? • Has and independent validation and verification been deemed advisable?		
Definition	• Have all quality characteristics for the system under development been defined and specified (i.e., accuracy, timeliness, etc.)? • Are there quality characteristics measurable and therefore testable? • Is each quality characteristic and its measurement criteria fully documented as a requirement?		
Design	• Are periodic quality reviews scheduled to ensure that "structured" methods are being adhered to by the developers? • When discovered, are design defects being recorded, resolved, and entered into a QA metrics database? • Are test cases and test data being designed by the QA group as the system is being designed?		
Development	• Are documentation and code reviews being conducted independent of the original programmer? • Is unit, program, and systems testing being conducted? • Are coding and other defects being recorded, resolved, and entered into the QA metrics database?		
Deployment	• Are system integration and workplace acceptance tests being conducted? Are performance tests being conducted? • Has all development and testing documentation been through a quality review? • Are all test cases and other test materials finalized before system release to production status?		
Maintenance	• Do quality reviews continue for all changes to the production system? • Are all test cases and other test materials under configuration management? • Is all documentation up-to-date?		

Exhibit B.6 Quality Assurance and Testing Plan

MANAGEMENT REQUIREMENTS

Life Cycle Phases	
	CONFIGURATION MANAGEMENT (CM): This is a project control plan that focuses on the identification and management of work products, or "artifacts," being produced by the development effort. The plan defines how an inventory of all work products (i.e., requirements, designs, code, tests, and documents) will be recorded and accurately maintained for the life of the system. Without CM, work products cannot be monitored properly and confusion results.
Preparation	• Has a CM process been defined for this project? Is it consistent with best practices and corporate policy? Will CM be accomplished manually or using automated tools? Will CM-trained employees be ready on the first day of the project? • Has an individual empowered to enforce CM been identified? Does the person independently report to the project manager? • Does the person monitoring CM have the authority to stop project activities until CM deficiencies are resolved?
Definition	• Do all participants on the project understand the CM process to be used? Is training in automated CM tools complete? • Upon completion of the definition phase, are all requirements identified and under configuration management before proceeding with the system design? Are all changes to requirements being reviewed for overall impact on the project?
Design	• Are all work products from the design being placed under CM? • Are changes to the design being properly brought under CM? Are changes being evaluated for overall impact on the design? • Have test cases and test materials been brought under CM? Are documentation and training materials under CM? • Does the person monitoring CM report to the project manager any deviation from CM policy or process?
Development	• Is all programming documentation and code under CM? Have any spot audits of the CM process and the daily baseline been conducted? Do all program changes undergo an impact analysis to determine effect on the system? • Are all test materials remaining under CM? Are all documentation and training materials still under enforced CM?
Deployment	• Are all system documents, code, reports, testing, and training materials under CM, in their final form, before release of the system production or for sale? Are all baselines final?
Maintenance	• Are all system documents, code, reports, testing, and operations materials maintained under CM consistently updated to reflect the production system accurately? Have any audits been performed to confirm this?

Exhibit B.7 Configuration Management

Life Cycle Phases	MANAGEMENT REQUIREMENTS
	DOCUMENTATION PLAN: This plan concentrates on producing sufficient and comprehensible documentation that accurately depicts the work products of all developmental actions that occur in each life cycle phase such that each document guides the work to be done in subsequent phases
Preparation	• Have all system-level and business-level documentation requirements been identified? Have all legal, regulatory, and best-practice documentation requirements been identified? Has documentation production during systems development, and the maintenance of such documents over the anticipated life of the system been budgeted?
Definition	• Are system requirements being documented in a manner that will facilitate future changes and maintenance by people not involved in the original development effort? • Will human factors be considered in the development of documents and their presentation to employees or customers? • Have documentation requirements been reviewed for comprehensiveness and clarity of purpose?
Design	• Are system design documents being generated using one of the best-practice structured approaches? • Are system test design documents complete? • Are all documents complete and have they been reviewed for quality and clarity? • Are all documents under configuration management (CM)?
Development	• Are program flows being documented so that system interfaces and inputs and outputs are clear and understandable? • Is all programming logic being documented? Are databases and their structure documented? • Are all test plans and test data fully documented so that they can be utilized again for the life of the system? • Is there, under CM, an accurate daily baseline of all programming, database, and testing documentation?
Deployment	• Is all finalized documentation printed or available electronically to all users or customers before release of the system? • Are all final documents, in whatever media, under CM, and do they accurately reflect all other work products under CM?
Maintenance	• Are system and user documents kept current, reflecting changes to the system or to workplace operating procedures? • Are test materials and documents kept up-to-date?

Exhibit B.8 Documentation Plan

Life Cycle Phases	MANAGEMENT REQUIREMENTS		
	TECHNOLOGY TRANSFER PLAN: This plan ensures that "new" technology and features of the "new" system are thoroughly understood by employees/customers who must use and maintain them. This is true even if the system's operation is to be outsourced. Usability, maintainability, and sustainability are the objectives of this plan.		
Preparation	• Is the system's proposed technology consistent with approved corporate standards? Are new standards needed? Have the issues of usability, maintainability, and sustainability been evaluated during the feasibility study? • Should a "pilot" project for this "new" technology be considered?		
Definition	• Have all technical interfaces and sociotechnical interactions been identified for this system? • Are workplace procedural changes needed? Who will modify those procedures? Have necessary employee/customer skills for training been identified? Have technology transfer activities been funded? Are any acquisitions required?		
Design	• Has a strategy for the transfer of technology from developers/contractors to users/employees been developed? • Has a strategy for the transfer of the systems from developers/contractors to users/employees been developed? • Has each strategy been funded?		
Development	• Has the technology transfer strategy been approved by all stakeholders to the project? • Are all system design and development work products ready for transfer? • Have acquisitions to support the transfer of technology been completed? Are site surveys and transfer plans required?		
Deployment	• Are all physical office locations ready for the insertion of the technology? • Are early deployments being audited to obtain feedback that may influence the remainder of the deployments? • Are all management requirement categories of this framework completed prior to full fielding of the system?		
Maintenance	• Have all elements of the system needed for effective and efficient maintenance been turned over to maintenance personnel? • Have operations and maintenance personnel accepted responsibility for the system? • Are support contracts with suppliers in place?		

Exhibit B.9 Technology Transfer Plan

Life Cycle Phases	MANAGEMENT REQUIREMENTS		
	TRAINING PLAN: This plan directs the identification, preparation, and dissemination of training and instructional materials needed for the successful deployment, use, maintenance, and operation of the final developed system. This includes modified workplace procedures and forms for use by employees.		
Preparation	• Do mandated training requirements exist? Are there industry-related standards for instructional or training materials? • What are competitors providing their customers or employees? Is professional training contractor support needed? • Is training included in the initial budget projection?		
Definition	• Are criteria to ensure successful learning being incorporated into the specifications for technical training materials? • Does the company have the expertise to do this? • Have the training's presentation media been determined and included in the project's budget?		
Design	• Are training materials being designed concurrent with the design of the system? Does the system's design team include instructional design experience? Will training materials test user interaction with security features? • Do supporting contractor's training design and presentation abilities meet professional standards?		
Development	• Are training materials being prepared as systems near completion of programming and testing? • Are training materials in agreement with actual design and programming documentation? Do training materials reflect how the system really will work? Are anticipated error conditions and resolution procedures included in the training? • Have training materials been reviewed independently by the business units implementing the system?		
Deployment	• Are training materials being evaluated as part of scheduled pilot projects before full deployment? • Have training materials been completed and checked for quality before full deployment of the system or before sale?		
Maintenance	• Are training and other instructional materials updated as system changes occur? • Are training and instructional materials kept under configuration management?		

Exhibit B.10 Training Plan

227

Life Cycle Phases	MANAGEMENT REQUIREMENTS			
		Infrastructure and Risk Monitoring		
		Hardware	Software	Networks
	INFRASTRUCTURE AND RISK MONITORING: As part of a systems development or systems integration effort, this activity monitors all other management requirement plans and the hardware, software, and network support infrastructure for risks that may adversely affect the success of the project. This focus on risk management is done in conjunction with Appendix D.			
Preparation	• What risks, identified during previous projects, may pertain to this development or integration effort? • Are processing support infrastructures stable and sufficient for this effort or must new hardware, software, and networks be acquired and implemented? Are these acquisitions budgeted?			
Definition	• Have risks, identified during the feasibility study, a formal risk analysis, or through use of Appendix D, been factored into this project's plans? Has a mechanism to monitor these risks been determined? • Have mitigation plans for unresolved risks been developed for later use if need be?			
Design	• Are system designs being reviewed for risks to information security, processing integrity, and customer acceptability? Is the need for this system still valid? • Is the development schedule still valid? Is the budget still sufficient? • Are all management requirement demands being satisfied or is the project at risk due to lack of SDP enforcement?			
Development	• Are all development work products in synch and fully documented? Are project work products under CM? • Are contractors delivering according to their statement of work? • Have identified security and integrity risks been addressed during development? Are they fully tested and documented?			
Deployment	• Have necessary infrastructure upgrades been received, installed, and tested to determine their stability? • Are employees prepared to operate and maintain the system? Is the workplace ready? Is the product ready for sale? • Have support vendors and/or business partners delivered according to plan?			
Maintenance	• Are all the management requirements needed for systems operation and maintenance complete? • Have any necessary risk mitigation changes been fully incorporated into the final system? • Are disaster recovery and business continuity plans in place and tested? Will they be updated as changes occur?			

Exhibit B.11 Infrastructure and Risk Monitoring

A Corporate Plan of Action for Securing E-Business Systems (Sample)

Having examined the growth of e-business systems, the common vulnerabilities facing such systems, the threats posed to the business by such vulnerabilities, and the types of information security solutions that are available, an organization is faced with developing a plan of action that will correct current security deficiencies while creating an environment where future security threats are managed as a normal course of business. This appendix is a sample of such a plan.

After reading Chapters 1 through 4, which defined the breadth and depth of information and computer security concerns, it should be clear that discipline and dedication will be needed to secure the e-business environment. E-business security will not be realized because of good intentions and it will not happen because a few security "aficionados" in the corporation see the need and take the initiative. And it will not happen as long as management is willing to absorb security-related losses or pass them along to the consumer rather than take actions to secure vulnerable systems. Security will only come about through the direct involvement of executive management and the governance they bring to all enterprise-wide undertakings. Their perspective provides the balance needed for such programs to be realistic in expectations and practical in implementation. E-business security initiatives run a fine line between enabling or stifling e-business and must be managed in such a way that the line is continuously scrutinized. The methodology for striking the balance between enablement and the stifling of business is the process of risk management, and corporate risk management is a function of executive management. As has been shown, there are many potential threats to the corporation that must be analyzed on a continuing basis, with such analysis providing the fundamental justifications required to adequately fund future e-business security initiatives.

This corporate plan of action provides a sample, for executive purposes, of the steps commonly required of most organizations to establish and administer a cost-effective e-business security program. A plan that can function on a continuing basis in the years ahead even as technologies and business objectives change. A security plan of action is a management program that enables a business to thrive within a framework of risk that is deemed acceptable to all those who have a stake in the success of the organization. As the interdependencies of e-businesses grow, this list of stakeholders will expand and the framework for analyzing and accepting risk must be periodically revisited to ensure proper coverage.

Likewise, as e-business grows, the complexity of business operations increases to the point that the management of IT system activities and the management of security merge such that a failure in systems management can result in an increase in business vulnerability and the creation of potential breaches of security. *As an example: one of the most common system management problems is the challenge of keeping accurate inventories of corporate personal computers, laptops, software licenses, and up-to-date knowledge of software running on corporate host computers and servers.* In fact, by encouraging the entrepreneurial behavior of employees, many companies have unwittingly contaminated their processing environments with all sorts of "homegrown" software brought into work by those same employees. This reality was largely substantiated by many organizations as they attempted to identify software that needed Y2K remediation or replacement. It was often discovered that unknown software resided on critical processing systems and no one was sure what it did, much less whether it was Y2K-compliant. Since Y2K, companies have hopefully not allowed this situation to be recreated through inattention to the fundamental system management discipline of software configuration management.

This plan of action assumes that certain fundamental IT system management disciplines and "best practices" either are missing entirely or are poorly applied and enforced.

This plan, unlike many computer security plans, first addresses the adequacy of fundamental IT and system management activities and then lays out a likely series of security actions needed to secure an e-business. The starting point, however, will not be the generally publicized actions for establishing and managing confidentiality, integrity controls, and infrastructure availability/reliability for the e-business. The starting point will be the assessment and "shoring up" of fundamental IT and system management practices on which secured systems and processing environments depend. There is an added value to this approach in that if the e-business elements of the company are in confusion and are being mismanaged, a focus on security management alone will not greatly improve the security posture of the business. This is because integrity, confidentiality, and the ready availability/reliability of system processing assets are to be found primarily in "good" overall IT management, not just in "firewalls," encryption, and other security techniques. The proper functioning of security techniques and controls depend instead on the structured and disciplined management of all facets of IT and will necessarily be ineffective and subject to subversion in an unmanaged system environment.

E-BUSINESS SECURITY CORPORATE MANAGEMENT PLAN

Prepared By
The Office of Chief Information Officer

TABLE OF CONTENTS

Note: Items listed in this plan are illustrative and not exhaustive. Actual action plan items can be determined only after detailed analysis of the current state of security of an enterprise.

EXECUTIVE SUMMARY

This plan of action describes the actions required for an accelerated, enterprise-wide improvement of the corporation's information security posture, with special emphasis on our e-business systems and their operation. Since the summer of 2001, the chief information officer has been initiating efforts to strengthen the corporation's information security function. As a result, the board of directors recently approved the creation of a capital investment fund to secure our vital e-business systems and operations. This fund will finance a comprehensive effort to assure the confidentiality, integrity, and availability/reliability of corporate information, business application processes, and the computing infrastructure. This security initiative has already launched several sub-initiatives to rectify security and systems management deficiencies reported by last year's audit review.

Actions in this plan respond not only to vulnerabilities in the security posture of our vital e-business systems, but also to weaknesses that have been noted in our overall IT and systems management practices on which effective security controls are anchored.

This plan recognizes that some dramatic improvements can be immediate and inexpensive (i.e., by simply enforcing existing security controls), while others will depend on considerable investment and will take time.

For security to work, there must be accountability. For that reason, the plan states in unambiguous terms the responsibilities of "key" officials and executive committees. Individuals directly responsible for this plan and individuals directly responsible to support the actions in this plan will have their performance contracts modified accordingly.

This plan is suitable for release to oversight entities on a need-to-know basis.

Signed
Chief Executive Officer

1. Purpose

This plan prescribes actions for the accelerated enterprise-wide improvement of the corporation's information security posture, with special emphasis on our vital e-business systems and their operation.

2. Background

Since the summer of 2001, the chief information officer, at the request of the "board," has been initiating efforts to strengthen the corporation's information and electronic business processing security function. As a result, the following actions have already been taken, leading up to the publication of this action plan:

a. There has been created a center for information security (CIS) within the office of the CIO.

b. The board of directors have been briefed on the cyber-security threat facing the corporation and are in full support of this initiative.

c. A capital investment "revolving" fund has been established to finance those enterprise-wide security actions that are common to all operating divisions. The fund will also provide fast-track financing of those unique security measures that are requested and justified by each business unit.

d. A subcommittee for e-business security has been created to advise the executive committee on e-business initiatives.

This strategic plan for improved information and e-business security will have lasting effect, because while it addresses today's immediate risks, it has an eye for tomorrow by viewing security as a business "enabler" and by requiring that a "due diligence" attitude be brought to all future IT and e-business projects. Past corporate efforts have often pursued the correction of isolated audit findings, with little attention given to the root causes of control weaknesses. While this plan describes actions that correct the security deficiencies reported in our recent annual audit, the plan also requires that the corporation view the securing of IT and our e-business systems as essential to the success of the business. To achieve an environment of manageable risk, our focus must be not only on security technologies but also on the e-business and system management policies and practices on which effective security depends. This plan will address both short-term and long-range actions designed to achieve an integrated state of security across all aspects of the corporation, with an immediate concentration on our e-business operations.

3. Planning Principles

This plan was prepared according to the following guiding principles:

a. This plan is in agreement with the corporation's five-year capital investment plan for the years 2002 through 2007. A newly established "revolving" fund provides immediate financing for critical short-term security
actions and allows business units to reimburse the fund over a three-year
period.

b. The plan acknowledges that some dramatic security improvements may be
immediate, requiring only the enforcement of existing security policies
and the adoption and enforcement of system management "best practices,"
and need little or no out-of-pocket expenditures. For example, major
improvements may be gained simply by requiring that security access
"rules" on security software and existing "firewalls" comply with existing
corporate policy. Also, great gains may be realized by installing system
"patches" as soon as they are available from vendors.

c. The plan acknowledges that other improvements will come only after the
implementation of a risk management program and the execution of commercial contracts for certain managed security services and security con-
sultations. There is also an acknowledgment that investment in corporate
security personnel and training will be required.

d. The successful implementation of this plan will also require that the CIO,
business unit managers, and other appropriate "line" and "staff" managers
be evaluated annually on their degree of support for the goals of this plan.

4. Roles and Responsibilities

a. *Chief Information Officer (CIO)*. Under the authorities creating the position of CIO, this corporate officer is ultimately responsible for the accom-
plishment of all actions in this plan. The CIO will:

   (1) establish a corporate security program,

   (2) chair the Subcommittee on E-Business Security reporting the Executive Committee on E-Business Initiatives,

   (3) chair an executive security group to assure senior staff and business
   unit manager involvement in security improvement,

   (4) report quarterly to the CEO and annually to the board of directors on
   the "state of corporate IT and e-business security,"

   (5) review this plan for adequacy and update it annually.

b. *Senior Staff and Business Unit Managers*. Because security challenges cut
across the entire corporation and affect the bottom line, the major burden
of implementing security improvements rests with those officials who
have direct control over business function and staff resources. Therefore,
senior staff and business unit managers must:

(1) give sufficient emphasis and support to this plan to assure consistent achievement in their respective business areas and at all facilities;

(2) dedicate sufficient staffing and resources to accomplish necessary security functions;

(3) justify the need for additional resources;

(4) enforce existing and future IT and e-business security policies and procedures;

(5) certify in writing the completion of System Security Certifications; and

(6) certify in writing requests for "waiver" from any part of this plan.

c. *Executive Security Group*—chaired by the CIO will champion this corporate initiative and provide support for the achievement of these planned actions. The group will:

(1) receive periodic briefings from the CIO and the subcommittee on e-business security about progress against this plan and about any "new" risks that threaten the successful implementation of e-business initiatives,

(2) approve significant additions, deletions, or modifications to this plan,

(3) assist in solving any cross-organizational barriers to security improvement,

(4) facilitate the funding necessary to execute this plan.

d. *Subcommittee on E-Business Security*—will assure that the corporation deploys only e-business applications and computing infrastructures exhibiting a degree of security commensurate with the risk facing the company and consistent with "due diligence" principles.

e. *Computer System Security Officers (CSSO)*—will assure that security actions for their respective organizations are implemented and enforced.

f. *Corporate Audit Committee*—will periodically conduct independent audits of the effectiveness and adequacy of the security measures taken to protect corporate IT assets and e-business systems.

5. Short-Term (Accelerated Actions)

a. Correct Deficient System Management Practices

Description: Since effective IT and e-business security is largely anchored in the fundamental management of IT, it is important to identify and correct any deficiencies in this area before spending large sums on sophisticated security controls and techniques. Many threats to information processing *integrity* and system *availability* stem from a lack of enforcement of standards, structured analysis and programming practices, the lack of testing, the inability or unwillingness to manage configurations, a failure to keep documentation current, and other failures. Until these deficiencies are corrected, we can expect only marginal improvement from the implementation of other, more expensive security controls.

Indicator of Problems: A recent internal audit report indicates that the corporation has failed to keep current our Y2K baseline inventory data (i.e., configuration control data). After the thousands of dollars expended to create this database, and knowing that similar data are needed for securing our e-business systems, the failure to keep it current demonstrates disturbing shortcomings in our management of IT. What other basic IT management controls are being poorly administered?

Action: Each business unit manager will cause an independent review of the adherence to "best practices" of the system management of the IT and e-business systems upon which their unit depends. The results will cause, in coordination with the CIO and the operational IT support unit or contractor, the correction of identified deficiencies.

Funding Considerations: Possible contracts for independent review by external experts. No expense is anticipated to correct deficiencies unless the noted deficiency is outside the scope of a management function already associated with good IT management practices.

b. Update IT Asset Inventory Data

Description: Before serious risk assessments can be conducted, the corporation must possess complete inventories of all electronic information files, hardware and software locations and licenses, network components and connections, and the operational topologies of our e-business operations. Furthermore, it is imperative that such inventories be kept up-to-date. The adequacy of the procedural mechanisms to accomplish this will be reported as an output from the previous action—Correct Deficient System Management Practices.

Indicator of Problems: It was discovered during the company's Y2K remediation effort that IT inventories were grossly inaccurate and in some cases were not kept at all. Corrective action was ordered at that time to establish and enforce stringent configuration management for all IT assets.

Action: Each business unit manager will cause a review to determine the accuracy of exiting IT inventories. Reports will be made to the appropriate business unit manager and the CIO.

Funding Considerations: No additional expense is anticipated to perform this action. The resources needed to keep inventories current should already be included in the operating budget.

c. Review and Update E-Business Application Profiles

Description: Equally important to keeping IT asset inventory data current is the requirement to have accurate, complete, and timely documentation describing each corporate e-business application. This "profile" must include all the "best practice" documentation prescribed as standard for an automated application developed using structured techniques. Also important is the ability of support system organizations and contractors to maintain such documentation such that at a moment's notice a complete and fully accurate accounting of an application to include its design, hardware requirements, files, uses, and software version/release can be made. It is also critical that the application's processing "path" to and through other software applications be up-to-date.

Indicator of Problems: Recent computer management reviews have shown that much of the information required to perform an "internal consistency audit" is not available. Too much information is in the "heads" of employees, thus putting the company at risk.

Action: Each business unit manager will cause an independent review of the condition of e-business application support in their business area. The CIO will provide guidance for the conduct of this review.

Funding Considerations: Since this type of documentation is necessary to perform systems maintenance, it should be covered by the existing operating budget; no additional funding will be provided.

d. Implement Windows NT Enterprise Security Policy

Description: This action implements a security policy recommended by the CIO as a "due diligence" course of action for any organization using Windows NT. The policy strengthens the formula for passwords (particularly those for network authentication) and for the protection of system administrator privileges.

Indicator of Problems: Sampling of thousands of accounts during several different penetration tests conducted last summer document that weak passwords, poor user account housekeeping, and unprotected system administrator privileges are chronic and widespread problems for the corporation. Unacceptable password strength and administration was called "the most mundane yet all-important countermeasure" by the authors of the security text *Hacking Exposed.*

Action: Business unit managers and staff directors will certify completion of this action by the end of the year.

Funding Considerations: No additional expenditures are required.

e. Remove Unsecured Dial-Ups

Description: This action is to implement the prohibition on all unsecured dial-in connections by employees, contractors, or other individuals with access to corporate data. This policy was established last year by the CIO and was approved by the executive committee. The most common case of this vulnerability is where an individual attaches to his or her workstation or laptop a dial-up modem and operates a remote access product such as PCAnywhere. Free utilities are available that permit facilities to scan their analog phone connections to find unsecured connections. This action is to initially disable each unsecured connection and take measures to assure that the individual who installed the connection is educated about the corporate policy. Repeat offenders will be disciplined.

Indicator of Problems: Our Y2K readiness planning in November 1999 uncovered a significant number of PCAnywhere connections in certain organizations. Those connections were disabled. Undoubtedly, other organizations have similar problems.

Action: Each business unit manager and staff director will require that all workstations, laptops, servers, routers, or other network-connected devices having a modem connection be inventoried. Modems will be removed if feasible or their continued use will be authorized in writing as mission-critical and approved for continued operation on an adequately secured basis by the end of 2002.

Funding Considerations: No expenditure of funds is required.

f. Implement Configuration Standards for External Connections

Description: All corporate external electronic connections, such as Internet gateways, must incorporate the controls prescribed in Corporate Instruction xxxx, *Security of External Electronic Connections.* This action requires the system administrator for each connection to set certain devices and software switches to harden the connection against tampering or attack. These controls are considered minimum for "due diligence" attention to such connections.

Indicator of Problems: Two recent penetration tests documented widespread configuration weaknesses in numerous external connections with the Internet. For example, during 2001, several connections at a corporate facility were found to be a "zombie" device for suspicious traffic originating from out of the country and appeared to target one of our principal suppliers.

Action: All corporate external electronic connections must be configured to conform to the controls in the Corporate Instruction. Business unit managers and staff directors will certify completion of this action by the end of 2002, including any deferred actions resulting from the need to acquire upgraded devices for certain locations.

Funding Considerations: Some organizations may find their connection device too obsolete or underequipped to satisfy all controls. Replacement equipment may have to be procured; these products are moderately priced.

g. Audit Personal "Clearances" of Systems Staff

Description: Offices are expected to examine the security clearances of incumbent computer staff, especially those having system administrator privileges. These staff (employees or contractor) should be in positions having a sensitivity designation of no less than "critical-sensitive" and must have a background investigation commensurate to the sensitivity designation. Employees or contractors who have system administrator privileges and permissions have enormous technical capabilities to affect the broadest range of security for the corporate system.

Indicator of Problems: The full extent of this problem is not known, but it is likely that because of the speed with which the corporation has expanded its e-business infrastructure, some percentage of system administrators are not covered by these controls.

Action: Business unit managers and staff directors will initiate this action for clearances of personnel supporting their business area. The Office of Corporate Security will request and coordinate background investigations for the business units.

Funding Considerations: A background investigation for a critical-sensitive position costs less than $3,000. Since each facility should have only two staff members with system administrator privileges, the cost per facility is negligible.

h. Require Incident Reporting as a Standard Practice

Description: Many corporations maintain a computer incident response capability (CIRC) to assure that suspected security breaches and vulnerabilities, such as viruses, are detected, reported, and corrected as quickly as possible and with minimal impact on e-business operations. It is the intent of this action to establish a corporate CIRC as a "key" element of our e-business security initiative.

Indicator of Problems: In August 2000, the *Fun Love* virus caused a six-hour denial of service to e-mail across parts of the corporation. In February 2001, the *Anna Kournikova* virus caused an additional four hours of downtime for e-mail services. E-mail is essential to the operation of the corporate e-business and such episodes must be minimized.

Action: A corporate CIRC will be established out of the office of the CIO, with all system support organizations reporting all incidents as soon as they are detected. The CIRC has the responsibility to disseminate incident data, whether substantiated or not, to all system support organizations. (Detection of suspicious activities at the system or network level will be addressed in the next action item.) Business unit managers will require reporting to the CIRC.

Funding Considerations: Funding for the corporate CIRC will come from the office of the CIO. Instructions will be generated on how to determine local expenses for each system's support organization.

i. Install Intrusion Detection Systems (IDS) on Critical Systems

Description: It is imperative to know when corporate networks and host computer systems are being "attacked" from the outside. It is equally important to know when employees are abusing system and access privileges. To date, the corporation has "built out" our entire e-business infrastructure without the ability to detect intrusions. This action requires that IDS be applied to critical networks and "backroom" host computers as soon as possible.

Indicator of Problems: The Federal Bureau of Investigation estimates that approximately 30 percent of system intrusions originate from outside an organization while the remaining 70 percent are "insider" jobs. In our highly competitive marketplace neither situation can be tolerated. While other actions in this plan are intended to help prevent security problems, they will not always be successful. At a minimum, the corporation must know when it has been "attacked" and possibly penetrated and when the trust we place in our employees has been violated.

Action: Each business unit manager will initiate an analysis to determine, based on the criticality of systems, where intrusion detection sensors should be placed to detect attempted intrusions of our e-business systems. Placement of recommended IDS should be completed one year from the effective date of this plan.

Funding Considerations: An IDS placement study will be performed through a contract being administered by the Office of the CIO. Funding for actual IDS procurement, placement, and monitoring will be the obligation of the business units served by the network or "backroom" host computer system. This cost may be significant, but given our e-business systems dependence, it is considered a "due diligence" measure.

j. Conduct Local Focus Security Reviews

Description: Security review teams will be established at each facility to correct a small but pervasive set of vulnerabilities in a few systems and at locations that are considered most critical to our e-business operations. These are operational day-to-day problems; for example, a security check of a "secured area" at the end of the day. These vulnerabilities are easily exploited and may lead to cases of unauthorized disclosure, fraud, and damage to business data and confidential customer and business partner data.

Indicator of Problems: Internal audits by the corporate audit staff, as well as contracted security testing, have documented that these vulnerabilities are commonplace.

Action: (1) All accounts of separated employees, contractors, and others no longer needing access will be removed. Accounts unused for more than 60 days will require reauthorization certifying the need for account continuation. (2) Beginning immediately, all account holders will have newly signed security agreements detailing their privileges and acknowledging their responsibilities and allowing the corporation to monitor their system activities. (3) All client workstations, servers, routers, and any other network-connected devices will install all security patches immediately. (4) All client workstations, servers, routers, and any other network-connected device will have "security banners" displayed for all necessary e-business services. (5) All unnecessary services will be disabled or waivers will be authorized by the business unit manager.

Funding Considerations: These weaknesses are inexpensive to correct, but they do require enforcement vigilance at the local office level. Suffiency of current funding levels to perform their action will be reviewed every six months.

k. Conduct Awareness Training

Description: A corporate Intranet web-based security awareness curriculum now exists for orientation and annual refreshment in security practices applicable to the average employee using or accessing e-business applications.

Indicator of Problems: A number of symptoms associated with employee ignorance of basic security practices are regularly observed across the corporation and are especially troublesome in our e-business operations. These include:

- opening unsolicited virus-infected e-mail, which causes rapid proliferation of viruses across the corporation or a resurgence of prior extinguished viruses,
- poor choice of passwords or not protecting their password,
- careless handling or disposal of sensitive company or client information,
- dissemination of sensitive information beyond the practice of "need to know."

Action: Business unit managers and staff directors are responsible for this action and will assure that all local office staff are administered the security awareness training.

Funding Considerations: This action requires no funds.

l. Perform System Penetration Testing

Description: Conduct periodic penetration tests of the corporation's e-business infrastructure and "back-office" host computer systems. These tests include network, dial-up attempts, and physical penetration of "key" corporate facilities housing the components of our e-business infrastructure.

Indicator of Problems: Enforcement of best security practices has suffered because of the lack of assigned security personnel and resources at each of our major corporate facilities housing our e-business infrastructure. It has also been noted that corporate VIPs get special treatment when it comes to security enforcement. This must end!

Action: (1) A contract for independent third-party penetration testing will be provided by the CIO for the purpose of providing support to the CSSOs in their enforcement task. (2) Results of tests will be reported to CIO and CEO quarterly. (3) Business unit managers and staff directors will present "get well" plans and progress against those plans as needed.

Funding Considerations: This action will be funded by the office of chief information officer and the office of corporate security.

m. Enterprise-Wide Antivirus Regimen

Description: An antivirus "regimen" will provide stronger protections against virus outbreaks. The "regimen" will include services for rapid virus product updates to all field locations, reduced manual intervention to distribute and install product updates, automated policy setting, and feedback assurance reporting to management that installations have in fact been made.

Indicator of Problems: Over the past two years, the corporation has been attacked by numerous viruses that have cost millions of dollars in disturbance to workforce productivity, diversion of scarce technical staff resources, and some denial of services to our e-business operations. Even small amounts of "downtime" must be avoided if at all possible.

Action: The office of the CIO will award a contract for the deployment of a corporate-wide antivirus "regimen" by the end of 2002. Each business unit manager and staff director will ensure proper staffing for this effort in their support IT units.

Funding Considerations: The office of the CIO will fund the contract. Business unit managers and staff directors will fund necessary supporting staff positions.

n. Install All Vendor Security Patches

Description: Vendors are continuously fixing security flaws in their software. These fixes are released as "patches." To be effective, they must be installed as soon as they are received.

Indicator of Problems: Recent findings by internal audit indicate that patches often go days and even weeks before being installed on our production systems. At times, security patches have been among these delayed installations. This may leave the corporation open to unnecessary risk.

Action: Business unit managers and staff directors will ensure that all security patches received from support vendors are installed immediately. If such installation would interfere with production work, patch installs must be scheduled to be operational within a time frame approved by the appropriate operations manager.

Funding Considerations: No additional funds are required for this action.

6. Long-Range and Continuous Actions
   a. Appoint Computer System Security Officers (CSSOs)

Description: Every corporate facility and office must staff a skilled and qualified CSSO who works on e-business and other IT security matters at least as a primary duty. In some cases, it may be possible to time-share the CSSO across several locations in a commuter area, but coverage should not be rendered ineffectual because of this concept.

Indicator of Problems: The prestigious SANS Institute cites "assigning untrained people to maintain security, and providing neither the training nor time to make it possible to learn and perform" as number one in the institute's Top Ten security mistakes made by senior managers.

Action: Business unit managers and staff directors will cause the assignment of a CSSO to each facility and/or office. The OCIO, in coordination with the corporate director of personnel, will establish a career path for CSSOs. They will also define policies and standards for CSSO duties and create a developmental program for continuous CSSO education and training.

Funding Considerations: The OCIO will fund the initial analysis to determine career path actions and curriculum identification. Business unit managers and staff directors will fund additional personnel to perform the CSSO function as required.

b. Deploy Security (CSSO) Training

Description: CSSOs require a comprehensive and continuous training program not dependent on travel or attendance in classroom settings. Web-based training media makes effective remote learning possible.

Indicator of Problems: Associated with untrained and insufficiently skilled CSSOs are:

- ignorance of security principles, fundamentals, and security control techniques,
- inability to perform significant elements of local security programs,
- inability to properly document facility security, and
- ineffective management and oversight of aspects of local security.

Action: The corporate security program will establish the contractual vehicle for CSSO training and establish the initial corporate-wide training program for CSSOs. This will be completed within six months. Fifty percent of incumbent CSSOs will complete the training course within six months of course availability; 100 percent will complete training within one year. Business unit managers and staff directors will direct training at the local level.

Funding Considerations: This action is funded by the corporate security program.

c. Practice Risk Management

Description: Risk management is the process whereby the corporation institutionalizes e-business security. Risk management is also the process whereby security is continuously scrutinized and adjusted as technologies, vulnerabilities, and risks to the corporation and our business partners change.

Indicator of Problems: Historically, every few years the corporation has been advised by the audit committee to perform computer security vulnerability assessments to determine risks to the corporation and to assist in making intelligent decisions about corrective security actions. E-business processes require a much more aggressive approach because e-business systems are in a constant state of change. Because of this, computer security risk management, as a business discipline and process, must become integral to corporate decision making.

Action: After due consideration, the CEO and the executive committee, and in full recognition that costs will be incurred, the following risk management actions will be initiated over the next several months:

(1) E-business security risks and recommended corrective safeguards will be presented to and reviewed by the CIO and the executive security group monthly for the next six months and quarterly thereafter.

(2) E-business security risks and corrective and mitigating actions will be reported to the CEO and the executive committee quarterly.

(3) Each existing e-business application, legacy system, and support infrastructure will be analyzed for security risks (i.e., threats to integrity, confidentiality, and availability/reliability) by the end of this year, with next year's budget reflecting necessary corrective and mitigating actions. All planned actions and budget requests will be coordinated through the CIO to eliminate duplication of actions.

(4) All "new" e-business systems in development or being procured and integrated will be subjected to a thorough security assessment to determine risk and corrective actions.

(5) All e-business systems being planned will require a full security assessment of their design, and decisions concerning security controls will be made before development continues.

(6) All e-business systems in development will adhere to "structured" analysis, design, development, testing, and documentation techniques to ensure that security is maintainable during the life of the system.

Funding Considerations: Security risk management and adherence to "structured" system development techniques have been the policy of the corporation since the mid-1990s. Methods and techniques to carry out this action are assumed to be in place. If not, each business unit manager and supporting IT organization will execute this action out of existing budget. This area will be audited for compliance beginning with our next series of biannual audits.

d. Deploy Security Training

Description: Security training, beyond general employee awareness, has as its target three classes of corporate employees: users, managers, and system administrators. This planned action addresses the need to obtain and conduct "platform"-specific training for each of these classes. While there are many sources of off-the-shelf training available from vendors and security associations and special interest groups, the corporation chooses to tailor security training to our particular e-business applications and operational environment.

Indicator of Problems: A lack of standard "platform" and e-business application security education and training exists in the corporation. Until now, personnel have performed security functions based on common sense, their own readings, or their experience in prior jobs. This has led to uneven security at best and chaos at worst. We cannot expect corporate personnel to practice security "best practices" if they are not cognizant of those practices and are not trained in their execution. The corporation wishes to remedy this situation.

Action: The executive committee on recommendation of the executive security group approves the development of the following types of security training for employees of the corporation.

- "platform"-specific security training for business operators of each of our e-business applications,
- "platform"-specific security training for managers, and
- "platform"-specific system administrator security training in how to "harden" our infrastructure.

Business unit managers will fund development of such training and presentation of courses in the most cost-effective manner so long as the goal of corporate security training is met by this time next year. Training will also meet with the independent approval of the corporate audit committee. Other training in such topics as contingency planning and disaster recovery will be sponsored corporate-wide by the CIO. All training development and presentation will be coordinated through the office of the CIO.

Funding Considerations: A contract for security training will be established by the CIO. Initial budgets will be determined as requirements are defined by each Business Unit Manager and Staff Director. Training budgets will cover periodic and refresher training as determined by employee attrition, rate of turnover, and new assignments.

e. Implement Enterprise-Wide Intrusion Detection (ID)

Description: This action will coordinate an effective and integrated enterprise-wide intrusion detection capability. Because of the corporation's dependence on real-time e-business communications, ID will be considered our first line of security defense for all e-business operations and will be consulted continuously as we adjust our preventive security measures and policies. It is important that networks, servers, host mainframes, and storage devices housing sensitive corporate and customer data be monitored.

Indicator of Problems: Many CIO-sponsored penetration tests have been conducted with none having been detected by the facilities that were targeted in the tests.

Action: The CIO and the Subcommittee on E-Business Security will cause network and legacy host computers to be monitored by state-of-the-art ID systems manned by analysts experienced in interpreting ID data and responding so as to limit damage should an intrusion occur. Networks, especially those with external links to the Internet, will be monitored by this time next year. Mainframes and storage devices will be under ID within 18 months.

Funding Considerations: The executive security group will fund ID acquisition and support staff recruitment. Ongoing maintenance of an ID capability will be the responsibility of business unit managers and staff directors.

f. Implement Public Key Infrastructure (PKI) and Digital Signatures

Description: Several of our existing e-business applications and many of our systems now in design and implementation require an implementation of PKI and digital signatures to satisfy the corporate and industry goal of access with trust. Access with trust requires strong authentication and non-repudiation to guarantee the integrity of business transactions and ensure the confidentiality of customer or corporate data when in transit over the Internet.

Indicator of Problems: Increasingly, the corporation is transmitting "in the clear" and without proper authentication codes business transaction data and customer information over the Internet and the corporate Intranet. E-mail is often being used to exchange corporate proprietary information with business partners where electronic signatures and text encryption is merited. Other security techniques, such as shared secret passwords or personnel identification numbers, are not sufficient; they do not scale up to large user communities, are difficult to administer, and are more susceptible to compromise than when using public key encryption and digital signatures.

Action: A corporate directive on the use of public key encryption will be coordinated, approved, and become policy by 01/01/03. Digital signatures will be implemented for transactions and documents that require authentication by 01/01/04. Certificates will be managed through a third-party certificate provider under contract to the CIO.

Funding Considerations: This action will be funded by the corporation and administered through the office of the CIO.

g. Implement Simplified Sign-On

Description: This action will implement more secure and efficient sign-on capabilities for employees. Technologies that enable more secure identification and authentication and that simplify the sign-on event have become economically advantageous.

Indicator of Problems: The need for more positive and secure identification and authentication has been the subject of two internal audit reports. Evidence that employees are increasingly frustrated about the difficulties with the sign-on process surfaces in all corporate discussions and surveys about security.

Action: The CIO will contract for an assessment of problems facing the corporation in implementing a simplified sign-on capability. Following the assessment, the CIO, in coordination with business unit managers and staff directors, will prepare a concept of operations document and a business plan for implementation.

Funding Considerations: The office of the CIO will fund the initial assessment of this effort.

h. Implement Security Testing

Description: In the future, it is imperative that the corporation deploy only fully secured e-business applications. This action requires that all e-business applications and other systems under development be tested for anticipated security vulnerabilities before being fielded.

Indicator of Problems: The corporation, like most technology-dependent organizations, has been playing catch-up when it comes to security. Business applications and networks have been deployed with little thought given to secured transactions. "Due diligence" requires that we test for security.

Action: Each business unit manager and staff director will require that all future e-business systems and support networks be thoroughly tested for security "defects" before deployment. The office of the CIO will incorporate security testing procedures into the corporate systems development standard and the audit group will review for compliance.

Funding Considerations: The office of the CIO will fund this action and implement it in each business area IT support department. Costs should include training for all systems analysts designing and supporting e-business applications and networks.

i. Certify and Accredit E-Business Applications

Description: All future e-business applications and supporting infrastructure projects will be certified and accredited by an independent third party to be secure per the design, development, and testing specifications for the system. Certification will be planned for all e-business systems and infrastructure projects now under development or in acquisition. This includes in-house as well as contractor-developed systems and managed services contracts. Without this critical action, corporate management, stockholders, the board, and our business partners have no assurances that appropriate security safeguards are implemented in an e-business system or application.

Indicator of Problems: The corporation has never required that e-business or other IT systems be certified compliant with a prescribed set of security specifications. The practice has been to consider security "after the fact" and usually after an incident has occurred or an audit has discovered security defects.

Action: A professional service contract will be awarded by the office of the CIO for long-term assistance in implementing a certification and accreditation (C&A) program. Policies requiring C&A will be issued by the office of the CIO. A plan for retroactive C&A and for C&A of all systems in development will be completed before the end of the year.

Funding Considerations: This action is funded by the corporation and administered by the CIO.

E-Business Risk Management Review Model Instructions for Use

This e-business risk management review model provides executive management with the ability to monitor several categories of IT project and e-business operational risks that are often overlooked and underappreciated by the IT staff and the sponsoring business unit due to a tendency to focus on the technology of the system under development. These risks generally fall outside the scope of the typical security vulnerability and risk assessment and therefore are often not taken into account until too late. Some of these risks may have surfaced during the feasibility study while others may not.

The areas of risk suggested for monitoring in this appendix require access to information and expertise that commonly goes beyond that of the technology staff. Thus, other corporate staff groups must be involved, as necessary, to ensure that all potential risks are being adequately addressed.

The risks being recommended for special executive oversight include, but are not limited to:

- Failure of an underlying e-business technology
- Likelihood of support vendor failure
- Likelihood that labor market can support the planned e-business initiative
- Likelihood of losing competitive advantage due to project delay
- Risks posed by "creeping" requirements
- Risks posed by the emerging liability challenge
- Risks associated with meaningless warranties
- Likelihood of new law and regulations governing IT
- Risks of project delay, abandonment, marginal success rate

The methodology best used to identify risks and assess their impact is the "Delphi" approach, where knowledgeable individuals and outside experts who monitor special risk areas are polled as to the impacts of a particular category of risk. A consensus is reached, it is accepted or rejected by management, and appropriate action is taken. From time to time, other risks may become known and may be added to this initial list.

The executive IT management committee responsible for e-business development projects is the appropriate place to periodically review the risks addressed by this appendix.

What follows is a short description of each listed risk, and Exhibit D.1 (shown at the end of this Appendix) provides a form for tracking changes in risk status at periodic reviews.

RISK AREA 1: FAILURE OF AN UNDERLYING E-BUSINESS TECHNOLOGY

This risk deals not so much with an outright failure of a fundamental technology but rather with the gradual erosion of the anticipated performance characteristics of a particular product's manifestation of technology that does not live up to expectations. This risk can affect an e-business project adversely because two things happen as expectations are changed. First, the original system's concept will alter as the realization of technological shortcomings force a reexamination of what can actually be attained. This forces an undesired change to the e-business system as finally implemented. Second, if the technology's promise is too seriously missed, the entire project is likely to be scrapped until a proven technical solution can be found or developed. When this occurs, project momentum is often lost and new technology and events may overtake the system's original concept.

If the failure of the technology is not discovered until late in a project's development cycle, the adverse effects will be very severe as the future of the business may have been depending on this particular e-business application and its implementation. Historically, to make "something work," corners are cut and security is usually the first thing cut.

The anticipated and probably hyped future of an underlying technology must be monitored very carefully so that early warnings of problems are discovered in time to adjust e-business system plans.

RISK AREA 2: LIKELIHOOD OF SUPPORT VENDOR FAILURE

New technologies being employed in e-business applications and systems (i.e., hardware devices, components, support software, security tools, etc.) are often initially developed by start-up companies comprised of talented engineers, entrepreneurs, and with support by venture capitalists. Early sales are imperative for the future viability of such start-ups. To achieve such sales, companies often employ, at very lucrative commission rates, professional sales personnel noted for success at delivering high-volume orders. They are motivated to sell and may have little regard for the actual condition or performance of the product, the software, the service, or after-sales service. In fact, with many start-up companies that are striving to be one of the first to market with an implementation of a new technology, the product may still be in the prototype phase, and after-sales service does not exist beyond a phone call to the "creator" of the product. These are facts of life in the rapidly expanding world of information technology.

Caveat emptor is alive and well when dealing with technology start-ups. The degree of corporate stability and solvency that business executives have come to expect of their other business partners may not exist with IT companies, and this poses a special business and security risk to a corporation's foray into e-business. Information technology companies, especially those associated with cutting-edge technologies and their implementations, are extremely volatile and susceptible to financial problems or acquisition. This risk area calls for special monitoring to preclude any "surprises" as a project progresses along its development cycle.

RISK AREA 3: LIKELIHOOD THAT LABOR MARKET CAN SUPPORT THE PLANNED E-BUSINESS INITIATIVE

This risk is extremely important and difficult to assess. Recently, the U.S. Commerce Department's Office of Technology Policy estimated that there would be a need for approximately 1.3 million new computer engineers, programmers, and systems analysts over the next decade. At the same time, the Department of Education reports a decline of 40 percent in computer science graduates. If the United States cannot fill this need for IT workers, U.S. innovation, competitiveness, productivity, and economic growth could be undermined. Even after the .com meltdown, shortages in IT workers exist across all industries.

The probability that a corporate e-business initiative could be adversely affected by a shortage of skilled IT workers is a function of many factors, including:

- popularity of the technology or product—is the technology viewed as having "resume value" by prospective employees?
- estimated local population of people trained and skilled in the technology or product
- ability to meet salary requirements of skilled personnel—new technologies often start bidding wars for qualified people
- creativity of compensation packages—nonmonetary items and issues
- willingness to offer contracts to critical personnel to better ensure their longevity on projects
- willingness to subsidize employee non-IT education
- reputation of the company as a good place to work.

Many of the conditions of employment needed to build and retain a competent and reasonably loyal IT workforce may seem, to non-IT employees, to create a special group—an elite class of employees; but, remember the more esoteric a chosen technology, the more specialized and scarce the workforce required to support it.

This, of course, can create problems not worth the advantage gained by adopting a too esoteric technology. In the worst case, it can lead to a situation where the company is held hostage by the *only* people who understand the company and how its cutting-edge e-business systems work. This then creates a special category of e-business security risk—one that is very difficult to deal with unless anticipated. Executives must consider very carefully whether they want to give that kind of power to their technicians. Note that outsourcing does not necessarily solve this problem; it just moves the point of risk farther from direct corporate control.

RISK AREA 4: LIKELIHOOD OF LOSING COMPETITIVE ADVANTAGE DUE TO PROJECT DELAY.

The difficulty with assessing this risk lies in attempting to correlate a perceived window of competitive opportunity with the actual, not the scheduled, progress being made on the e-business project being developed to capitalize on the opportunity. A project of this nature (i.e., one being developed to gain competitive advantage), even when rushed, must be under tight project management control (Appendix B) with effective metrics being captured and reported accurately to management. The first reaction of many will be to "cut corners" when such projects are delayed in order to get to market quickly. Also, some in the IT group may view this type of project as a "fast track" to promotion and influence within the corporation. They are simply responding to what they have probably seen work for others under similar circumstances—quick deployment regardless of the quality or security of the system delivered.

Corporate executives, because of their "due diligence" responsibilities, must insist that shortcuts in building a quality and secure e-business system not be taken. They, above all others, must require that an appropriate and structured SDP (see Chapter 6 and Appendix B) be followed or the company may unwisely "seize" the opportunity from a competitor but do so with a half-baked system that will eventually do more harm than good to the reputation of the corporation. While your company is backtracking, exercising "damage control," and attempting to make the system work, the competitor is capitalizing on your mistakes and your bad press and taking control of the market opportunity.

A final word or caution: Without senior executives championing a sound development approach during times such as this, the chief information technologist stands little chance of overcoming pressures from other less understanding executives to get the system up quickly, even at the expense of ending up with an unsupportable and insecure e-business system.

RISK AREA 5: RISKS POSED BY "CREEPING" REQUIREMENTS

One of the most frequent complaints from IT professionals when attempting to construct an automated business system is that customers/users/management keep changing the requirements—they do not seem to know what they need or want from the system. Often, the complaint has merit and is especially likely to be true if the underlying way of doing business is changing because of automation, as it is with an e-business system. This represents one of the greatest risks to a project's success and therefore its security. Without a clearly documented set of business requirements, which function as blueprints, the subsequent phases of systems development will likely be a waste. A wonderfully engineered system may result, but it is not what was needed and did not solve the business problem or capitalize on the perceived opportunity.

From the perspective of e-business security, a gradual "creep" in requirements has two possible effects. First, continually changing and expanding requirements indicates an instability in the business concept being automated. It demonstrates a lack of knowledge and understanding about how the business function is to be carried out. Such lack of understanding makes securing the e-business system next to impossible because security and integrity controls must be applied to well-analyzed application and supporting technical infrastructure to be effective. Second, continually changing requirements are likely to delay the project schedule to such a degree that corners will be cut to make target dates. Once again, security is one of the things that is bound to be cut, the rationale being that security can always be implemented after the system is up and running. The truth is that security and integrity controls are essential to the e-business process being deployed for user or customer acceptance—if controls are not included at this time, there can be no objective judgment about how well the system actually works.

Creeping requirements become a risk when a disciplined requirements definition and validation period is not enforced. A continued vagueness of system goals means that no baseline of requirements stabilizes and systems programming and integration cannot proceed in an orderly fashion. Each time additional requirements creep into the statement of specifications, systems developers should pause and reevaluate the design in light of the "new" requirement. They should then reconcile any design inconsistencies, conduct quality assurance and security reviews, and then proceed with development. If requirements change too frequently, these steps are not likely to be performed with any consistency and attempts will be made to simply fold the "new" requirement into the developing system as best they can.

Each time a "new" requirement creeps into a system already under development, either the scheduled time to completion must be adjusted to reflect additional analysis or management should be informed that they are assuming the risk of modifying a system without the benefit of a thorough impact analysis. Much is sacrificed when system requirements are not locked down, at least until a system satisfying initial requirements is completed.

RISK AREA 6: RISKS POSED BY THE EMERGING LIABILITY CHALLENGE

Liability, an area of emerging risk, will require concentrated executive awareness and attention for the foreseeable future as various legal challenges rewrite the landscape for developers, service providers, value-added resellers, system integrators, and consultants. Also likely to be further defined will be the "due diligence" responsibilities of accounting, consulting, and legal firms when participating as advisors to mergers and acquisitions. Additionally, as the pace of IT-related business failures mounts à la the dot-com meltdown, there will be many stockholder and investor suits against technology companies and investment brokers who advised in favor of such investments.

Managing this area of risk will require the involvement of the corporate legal staff to monitor changing developments as various liability scenarios unfold over the next few years. Regardless of the fact that "safe haven" limitations were enacted for Y2K failures, the type of cases that were under consideration before that legislation was passed will herald the future for software and systems litigation for the next decade. Corporate legal staffs must track developments in the following areas.

- *Product Liability Claims.* Opposing lawyers will collect product information including technical documentation, manuals, advertising materials, "bug" notifications concerning products, and internal e-mail concerning products or systems while they were in development and/or being marketed. Opposing lawyers will try to establish early corporate knowledge of product malfunctions that may or may not have been corrected before release for sale or contract delivery. Intentions of "fixing" malfunctions, as has been the practice, may not stand up as a defense, depending on severity and the adverse impact on customers.

- *Breach of Contract.* This is the first line of litigation in cases where written contracts and implied warranties and promises come into conflict with the actual performance of the software or system. This is where the concept of duty of the "expert" to the "non-expert" may be tested regardless of counter-charges of contributory negligence.

- *Fraud and Misrepresentation.* Lawyers in discovery will uncover exaggerated product claims, hyped advertising, overoptimistic development schedules, inflated résumés, evidence of shortcuts and deviations that were taken from best practices, and employees willing to testify about how warnings were not heeded by management. Outsource firms and consultants may be particularly vulnerable if their advertising claims or past performance statements turn out to be false or inflated.

- *Insurance Claims.* Even though most state insurance commissions ruled that Y2K could be excluded from coverage, do not expect this to hold true for future claims against *errors and omissions* coverage. Look for insurance companies to become much more inquisitive about software and systems development practices, especially testing, before continuing to offer coverage and in the determination of premiums.

- *Officers' and Directors' Liability.* When future software and system failures are litigated, lawyers will want to know when senior management was first aware of a potential problem (i.e., the one for which the company is being sued) and what they did about it. Counsel will argue that such notification started a clock running during which time directors and officers were to have exercised "reasonable care" in performance of their fiduciary responsibilities. Under such circumstances, testimony from employees and copies of warning memoranda and e-mails will be damaging. The presence of warning messages may indicate a project that was being properly managed or one that was out of control, depending on what actions were then taken. Attempts to destroy warning messages would indicate a cover-up and may constitute a crime in itself.

There are serious management implications associated with any possible scenario. Simply blaming IT employees for defective software and systems will not stand up in court. With such cases, it will be demonstrated that the defective systems in question were the result of a trade-off decision concerning quality and/or security management. Or it will be shown that no SDP was in place or enforced and therefore known IT best practices were not employed. Developing systems under no controlling discipline and/or making trade-off decisions among cost, schedules, and systems quality and/or security requires at least the passive participation of senior executives and cannot be relegated to subordinates, as a defense, without incurring even greater personal risk as an officer or director. Chief information officers will be especially vulnerable in the years ahead and in many organizations will be forced to take unpopular positions regarding the quality and security of IT products, services, and internal systems. Without senior executive support and protection, CIO will all too often stand for "Career is Over."

Some will argue that as soon as the first director or officer is held personally liable for a software or system failure, the rest of corporate America will simply isolate themselves from situations and decisions. Such a strategy, however, could backfire, resulting in charges of negligence.

RISK AREA 7: RISKS ASSOCIATED WITH MEANINGLESS WARRANTIES

For those organizations that are greatly dependent on information technology and on the IT industry for software systems and support, there is an emerging special category of risk that must be monitored. This risk centers on the industry's continuing attempts to further limit its liability for defective products. This potential threat comes as part of an initiative being spearheaded by the software industry and is found in the Uniform Computer Information Transactions Act (UCITA). The UCITA is a proposal for applying consistent rules to computer software licenses across all 50 states. The UCITA would amend the Uniform Commercial Code (UCC). The UCITA would essentially:

1. Give vendors the right to repossess software by disabling it remotely
2. Make the terms of off-the-shelf licenses more enforceable
3. Prevent the transfer of licenses from one party to another without vendor permission
4. Outlaw reverse engineering of software
5. Allow vendors to disclaim warranties
6. Allow vendors to *not* be held accountable for *known* defects

While the first four provisions may seem petty or even onerous to some, they are understandable attempts by an industry, besieged by piracy, to protect its intellectual property and revenue stream. The fifth and sixth provisions, however, are far more troubling from the perspective of a corporate or individual software buyer. It would seem that these provisions allow vendors not only to disclaim warranties for what is later found to be defective, buggy, or virus-infected software, but also to escape accountability for defects that the vendor knew existed at time of sale. According to Watts Humphrey, a fellow at the Software Engineering Institute at Carnegie-Mellon University, "the provisions say that software publishers are not liable for the poor quality of their products. Today, any feature that a vendor demonstrates at a trade show or writes about in a product manual must be a working part of the product. The proposed law would seem to change that."

The UCITA, it is feared, will cause a lowering of standards for software performance and will cost users more money because, having reduced faith in warranties, they will have to take extra steps to ensure that software products work properly before buying them.

Risk of this nature calls for executive attention to ensure that corporate interests are well represented during all dealings with the IT industry. Corporations also must participate when legislative agendas of this nature are being proposed. Do not assume that when people are drafting laws such as the UCITA that they are ensuring balance and watching out for everyone's best interest.

RISK AREA 8: LIKELIHOOD OF LAW AND REGULATIONS GOVERNING IT

In opposition to increases in "safe haven" protection being sought by IT vendors, there are likely to be demands for "new" laws and regulations to ensure the proper management, confidentiality, and accurate uses of private information. Already, the health care industry is implementing legislation governing the confidentiality and integrity of patient data. This particular law, the Health Care Information

Portability and Accountability Act (HIPAA) affects all patient data, whether in manual or automated form.

A model for future laws governing the confidentiality of customer data will likely be the Privacy Act of 1974, which pertained to federal record keeping. Enacted years ahead of its time, the Privacy Act set a standard for required record accuracy before making any determination about an individual citizen. The law prescribed procedures for citizens to gain access to their records, procedures for contesting record content and accuracy, and procedures for ensuring that corrected record data would be passed along to any government agency in possession of the originally inaccurate data. The law also called for civil sanctions against the government for making adverse determinations about a citizen based on inaccurate information or violations of confidentiality, and it allowed criminal penalties for individuals who violated the confidentiality rules of these record systems.

It is advised that the corporate legal staff monitor developments in this area and ensure that technical staff and management account any such requirements in future e-business systems. Appendix B has special instructions for ensuring privacy, and confidentiality requirements are addressed as part of the security, internal controls, and quality assurance (QA) management plans governing systems development.

RISK AREA 9: RISK OF PROJECT DELAY, ABANDONMENT, AND MARGINAL SUCCESS RATE

Without a doubt, the most serious risks that must be overcome are those associated with continuing to conduct business in light of the vast number of IT projects that are delayed, abandoned, or considered finally to be only marginally successful. Generally, the following statistics are accepted:

- 25 percent of all IT projects are abandoned
- At least 15 percent are delayed seven months or more
- 40 percent of new systems are considered failures
- 40 percent are considered to have made marginal improvements
- finally, only 20 percent are considered to be unqualified successes

Unless and until this ultimate risk is recognized, accepted as a business fact, and managed from the executive suite, many of the anticipated e-business advances of the next decade will not be realized.

It is feared by some that IT is rapidly approaching the point where system delivery statistics can only get worse. IT complexities, uncertainties, lack of methodological enforcement, skill shortages, and business partners experiencing the same problems, indicate that we may be approaching a state of crisis that only the most intense involvement by senior executives can turn around. Only under executive leadership can the persistent and escalating conflict between IT and business goals be brought under control.

For at least a decade, a major reported goal of CEOs has been to better align the goals of IT and business. The very fact that these two sets of goals are perceived to be out of step evidences the problem both groups are having communicating. It should be obvious that IT systems and other related computing assets exist to support the conduct of business and not the reverse, and yet many CEOs see lack of mutual alignment as a major problem. What is wrong with this picture? Is the IT group or the IT contractor running the corporation? How could that be? It can be true only if an information technology leadership vacuum exists at the top of the company. And this can be true only if senior corporate executives, not understanding the critical nature of their IT dependence, have delegated systems responsibility too low in the organization to effect coordinated, enterprise-wide action. Some will contend that IT is too complex to be managed from the executive suite. Others will hold that this approach will result in micromanagement and that e-business projects will be delayed more frequently and be more expensive because of it.

This last criticism may be true if senior executives are monitoring the wrong activities or too many activities and managing against the wrong success criteria. But it is *not true* if appropriate IT project activities are selected for executive review and if success criteria for an IT undertaking are consistent with the success criteria of the business unit that the e-business project supports. Appendix B presents a model for an appropriate level of executive engagement in e-business projects. It outlines a general-purpose systems development process model that includes the critical areas of development and project management activity that must be reviewed periodically by oversight management.

RISK AREA:	Insert Description of Risk

Original Need or Opportunity for This Project;	_____ _____ _____
Change Summary Posted by Risk Category:	_____ _____ _____
Change Summary Posted by Risk Category:	_____ _____ _____
Change Summary Posted by Risk Category:	_____ _____ _____
Impact on Project:	_____ _____
Dollar Change: Impact on Project:	_____ _____ _____
Dollar Change: Mitigating Actions:	_____ _____ _____ _____
Continued Project Viability:	_____ _____ _____

Exhibit D.1   IT Risk Management Review

Appendix E

Resources Guide

Staying up-to-date with e-business security developments is a daunting task. Today's solution may be the Achilles' heel of your system tomorrow. Adequate security programs require the constant updating of knowledge and the tireless research such currency demands. In the following pages, a number of information research sources are provided to speed and ease the task of staying current.

WHERE CONSOLIDATED LISTS OF SECURITY VULNERABILITIES ARE MAINTAINED

http://cve.mitre.org

http://xforce.iss.net

www.cs.purdue.edu.coast/projects/vdb.com

www.rootshell.com

http://seclab.cs.ucdavis.edu/projects/vulnerabilities/#database

WHERE PUBLIC DOMAIN SECURITY TOOLS CAN BE FOUND

ftp://ciac.llnl.gov/pub/ciac/sectools/unix

ftp://coast.cs.purdue.edu/pub.tools

http://cert.org/other_sources/tool_sources.html

ftp://porcupine.org/pub.security.index.html

ftp.funet.fi/pub/unix/security

WHERE VENDOR-SPECIFIC SECURITY PATCHES CAN BE FOUND

BSDI	ftp.bsdi.com/bsdi/patches
Caldera Open Linux	ftp.caldera.com/pub.OpenLinux/security
Debian Linux	ftp.us.debian.org/debian
Compaq	ftp://www3.compaq.com/support/files

FreeBSD	ftp.FreeBSD.org/pub/FreeBSD
HP	http://us-support.external.hp.com
IBM	http://service.software.ibm.com/support/rs6000
NT	www.microsoft.com/security
OpenBSD	www.openbsd.com/security.html
RedHat Linux	www.redhat.com/corp/security.html
SCO	ftp.sco.com/SSE
SGI	ftp.sgi.com/patches
Sun	http://sunsolve.sun.com

SECURITY INCIDENT RESPONSE CENTERS

Australian Computer Emergency Response Team (AUSCERT)	www.auscert.org.au auscert@auscert.org.au
CERTSM Coordination Center	www.cert.org cert@cert.org
Computer Incident Advisory Capability (CIAC)	ciac.llnl.gov ciac@llnl.gov
Defense Information Systems Agency Center	
For Automated System Security Incident Support Team (ASSIST)	www.cert.mil cert@cert.mil
Federal Computer Incident Response Capability (FedCirc)	www.fedcirc.gov fedcirc@fedcir.gov
Forum of Incident Response and Security Teams (FIRST)	www.first.org first-sec@first.org
The German Research Network Computer Emergency Response Team	www.cert.dfn.de/eng/dfncert dfncert@cert.dfn.de
NASA Incident Response Center (NASIRC)	www-nasirc.nasa.gov/incidents.html nasirc@nasire.nasa.gov
Federal Bureau of Investigation (FBI) - National Infrastructure Protection Center (NIPC)	www.nipc.gov nipc@fbi.gov
A full list of European CERTs can be found at	www.cert.dfn.de/eng/csir/europe/certs.html

GENERAL SECURITY WEB SITES

http://java.sun.com/security
www.telstra.com.au/info/security
www.sans.org/giac.html
http://ntbugtraq.com
www.cerias.purdue.edu/coast
www.nsi.org/compsec.html
www.boran.com/security
www.securityportal.com
www.tno.nl/instit/fel/intern/wkinfsec.html
http://10pht.com
http://xforce.iss.net
www.packetstorm.security.com

GOVERNMENT SECURITY WEB SITES

www.itpolicy.gsa.gov
www.nswc.navy.mil/ISSEC
www.cit.nih.gov/security.html
http://cs-www.ncsl.nist.gov

BULLETINS, NEWS GROUPS, AND ARCHIVES

Bugtraq Full Disclosure List	listserv@securityfocus.com
CERT Advisories	cert-advisory-request@cert.org
CIAC Advisories	Majordomo@rumpole.llnl.gov
COAST Security Archive	coast-request@cs.purdue.edu
Firewalls Digest	Majordomo@list.gnac.net
Firewalls Wizards	Majordomo@nfr.net
FreeBSD Security Issues	Majordomo@freebsd.org
Intrusion Detection Systems	Majordomo@uow.edu.au
Linux Security Issues	linux-security-request@RedHat.com
Legal Aspects of Computer Crime	Majordomo@suburbia.net
NT Bugtraq	listserv@listserv.ntbugtraq.com

The Risks Forum	risks-requests@csl.sri.com
WWW Security	Majordomo@nsmx.rutgers.edu
The Virus Lists	LISTSERV@lehigh.edu
Security list FAQ located at:	http://xforce.iss.net/mailists.otherlists.php3

Free Computer Security Publications: National Institutes of Standards and Technology Publication List 91—Computer Security Publications U.S. Department of Commerce www.NIST.gov

Index

Printed and bound by CPI Group (UK) Ltd, Croydon, CR0 4YY
16/04/2025